Four Centuries Of Machine Knitting

*Commemorating
William Lee's Invention Of
The Stocking Frame In 1589*

Edited by John T. Millington and Stanley Chapman

Foreword by HRH The Princess Royal

Knitting International, Leicester, England.

A Message from
HRH The Princess Royal
Patron of the
William Lee Quatercentenary Committee

HRH The Princess Royal, The Princess Anne, Mrs. Mark Phillips GCVO.

BUCKINGHAM PALACE

The Willam Lee Quatercentenary Year, which marks the invention of the first stocking frame in the village of Calverton in the county of Nottinghamshire in 1589, is clearly a milestone in the annals of the Knitting Industry.

As President of the British Knitting Clothing & Export Council, my visits to knitting companies have provided me with many opportunities of seeing for myself how the legacy of Lee's ingenuity lives on in today's dynamic Knitting Industry. The explosion of creativity stimulated by the recent investment in computer aided design and harnessed to the new advanced electronic knitting processes, is contributing positively to the prosperity of the Knitting Industry for the benefit of future generations.

I extend my best wishes to everyone engaged in the Industry producers, suppliers and customers at home and abroad, that this Quatercentenary Year will be a truly memorable celebration of William Lee's undoubted genius.

Anne

©Knitting International 1989
First Published 1989

All rights reserved. No part of this publication may be reproduced in any form by any means, without permission from the Publisher.

ISBN 0 9514312 0 X

Printed in Great Britain by
Cradley Printing Group plc,
Warley, West Midlands
and bound by
J. W. Braithwaite & Son Ltd,
Woverhampton
for the publishers
Knitting International,
Eastern Boulevard,
Leicester LE2 7BN,
England.

A Message From The Sponsors

ICI (UK) Fibres is proud to be associated with the spirit of the William Lee Quatercentenary Celebration through this Commemorative Book. The contents form a permanent tribute to the genesis of a great industry, to its people and to its commitment to the future.

A Message From The Chairman Of The William Lee Quatercentenary Committee

Andrew Winkler, C.Text, FTI, FSDC.

IN 1989 WE CELEBRATE the 400th Anniversary of the knitting industry with an exciting programme of events produced after two years of sustained effort. William Lee was the founding father of this great industry with his invention, in 1589, of the hand knitting frame.

We are proud and grateful to be honoured by the patronage of HRH The Princess Royal, who, for many years, has supported and encouraged the knitting industry in its various endeavours.

On behalf of the Committee I wish to express my thanks and appreciation to the sponsors and supporters who, through their generosity, have made a dream come true.

I should like to give my personal thanks to Bryan Atkins, the director of the committee, who was appointed through the generosity of Marks & Spencer; to the hon. officers, Russell Kempton, David Elson and Barry Start; and the committee members, who, fuelled by endless enthusiasm have jointly worked very hard.

The celebrations offer an excellent opportunity for any organisation with vision to make use of the Quatercentenary programme as a launching platform for their own promotional projects.

In addition to the published programme, other events are being considered. They will be announced in 'Knitting International'.

It is hoped that sufficient funds will be retained at the end of the year to establish suitable lasting momentoes of the "Lee 400" anniversary.

Funding, Sponsorship And Support For The William Lee Quatercentenary

Contributors

John Air Ltd, Scotland; British Lace Federation; Calverton Parish Council; Calverton Preservation Society; Coats and Clark Inc, Albany and Toccoca, USA; Coats Viyella plc; Courtaulds plc; Cooper, Parry, Watson, Sooter & Co, Chartered Accountants; Du Pont (UK) Ltd; Gedling Borough Council; Edward W. Guy, Solicitor; Hatra; ICI (UK) Fibres; T. W. Kempton Ltd; Klitra; KIF; Knitting International/Ferry Pickering Publishers Ltd; Leicester and District Knitting Industry Association; Leicester Textile Society; Geoffrey E. Macpherson Ltd; Marks & Spencer plc; Midland Bank plc, West Bridgford, Notts; Midlands Section, Textile Institute; National Westminster Bank plc; Nottingham City Council; Nottinghamshire County Council; Nottingham Textile Society; Pasold Research Fund; Pretty Polly Ltd; Shima Seiki Europe Ltd; Textured Jersey plc; Understanding Industry; Viscosuisse Textured Yarns Ltd.

Sponsors

Du Pont (UK) Ltd ICI (UK) Fibres Viscosuisse Textured Yarns Ltd	Royal Fashion Spectacular
Marks and Spencer plc	Design Council Award
Grieve Ltd	International Technology Competition
Guilford Kapwood	Royal Society of Arts Award
International Wool Secretariat Parkland Textile (Holdings) Ltd	Royal Society of Arts Award
Branded Hosiery Group (Pretty Polly Ltd, Charnos plc, Berkshire Hosiery (UK) Ltd, Elbeo Ltd, Couture Marketing Ltd, Courtaulds Hosiery Ltd)	Various Hosiery Projects
Coats Viyella plc	Schools GCSE Resource Book
Profitex Ltd	Schools Essay Competition
Groz Beckert UK Ltd	Pictorial Tea Towel
Gedling Borough Council	Sponsored Painting
ICI (UK) Fibres	Commemorative Book
Karl Mayer Textile Machinery Ltd	Lee Jacquard Lace Panel
Courtaulds plc	20 Students to Textile Institute World Conference
Textured Jersey plc	12 "
Zellmanar Ltd	4 "
Stevensons Dyers Ltd	2 "
Precision Processes (Textiles) Ltd	2 "
St. Moritz Fabrics Ltd	1 "
Kirstol Ltd	1 "
Seton Healthcare Group	1 "
Richard Beardall & Co	1 "
R. Cresey and Sons Ltd	1 "
Maria Potempski Assoc	1 "
Profitex Ltd	1 "
Benjamin R. Vickers & Sons Ltd	1 "
Readicut International plc Brother Knitting Machines	Knit a Toy Charity Competition
Nottinghamshire County Council	Civic Reception and Lee 400 Keynote Speech

Contents

Origins and growth
    The hand knitting industry. Joan Thirsk **9**
    William Lee and the invention of the knitting frame. Negley Harte **14**
    From domestic to factory industry: hosiery statistics. Stephen C. Wallwork **21**
    A fashion history of knitting. Terry Brackenbury **26**
    Marketing and distribution: how today's system evolved. Stanley Chapman **32**
    Three centuries of knitting in Scotland. Clifford Gulvin **38**
    Salient features of knitting technology. Tony Nutting **58**
    Rise and fall of the knitting machine builders. Paul Stibbe **64**
    400 years of domestic machine knitting. Kathleen Kinder **69**

Industry leaders reflect
    Messages from industry leaders for the world of knitting **81**

Programme of events
    Wm. Lee quatercentenary programme of celebrations **94**
    Village that saw the birth of the knitting frame. Chris Peck **105**
    Some UK museums and places of knitting interest. Doreen Beardall **108**
    Quatercentenary projects and competitions **112**

Business prospects
    Impact of future change on makers of knitted products. Rodney Gunston **114**
    Future prospects for 1992 and beyond. John Harrison **118**
    Profits, exchange rates and enterprise in the 1980s. David Buck **129**

Fibre and yarn future
    Wool's current and future role in the knitting industry. Caroline Walker **131**
    Linen in knitting. R. R. Franck **136**
    Blossoming renaissance of world's oldest synthetic fibre. John Coleman **138**
    Courtaulds and knitting. Robert Aitkin, John Picker **142**
    New end uses in polyester's future. R. J. Woodward, G. D. Myers, J. G. Kilroy **153**
    A fibre giant's chlorofibre speciality. Terry Duncan **157**
    The expanding uses for Lycra in knitting. Margaret Jacob **159**
    A spinner's view of the future. Robert Shelton **162**

Technology update
    Fully-fashioned to seamless: productivity and fashion. Dennis R. Goadby **165**
    Into the weft knitting future. David J. Spencer **169**
    The warp knitting story. R. Wheatley **171**

Literary legacy
    The top 200 knitting books. Jack Smirfitt **177**

Directory of advertisers 184

William Lee Quatercentenary Executive Committee

Andrew Winkler, chairman: hon. treasurer, The Textile Institute; previously director, Nottingham Manufacturing Co. plc and Vantona Viyella plc; chairman Profitex Ltd.

Russell Kempton JP, vice chairman: chairman T. W. Kempton Ltd; past chairman of council, The Textile Institute; past president Mailleurop.

Bryan D. Atkins, director: consultant to Marks and Spencer plc, president, Home Laundering Consultative Council; knitwear consultant to International Trade Centre UNCTAD/GATT (United Nations) Geneva.

D. M. Elson, hon secretary: lecturer, Department of Fashion and Textiles, Trent Polytechnic; vice-chairman Midlands Section, Textile Institute; consultant to United Nations.

R. B. Start, hon. treasurer: director, Geoffrey E. Macpherson Ltd; chairman, Midlands Section, Textile Institute.

Mrs. D. Beardall JP: director, Richard Beardall & Co; trustee Ruddington Framework Knitters' Museum.

R. Bracegirdle: principal officer/curator, Science and Industry Museum, Leicestershire County Council, museum educational tutor, textile and industrial historian.

T. Brackenbury: principal lecturer, Department of Fashion and Textiles, Trent Polytechnic.

Dr. Stanley Chapman: Pasold Reader in Textile History, Nottingham University.

H. K. Dunkley: former deputy managing director, Geoffrey E. Macpherson Ltd; textile consultant.

Councillor Martin S. Hall: past president, Nottingham Textile Society.

John Harrison: director, The Knitting Industries' Federation.

Dr. R. Harwood: head of Fashion and Technology Department, Leicester Polytechnic.

John C. Haslam: director of Property Development & Tourism, Nottingham City Council.

Dr. S. J. D. Hay: marketing director, ICI Fibres.

T. D. Hennessy: branch director, UK and Ireland, International Wool Secretariat.

D. Hogg, marketing manager, Inward Investment, Economic Development Unit, Nottinghamshire County Council.

Councillor Oliver Kingdon: previously managing director, Elbeo Ltd.

John Kirkland: managing director, Pretty Polly Ltd.

David Lambert: president, National Union of Hosiery and Knitwear Workers.

Jimmie Lewis JP: director, Marketing Services, Courtaulds Clothing.

B. Loughborough: arts director, Nottingham City Council.

Dr. G. McLeavy: chairman of council, The Textile Institute; previously assistant managing director, PPT Ltd.

R. J. Meads: marketing director, Stevensons Fabric Dyers Ltd.

John Millington: editor and managing director, Knitting International; director, Ferry Pickering Group plc; president UK branch International Federation of Knitting Technologists.

R. W. Mills: technical author and consultant.

Professor D. Munden: former head of School of Textile and Knitwear Technology, Leicester Polytechnic; member CIM Centre, Leicester Polytechnic.

Mrs. K. E. Needham: clerk to Calverton Parish Council.

Professor E. W. Newton: dean of School of Art and Design, Nottingham Polytechnic.

M. J. O'Brien: managing director, Monk-Dubied Ltd.

Chris Peck: secretary, Calverton Preservation Society.

A. Reid: Employment and Economic Development Unit, Leicester City Council.

J. Smirfitt: librarian, Hosiery and Allied Trades Research Association.

The Rt. Rev. Richard Rutt: Bishop of Leicester; author of book "The History of Hand Knitting".

Glyn W. Smith: previously senior development officer, ICI Fibres.

J. Walker MBE: previously chairman, Basford Textile Group Ltd; past president, Lace Federation.

Mrs. Ivy Ward: chairman, Calverton Parish Council.

Dr. B. Wheatley: former joint acting head, School of Textile and Knitwear Technology, Leicester Polytechnic; consultant, lecturer and technical author.

The Hand Knitting Industry

By Joan Thirsk

IN THE LONG HISTORY of human inventiveness and ingenuity, it is fairly certain that knitting with needles is not as old a skill as weaving. A clue pointing in this direction is the fact that European languages lack a precise word for knitting: they make do with words that had an older meaning, like the verb 'to knit' in English. Spanish offers an even better example: knitting is called making stitches *(hacer punto),* and there is no satisfactory noun apart from *trabajo de punto* (the work of stitching). Nowadays the Spaniards borrow the French verb *tricoter* and turn it into *tricotar,* but that is relatively recent usage.

Medieval Origins

As for documents on knitting, they are few and far between until the later Middle Ages, although Papal Bulls refer somewhat earlier, in the eleventh and twelfth centuries, to the use of knitted gloves as part of the ritual of church services. Between 1200 and 1500 more precise references begin to accumulate, along with some pieces of actual knitting, but nearly all concern articles of clothing belonging to clerics. They were likely to be among the best preservers of such objects. The records of Cluny Abbey in France mention twenty-two pairs of gloves in 1382, and those of St. Paul's Cathedral three pairs in 1402. About thirty pairs of knitted gloves lie at present in church treasuries in southern and western Europe, and one pair of knitted leggings has also survived, of Bishop Konrad von Sternberg, dating from 1192. All these early examples show coarse knitting on stout needles, using silk, or sometimes linen thread. In a class apart are some knitted cushions of silk, with decorative patterns of high artistry, which have been found in tombs in Spain, dating from 1275 and 1283.

In short, we have examples between 1190 and 1290 of knitting, showing skilful shaping (for gloves) and intricate patterns (for cushions), executed in the service of the church and princes of state. We may reasonably guess from all this that knitting simple items like children's socks (unshaped) and adults' leggings was practised in scattered places in Europe at the same time, but that higher skills were usually found only in nunneries and in a few towns where clothiers catered for courtiers and the well-to-do.

Some kind of qualitative change seems to have taken place in the thirteenth century, as the unexploited potential of knitting as a craft began to be perceived. It was probably the result of an increasing trade between Europe and the Arab world, the beginnings of silk manufacture in southern Europe, which made silk threads more widely available than before, and the import of examples of patterned silk knitting. The silk cushions found in Spain, for example, have Arab decoration and could have been brought from Africa to Spain by the Moors.

Sixteenth century fashion: portrait of Richard Sackville, third Earl of Dorset, by Isaac Oliver. (Courtesy of the Victoria and Albert Museum, London).

Signs of knitting as a commercial occupation coincide with signs of knitting becoming a fashion, and between 1200 and 1400 both developments become more conspicuous, first in Italy and Spain, and then in France, Germany and the Netherlands. The Virgin Mary is depicted knitting in three Italian paintings of 1320-50, and in a German painting of about 1370-1400. A guild of knitters was in existence in Paris in 1366, and French documents soon after (between 1387 and 1392) refer to more varied knitted garments, namely, mittens, gloves, stockings and leggings. Knitting was becoming visible as it became a successful means of livelihood.

Capping

The first signs in England of commercial knitting occur in the early fifteenth century at Coventry, and, although no sure evidence has been found, foreign immigrants from the Low Countries may have been responsible for its beginnings. Knitted caps were becoming fashionable headgear, and the surname 'Capper' occurs in Coventry in 1435. The year 1448 may have been a significant milestone, signalling the increasing economic importance of the knitting industry in the town, for before that date the Coventry fullers were associated with the tailors; in other words, the fullers were concerned with the finishing of woven cloth. In 1448 they appear to have divided into two groups, one composed of walkers who fulled cloth, and the other of cappers, who felted knitted caps. The knitters were certainly an influential group among Coventry craftsmen by 1496 for a guild of Cappers was then formally incorporated. By 1500 many other English towns also had a capping industry. In Monmouth, which became famous for its knitted Monmouth caps, the industry may be more or less contemporaneous with that of Coventry, for cappers were numbered among its craftsmen in 1449.

The fifteenth-century industry of cap-making presented itself publicly as a male occupation. Almost certainly it employed many women knitters, but the finishing processes were in men's hands. The knitted fabric had to be blocked, either to make a beret-like top, or a bonnet shape, with brim, or peak, to which earflaps were sometimes added. The whole was then felted, thickened, and shorn, to improve resistance to rain. Many examples of finished caps survive in the London Museum and in the Victoria and Albert Museum, while Monmouth Museum has a Monmouth cap thought to date from the sixteenth century.

Capping was a town industry which prospered for between two and three hundred years. Monmouth caps continued to be worn into the later eighteenth century by Dutch seamen and American colonists, though in England reference to such a cap seems to have carried some pejorative meaning by the 1660s. But in Coventry and Monmouth signs of a decaying trade accumulated between 1550 and 1630, as caps lost their high place in fashion, and the industry evidently moved elsewhere. From Monmouth the industry moved to Bewdley, Worcestershire, while London took away much of the trade from other provincial centres. However, another branch of the knitting industry rose to prominence in its place — the knitting of stockings. Its success is again explained by a change in clothing styles in the sixteenth century, when long breeches or hose, formerly made of woven cloth, were replaced by short breeches, worn with long stockings that showed off the leg. The new fashion reached England when Henry VIII received a gift of knitted silk stockings from Spain. Next came fine worsted stockings from Italy, and by Elizabeth's reign, handknitters in England were copying both kinds. Furthermore, output was being enlarged in a third direction, by the knitting of cheap stockings of coarser wool.

Knitting Stockings In Tudor And Stuart England

The rapidity with which stocking knitting spread in England between 1560 and 1590, and became a commercial pursuit with a considerable export trade, strengthens the suspicion that knitting was already widely practised. At much the same time that Henry

Seventeenth century fashion: a pair of hand-knitted boot hose. (Courtesy of the Victoria and Albert Museum, London).

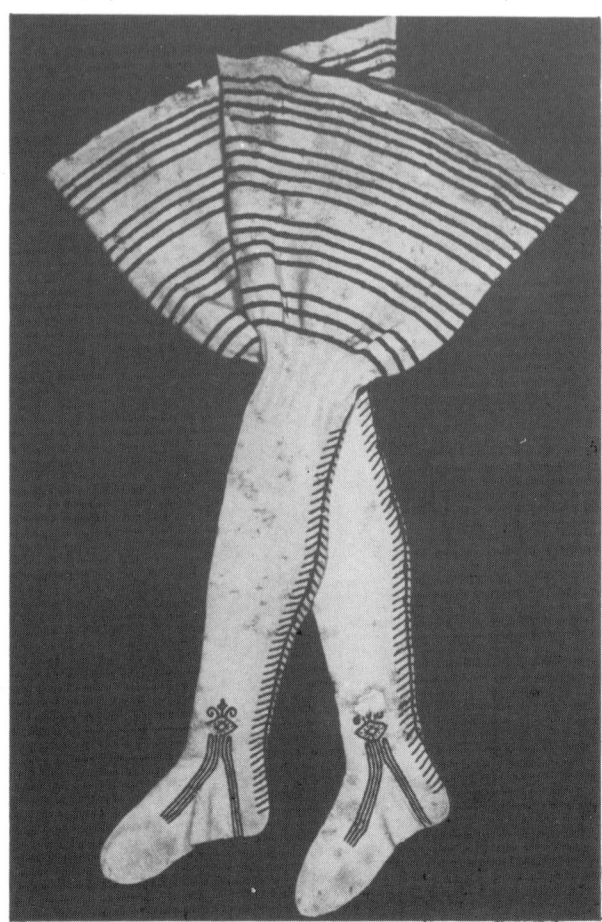

VIII was gloating over silk stockings from Spain, a crew member of the *Mary Rose* was wearing knitted wool socks, of which one survives at Portsmouth from the wreck of 1545. Knitted children's socks are also mentioned in household accounts of 1530. The change of clothing fashion among the well-to-do quickly caused a surge of demand for a cheaper version of silk and fine worsted stockings. Ready-made woollen stockings were needed for everyday wear, and events proved that country knitters could quickly provide them. We have other historical examples of peasant products that were drawn into the network of national and international trade at a certain moment when they fulfilled a need, perhaps because of their appearance, their cheapness, or because of changing fashions. A modern parallel might be Indian cheesecloth, which became for a time a fashionable blouse and shirt cloth in Western Europe, and in the process was much upgraded in quality.

The needs of the newly expanding stocking industry, unlike capmaking, did not oblige merchants to seek knitters in towns. Stockings needed no finishing, beyond washing and sometimes dyeing, and so merchants sought their knitters in villages where labour was cheaper. Knitting became a rural by-employment alongside farming, and was most successfully established in pastoral country where cattle and shop keepers (both male and female) could walk with their herds and flocks, or sit and guard them, and knit at the same time.

Between 1580 and 1630 the scale of the trade began to attract the taxman, and the main centres then identified were Norwich (a flourishing textile centre with varied products, including lace and many varied kinds of cloth), Northampton (with its forest country to the east), Doncaster (in the middle of the Ouse-Humber marshlands), Richmond, Askrigg, Middleham and Rotherham in the pastoral country of north and west Yorkshire, and Barnard Castle in Teesdale. But many other scattered places, unnoticed by the tax collectors, also had knitters, including Cornwall, counties in Wales, Cheshire, and Westmorland, where the inhabitants of Dentdale and Garsdale described themselves in one lawsuit as heavily dependent for a living on knitting because their farmholdings were so small.

Other places singled out for special mention were Yarmouth (indeed, all fishing ports were likely to be knitting centres), Tewkesbury in Gloucestershire, Pershore and Evesham in Worcestershire, Wells and Taunton in Somerset, and Tiverton in Devon. The naming of towns like these should not mislead, however, for they were the trading centres where stockings were washed, bundled and packed, whereas the knitters were found in the surrounding villages just as much as in the towns. The demand for knitters grew so rapidly that parish authorities from the 1580s onwards were teaching knitting to the poor in towns and villages alike. Despite the introduction of the knitting frame in 1589, the demand for hand knitted goods continued unabated.

The buoyancy of the handknitting industry is best understood when the full variety of its products, and the flexibility of its organisation is recognised. An Elizabethan list of stockings for export describes coarse white woollen stockings, men's stockings with scalloped tops, with large welts, of mingled colours, and children's coloured stockings. Stockings for the rich were made either of fine jersey wool or worsted, or silk, and had "quirks and clocks bout the ankles . . . sometimes haply interlaced with gold or silver threads".

Jersey and Guernsey were important centres for stocking knitting, exploiting the demand from both France and England, and in the 1670s one Guernsey dealer used thirty-three different code numbers for his wares. Another at St Peter Port offered marbled, fine marbled, striped with a fiery red colour, plain white, white striped with blue, greyish white, greyish white striped, greyish brown, iron-grey, blue and white, and black stockings. Prices also spanned a wide range of qualities. In the 1670s-1680s, they might cost 8d a pair, 1s 6d, 2s 6d, 10s 10d or for silk stockings worn at Charles II's court as much as 18s.

Continental Connection

By the end of the seventeenth century every country in Europe had its own hand knitting

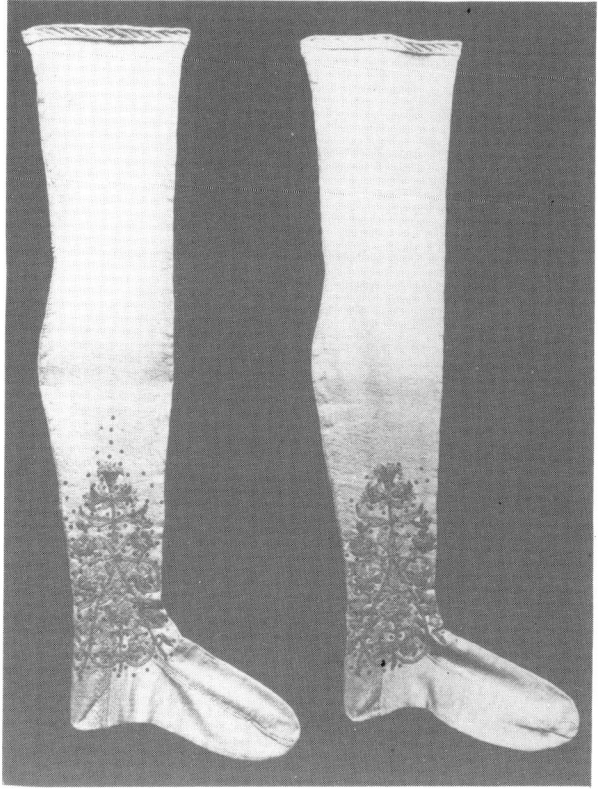

Machine knit fashion: a pair of boy's stockings with hand embroidered clocks, thought to have been made before 1625.

The English county of Yorkshire became one of the centres for stocking knitting and by the end of the sixteenth century was sufficiently flourishing to have attracted the attention of the taxman. George Walker's book, 'The Costume of Yorkshire' (1841), contains this picture of handknitters in Wensleydale. Four form a convivial circle out of doors on a fine day, while another woman knits as she walks and a man knits at the same time as he drives his sheep.

industry, with a defined market for stockings on which it concentrated its efforts. The pattern of specialisation in each country and region was, of course, constantly changing, but high demand sustained output despite the use of the knitting frame. In general, the frame seems to have been used to knit quality wares, especially stockings of silk, fine wool and later cotton. The handknitters held their own because of their wider competence: they fed the mass market for coarse stockings, but they could also produce fine quality work, such as waistcoats, children's dresses, and elaborately decorated stockings, of which some samples survive in our museums.

The mass market for English knitters of woollen stockings in the seventeenth century lay in Spain and Portugal (54 per cent of stockings exported from London between 1668 and 1669 went to these two countries), and it is likely that many of these imports ended up in South America. France, Holland and Germany took a fluctuating quantity of English stockings, but these countries also had their own industries, which were in direct competition with the English. French stockings, for example, found their way in increasing numbers into southern Spain in the later seventeenth century, but many were knitted on the frame and we do not yet know how, or if, they reshaped the English export business. The household accounts of the English gentry in the seventeenth and eighteenth century show them commissioning local people to knit clothing for them, and to alter and repair worn garments by re-knitting. Meanwhile the spread of handknitting in Scotland and Ireland suggests that there too a mixture of cheap and high quality hand knitted stockings continued to meet a market need.

Scottish Hand Knitting

In Scotland bonnet making was established almost as early as capmaking in England; in 1496 the bonnet makers of Dundee had a guild, and Edinburgh, Aberdeen, Perth, Stirling and Glasgow followed suit during the next hundred years. Stocking knitters in the villages drew one traveller's attention in 1615, and a decree of 1661 ordered the teaching of knitting in all the parishes of the kingdom. Alongside the knitting of workaday articles, fine knitting was encouraged in some places: during the 1650s and 1660s one Aberdonian, employing about four hundred knitters and spinners, was said to be especially encouraging fine work. The fine lace shawls of Shetland came much later, being a nineteenth-century innovation, but fine handknitting still had a modest future ahead.

The detailed differences between districts, and between hand and frame knitted wares elude us, and we are driven by meagre evidence to speculate. But all knitters were open to influences from elsewhere, and we should not underestimate the consequences. The origins of fairisle knitting, which is the distinctive characteristic of knitting on the Shetland island of Fairisle, have been much discussed. Does it owe something to the Spanish influence? One of the vessels from the Spanish Armada sank on Fairisle's rocks, and the shipwrecked Spanish sailors spent many weeks on the island before being taken to Shetland. Did they introduce colourful Moorish patterns to the islanders? We are unlikely to find an answer to this question, but it is worth emphasising that Fairisle lay in the path of vessels trading between Scandinavia and the Mediterranean, and was much visited by them. So throughout the centuries the islanders had opportunities to adopt ideas from elsewhere. As for purchasers, every knitting region of Britain had its own pattern of trade and its own clientele. Many Lancashire stockings in the later seventeenth century, for example, were exported to Ireland, while many Irish stockings went to the New World. The stockings of Shetland were readily bought up in the eighteenth century by Dutch fishermen arriving for the summer season off Lerwick, and yet Holland had its own knitting industry. Was it because of the soft wool or the patterning as well? We cannot be sure.

Long Survival

Handknitting retreated in the nineteenth century in the face of competition from the knitting frame, but it never disappeared altogether. It held out best in isolated rural communities, which lacked alternative occupations, and intermittently it revived stoutly wherever knitters by some change of practice caught a fashion and found a secure market, as did the Shetlanders with their lace shawl.

The social significance of knitting in more isolated places was often described in the nineteenth century, but we can reasonably guess that convivial knitting circles lightened the labour of knitting for the market in earlier centuries as well. A vivid account was given by William Howitt in *The Rural Life of England* in 1844. "As soon as it becomes dark", he wrote, "and the usual business of the day is over, and the young children are put to bed, they rake or put out the fire, take their cloaks and lanterns, and set forth with their knitting to the house of the neighbour where the sitting falls in rotation, for it is a regularly circulating assembly from house to house throughout the particular neighbourhood. The whole troop of neighbours being collected, they sit and knit, sing knitting songs and tell knitting stories. Here they often get so excited that they say 'Neighbours, we'll not part tonight', that is, till after twelve o'clock".

FURTHER READING

Bennett, Helen, Scottish Knitting, Shire Publications, 164, 1985.
Buckland, Kirstie, 'The Monmouth Cap', Costume, XIII 1979, pp 23-24.
Croft, Pauline, 'The Rise of the English Stocking Export Trade, Textile History, XVIII, 1987 pp 3-16.
Hartley, Maria and Ingilby, Joan, The Old Hand-Knitters of the Dales, Dalesman Publishing Company, Clapham, Yorks, 1969.
Henshall, Audrey and Maxwell, Stuart, 'Early Textiles Found in Shetland, part II. Clothing and other Articles from a late seventeenth-century grave at Gunnister, Shetland', Proceedings of the Society of Antiquaries of Scotland, LXXXVI, 1954, pp 30-41.
Rutt, Richard, A History of Hand Knitting, London, 1987.
Thirsk, Joan, 'The Fantastical Folly of Fashion: the English Stocking Knitting Industry, 1500-1700', in Joan Thirsk, The Rural Economy of England, London, 1984, pp 235-57.
Turnau, Irene, 'The Diffusion of Knitting in Medieval Europe', in N. B. Harte and K. G. Pontings, eds, Cloth and Clothing in Medieval Europe. Essays in Memory of Professor E. M. Carus-Wilson, London, 1983, pp 368-89.

Wm Lee And The Invention Of The Knitting Frame

By Negley Harte

'THE STOCKING KNITTING frame was invented in 1589 by the Reverend William Lee, Vicar of Calverton in Nottinghamshire'. This apparently straightforward statement of fact can be found in many historical works. Some such statement, or words to the same effect, is repeated in the textbooks of economic history and in all the literature on the history of the textile industries. It states a belief that is widely accepted, not just in Midlands lore, but as part of the British textile tradition. Yet to the historian, with his professional concern with evidence, it presents a problem. Four hundred years after the event, the question has to be posed: what is the evidence that so undeniably significant a technological development as the invention of the knitting frame, of major importance for the whole hosiery industry, was initiated by so improbable a figure as a provincial clergymen at so early a date as 1589?

The Legend Of William Lee

In fact, there is no evidence that William Lee was Vicar of Calverton, nor indeed that William Lee was in Holy Orders at all. There is, moreover, no contemporary evidence that it was in the year 1589 that he invented the stocking-frame. And there is no

The supposed romantic origins of the knitting frame are illustrated in this Victorian painting of William Lee and the woman in the legend. A copy of this picture hangs in the knitting department of Leicester Polytechnic and carries the date 1889, produced perhaps to commemorate the tercentenary of the invention.

evidence at all for the existence of the woman, whether girl-friend, fiancee, or wife, who is said to have inspired the invention in the more romantic versions of the well-known account. Nor is there for the involvement of the other woman, Queen Elizabeth herself, who plays a role in the oft-rehearsed legend of William Lee.

The legend developed early. It was established within the following century. By 1677, when Robert Thoroton published his history of Nottinghamshire, many of the component elements were clearly already present, if in somewhat garbled form. Thoroton's account reads:

> At Calverton was born William Lee, Master of Arts in Cambridge, and heir to a pretty freehold here; who seeing a woman knit, invented a loom to knit, in which he or his brother James performed and exercised before Queen Elizabeth, and leaving it to one Aston his apprentice, went beyond the seas, and was thereby esteemed the author of that ingenious machine, wherewith they now weave silk and other stockings &c.

A copy of Thoroton's book, examined by William Felkin nearly two hundred years later, contains a manuscript note that this evidence, with its plausible circumstantial details, had been provided by an account given by one 'Johannis Story, Gent'. How this gentleman was able to provide information about events ninety or so years previously, however, is not indicated.

Before 1677, though not published at the time, a rather different account of Lee and his invention had been provided by John Aubrey, the famous collector of seventeenth-century gossip. Sometime after 1656 he noted the following about William Lee:

> Mr William Lee, MA, was of Oxford (I think Magdalen Hall). He was the first inventor of the weaving of stockings by an engine of his contrivance. He was a Sussex man born, or else lived there. He was a poor curate, and, observing how much pains his wife took in knitting a pair of stockings, he bought a stocking and a half, and observed the contrivance of the stitch, which he designed in his loom, which (though some of the appendant instruments of the engine be altered) keeps the same to this day. He went to France, and died there before his loom was made there. So the art was, not long since, in no part of the world but England. Oliver Protector made an Act that it should be fellony to transport this engine.

Aubrey cited his source for this story as information he took from 'a weaver (by this engine) in Pear-poole Lane' in 1656, when 'Sir John Hoskyns, Mr Stafford Tyndale, and I, went purposely to see it'. A few years later, John Evelyn, the famous diarist, also provided an eye-witness account. On the 3rd May 1661 he recorded that he 'went to see the wonderful engine for weaving silk stockings said to have been the invention of an Oxford scholar forty years since'. The hearsay elements of this evidence are expanded elsewhere in Evelyn's writings, where he mentions 'Mr Lee or Leigh, a curate in some obscure part of Sussex' as the inventor.

These seventeenth-century accounts, evidently, are confusing. Thoroton in the 1670s firmly placed William Lee in Calverton in Nottinghamshire as a Cambridge graduate; Aubrey in the 1650s and Evelyn in the 1660s have him in Sussex as an Oxford man. Aubrey and Evelyn — perhaps not independent sources — have him as a curate, while Thoroton only has him as a Master of Arts. Both Aubrey and Thoroton set a woman central, in one case a wife, while only Thoroton has the other woman, Queen Elizabeth, figuring in the story. They were all writing a generation or more after the events they purport to record. They had to rely upon the sort of hearsay evidence that Gravenor Henson was to struggle with over a century and a half later. In Henson's *Civil, Political and Mechanical History of the Framework-Knitters,* published in Nottingham in 1831, he says that his account of Lee and his invention was derived

The romanticised vision of William Lee as a clergyman in a portrait of unknown provenance.

from old people that he had talked to. There was doubtless some embroidery of his own.

> The invention of the knitting machine (since better known by the name of the stocking frame, and the workmen as framework-knitters) owed its origin, as is universally agreed, to a singular circumstance, the disappointed love of the inventor, the Rev. William Lee, curate of Calverton, in the county of Nottingham. This gentleman, it is said, paid his addresses to a young woman in his neighbourhood, to whom, from some cause, his attentions were not agreeable; or, as with more probability it has been conjectured, she affected to treat him with negligence, to ascertain her power over his affections. Whenever he paid his visits, she always took care to be busily employed in knitting, and would pay no attention to his addresses; this conduct she pursued to such a harsh extent, and he vowed to devote his future leisure, instead of dancing attendance on a capricious woman, who treated his attention with cold neglect, in devising an invention that should effectually supersede her favourite employment of knitting.

And so on. Henson noted his sources for this romantic account.

The greater part of his information was obtained from Mr Hardy, Twister's Alley, Bunhill Row, London, who was apprenticed in London in 1711, and died, aged 90, in 1790 — from Mr Woods, Godalming — and from an ancient stocking maker who died in Collin's Hospital, Nottingham, aged 92, and who was apprenticed in Nottingham in the reign of Queen Anne, and all of whom gave a similar account. This is in some measure confirmed by the arms of the London Company of Framework Knitters, which consist of a stocking frame without the wood-work, with a clergymen on one hand and a woman on the other as supporters.

The historian cannot but note that Henson was himself only five years old when Mr Hardy died, aged 90, in 1790 and not much older when his 92-year-old informant died in Nottingham. By the early nineteenth-century, what Henson gave as the oral tradition was well established, and generations of repetition had made their own additions to the memories of Lee that had developed soon after his own lifetime. Such traditions cannot be dismissed out of hand. We are dealing with legend rather than myth. But the historian has to attempt to seek out first-hand contemporary evidence specifically dated to 1589 and the years immediately following. Much effort has been made to establish the facts of Lee's life and his invention, and — so far as has yet come to light — there are only six contemporary references to William Lee himself. These pieces of evidence, each with a clear provenance, need to be carefully examined.

The Evidence Concerning William Lee And His Invention

The first known reference to Lee is a very important one. It shows clearly that it was indeed William Lee who invented the knitting-frame. Dated 6 June 1600 was a partnership agreement between William Lee and George Brooke in which it was recounted that

> . . . William Lee hath by his long study and practice devised and invented a certain invention or artificiality being a very speedy manner of working and making in a loom or frame all manner of works usually wrought by knitting needles as stockings, waistcoats and such-like . . .

The agreement stated that William Lee and George Brooke were to be 'co-partners' in the 'forming and making of the said new artificiality or invention of knitting works' for a period of twenty-two years,

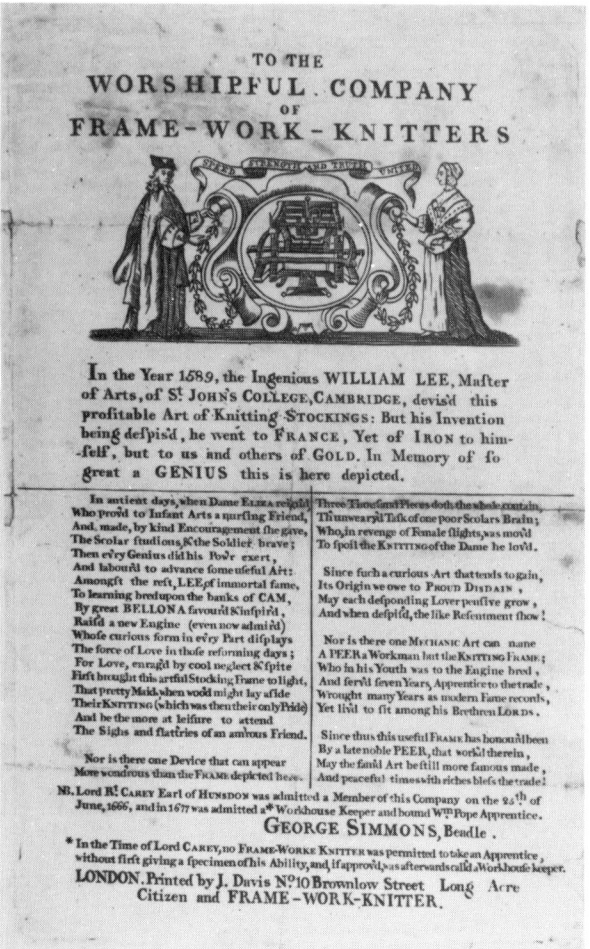

The late seventeenth-century arms of the Worshipful Company of Frame-Work-Knitters, supported by William Lee as a clergyman and the unknown female knitter.

sharing the resulting profits between them, beyond the first £200 which would be due to Lee himself. Brooke was to invest some £500 in the 'secret of the said invention' in order to develop the resulting 'knit works'. George Brooke was a well-connected potential patron for Lee, but there was little time for him to act as a sponsor or financier since in 1603 he was arrested on a charge of treason and was subsequently executed.

That Lee nevertheless continued to attempt to develop his invention is evident from the second contemporary reference. On 1 October 1605 he petitioned the Court of Aldermen of the City of London, describing himself as a 'Master of Arts' and as 'first inventor of an engine to make silk stockings'. He sought the freedom of the City of London by 'redemption' and also 'certain rooms to be granted unto him in Bridewell to work in'. ('Redemption' was the avenue to the freedom of the City by purchase open to those not entitled to the freedom — the right to pursue a trade — either by 'patrimony', i.e. inheritance, or by 'servitude', i.e. apprenticeship to a freeman). Lee's petition was referred to a committee, but there is no further reference to the matter in the minutes of the Court of Aldermen. If there was any result, therefore, it is not known. It seems likely that Lee did not press his request.

The third contemporary reference is to be found a few years later and indicates that Lee was still trying to develop his frame in London. In March 1609, the records of the Weavers Company of the City of London record William Lee, 'weaver of silk stockings by engine', as being admitted as a 'foreign brother' of the Company. He apparently paid £2 'in hand' for this privilege, and undertook to pay a further £1 'whensoever he shall set up any loom or sapyn (sic) to use the art of weaving'. The Weavers Company records do not record that the further sum of £1 was ever paid. It seems plausible to infer that Lee was having difficulty in establishing his invention.

The next two contemporary records of William Lee's activities both come not from London, but from Rouen in France. On 16 February 1612 a contract was signed between William Lee, 'an English gentlemen, at present a resident in this city of Rouen', and Pierre de Caux, citizen of Rouen, indicating that they had together 'organised a company for manufacturing stockings of silk and wool, upon a loom to be presently introduced into this country . . . '. The contract states that Lee was to 'supply four machines, in good condition, and ready for operation, besides the other four already delivered . . . ', and Lee agreed to teach the use of the machines to French apprentices as well as supplying six English workmen, 'skilled in the working and operation of these machines'. He also contracted to 'instruct and to teach one or more iron-

The late nineteenth-century monumental inscription to William Lee at Calverton: describing him as Reverend, as an MA, as of St John's College, Cambridge, and as vicar of the parish — all claims for which actual evidence is lacking.

workers the secret of manufacturing these looms and engines, without concealing anything whatsoever'. Money was to be advanced by de Caux to fund the establishment of Lee's knitting frame in Rouen. A further legal document, dated 1 March 1615, is less informative, but it confirms that 'Master William Lee, English gentleman' and two other Englishmen were still engaged in the 'occupation of knitting stockings' at that date.

These five pieces of evidence about William Lee, from London sources in 1600, 1605 and 1609, and from Rouen sources in 1612 and 1615, constitute the total known corpus of contemporary references

One of the earliest illustrations of the knitting frame, drawn by the Frenchman Hindret in the 1650s.

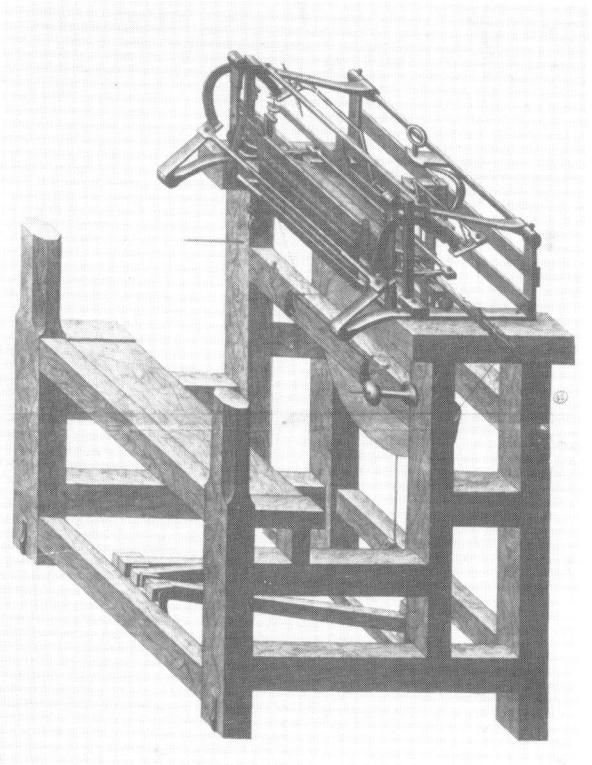

generated by the life and work of Lee himself. There is one other known contemporary reference to him, itself an important piece of confirmatory evidence, but unfortunately it occurs in two different forms. In 1607 Edmund Howes, one of the few contemporary writers to refer to technological change, noted in his edition of *The Abridgement of Summary of the English Chronicle:*

> This year 1589 was invented and perfected the art of knitting or weaving of silk stockings, waistcoats, coverlets and diverse other things by engines or steel loom by William Lee, sometime master of St John's College of Cambridge.

This reference appears to be the earliest indication that Lee's invention was made in 1589. A few years later, however, in 1615, Edmund Howes in a different work, his edition of *The Annals of England,* gives a different date and adds other information:

The stocking frame as it had developed by the end of the seventeenth century. (Science Museum, London).

> In the year 1599 was devised and perfected the art of knitting or weaving silk stockings, waistcoats, and diverse other things by engines or steel looms by William Lee, Master of Arts of St John's College in Cambridge, and after that he went into France, where he obtained a patent of the King, and there taught them that mystery, his servants were entertained in foreign nations as in Spain, Venice and Ireland and other places where they taught the secret of their art, and so it went through the world.

Three years later, in the 1618 edition of *The Abridgement or Summary of the English Chronicle,* Howes however returned to citing 1589 as the year of the invention, correcting his reference to Lee as 'sometime master of St John's College of Cambridge' to 'sometime Master of Art of St John's College, Cambridge', and adding:

> . . . and fifteen years after this he went into France and taught it to the French because he was not regarded in England.

Edmund Howes was evidently a well-informed writer. His second reference to Lee in 1615, giving the date 1599, could be read as a correction of his earlier account in 1607, especially since he adds information about Lee going to France and the early diffusion of the frame abroad, events that were very recent when he wrote. But then in 1618 he does correct a minor mistake and again re-asserts the 1589 date, though it cannot have been fifteen years later, i.e. in 1604, that Lee went to France, since the sources quoted earlier demonstrate that this must have been between 1609 and 1612. Perhaps the date 1599 in the 1615 account was simply a misprint, but it does add to the mystery of Lee.

The rest of Lee's life is very much a mystery. Milton and Anna Grass engaged in much amateur historical research for their book on Lee, and leapt to several conclusions, but they were able to throw little reliable light into the darkness. The parish registers of Calverton commence only in 1578, and so no record of Lee's possible birth there is confirmable. Many people by the name of Lee are to be found in Calverton in the late sixteenth century, including indeed several individuals called William Lee. One William Lee, yeoman, who died in 1607, had several sons, including a James and a William, and to William, the eldest, he left 'one ring of gold, in value worth 20 shillings'. The Grasses assume this William Lee to be *the* William Lee, resting heavily (though illogically) on Thoroton's remark that he was 'heir to a pretty freehold' at Calverton, combined with an imaginative leap of their own. A 'W. Leigh' matriculated at Cambridge as a member of Christ's College in 1579, but a further imaginative leap is needed to conclude that this was our man. The admissions registers at Christ's College, Cambridge

— where the Lee legend reaches its apotheosis in a commemorative stained-glass window — commences only in 1621, and that at St John's College, Cambridge, only in 1630, and so it is impossible to check on his possible membership of either of those colleges. 'W. Leighe' may have graduated BA in 1582 or 1583, but there is no record of his becoming an MA. At Oxford the trail is even weaker; the only William Lee there in the 1570s and 1580s has a well-documented career quite at odds with the known facts concerning our William Lee. Efforts to trace him in Sussex have not lead anywhere. There has been much speculation, especially on the basis of the possible Calverton and Cambridge bearings, but there are no more facts.

What is the historian to make of this evidence, such as it is? That William Lee was the inventor of a knitting frame in the late sixteenth century is clear. He described himself as a Master of Arts (though there is little to support this claim) and as a Gentleman (as a university graduate — and others — could), but it is improbable that he was ever a clergyman. He may well have come from Nottinghamshire, but it was London that was the scene of his first known operations. The London sources in 1600-09 show that he was struggling to develop his invention there, and the reference in the 1600 partnership agreement with Brooke to 'his long study and practice' could support the suggestion that Lee began work on the invention in 1589. But it seems clear that the invention cannot have been 'perfected' as early as that. The evidence from the City of London and from the Weavers Company in 1605-09 strongly suggests that Lee was having difficulty in bringing his invention into production — in turning, that is to say, his claimed invention into a practicable innovation. For reasons that can only be speculated about — the disapproval of the Queen, the lack of enthusiasm among the London vested interests, proto-Luddite prejudice, Lee's own lack of business experience — he left London between 1609 and 1612 and endeavoured to make a new start in Rouen. It seems likely that he did not benefit commercially from his invention in his own lifetime. Only in the following generation did his frame — or a development of it — come to be adopted as an actual innovation, with the resulting accretions of posthumous credit to William Lee.

The Historical Context of William Lee's Invention

Quite apart from the problems of disentangling fact from fiction in William Lee's own life, it has often seemed a puzzle to economic historians that so complex a piece of machinery was invented for knitting so far ahead of the mechanisation of spinning and weaving, the key changes in which did not take place until the industrial revolution period in the late eighteenth and early nineteenth centuries. In order to attempt to set the knitting frame in its proper context, it is necessary to understand the importance of hosiery in the sixteenth and seventeenth centuries in terms both of fashion and of production. The social and the economic context need to be appreciated.

From the late middle ages, men's legs were in fashion. The long flowing gowns common to both sexes and inherited from classical times gave way, for men (not women) to a new long-term fashion for shorter garments down to the waist and tighter coverings for the legs. In the sixteenth century the various forms of men's leg coverings were the subject of condemnation by moralists and attempted control by sumptuary proclamations. But the fashion gave rise to a new industry. Knitting, previously a household activity on a non-commercial scale, came to be undertaken for more than a purely local market. Originally producing knitted caps in the fifteenth century, the sixteenth century saw the fashioning potential of knitting being applied to leg garments, giving the term 'hose' a new meaning. By the last quarter of the century, a great variety of wool and worsted stockings were being knitted by hand in various parts of the country on a commercial scale, and indeed were finding export markets. Imported silk stockings were very fashionable and very expensive. They were beginning to be produced in England, and it was London which was the fashion centre.

Such was the buoyant market situation at the end of the sixteenth century which faced William Lee. Demand for all sorts of knitted goods was expanding, and the potential supply of hand-knitters was fully used up in many places, perhaps especially in London. If he began his inventive activity in Nottinghamshire, it would have been with the short fine wool produced by the sheep of Sherwood Forest. But the earliest recorded evidence places him in London, developing the frame for use with silk for

The model of Lee's knitting frame as re-created by Eric Pasold in the 1950s. (Pasold Research Fund).

stockings of the most fashionable sort. This is not altogether surprising, for, whatever his own experience of women was, their labour as a by-employment in the Midlands came cheap. It was a different matter in London with its rising wage rates.

It was a complex matter to produce a machine to knit, but knitting was essentially easier to reproduce by machinery than was either spinning or weaving. Nevertheless, how was it possible to create such a machine springing apparently precursorless out of sixteenth-century technology? This was a question which fascinated the late Eric Pasold, himself one of the leading hosiery manufacturers of the mid-twentieth century. It was his fascination with William Lee which stimulated much research on the subject and which led to his founding the Pasold Research Fund to stimulate further research into various aspects of textile history. In the 1950s he set himself the task of attempting to understand in a practical way how Lee had achieved his invention. It is worth quoting his own account:

> As a completed whole, Lee's stocking frame was an incredibly complex piece of machinery, but most great inventions rest on simple principles and only become complicated through application and improvements. Perhaps the machine of 1589 was simpler than the one we know. The earliest drawings we have of it are those made by Hindret in 1656. How much had it changed in the intervening sixty-seven years? I tried to find out by working backwards from Hindret's drawings, taking away every refinement, everything that was not essential to the basic operation of knitting, and in this way reconstructing a stocking frame resembling the one originally built by Lee.
> Using only the simple tools readily available to Lee, namely knife, hammer, saw, file, drill, chisel and scissors, and a frame for hardening the needles after they were filed and bent to the right shape, I built a simple model which functioned perfectly.

Eric Pasold thus proved that a mechanically inventive mind could create the knitting frame using the limited technology of the late sixteenth century. So complex a technological advance would not usually be expected to be made without preceeding partial achievements, but Pasold showed that it was actually possible.

That the new machine was not an immediate success is readily comprehensible in technological terms, and that the tinkerings of an outsider were unacceptable by vested interests is also easily understandable in economic and social terms. Yet by the end of the seventeenth century what has been described as the most complicated piece of machinery employed in the pre-industrial world was in increasingly extensive use in England and also in various European countries. Lee's achievement was marked by the rise of an industry on a new basis, as well as by the unfolding of a legend, and it is right that it should be the subject of anniversary celebration in 1989. The scope for further celebration, at various possible dates over the next few decades, should also be noted.

FURTHER READING

Gravenor Henson, History of the Framework Knitters *(1831; new ed. with intro. by S.D. Chapman, 1970).*

William Felkin, History of the Machine Wrought Hosiery and Lace Manufactures *(1867, new ed. with intro. by S.D. Chapman, 1967).*

Milton and Anna Grass, Stockings for a Queen: The Life of the Rev. William Lee, the Elizabethan Inventor *(1967).*

S.D. Chapman, 'The Genesis of the British Hosiery Industry, 1600–1750', Textile History, 3 *(1972).*

Joan Thirsk, 'The Fantastical Folly of Fashion: The English Stocking Knitting History, 1500–1700, in N.B. Harte and K.G. Ponting eds., Textile History and Economic History *(1973).*

E.W. Pasold, 'In Search of William Lee', Textile History, 6 *(1975).*

K.G. Ponting, 'In Search of William Lee...', Knitting International, 89, no. 1068 (Dec. 1982).

From Domestic To Factory Industry: Hosiery Statistics And Their Interpretation

By Stephen C. Wallwork

THE HOSIERY TRADE was for generations the staple industry for most of the East Midlands area, first as a domestic alternative or supplement to agricultural occupations, and then as a factory-based industry. Although there had been hand-operated knitting frames in workshops or small factories from the early nineteenth century, the factory system really started to develop in the mid-1840s, when steam power began to be applied to knitting machinery. Several accounts of the growth of the industry and its concentration in the East Midlands have already been published but none has adequately exploited the wealth of information available in various government publications of the nineteenth and twentieth centuries. This may be because, at first

Henry Doughty (c. 1830-1916), a Loughborough framework knitter who worked for Cartwright and Warner, a firm which was one of the pioneers of the factory system but used hand frames until the end of the last century.

sight, they appear to provide conflicting evidence. On further study, however, the data became largely reconcilable and are found to bring the long history of the industry into new and striking relief.

The history of the industry and the types of information available is best discussed in terms of four main periods. The first is the period of the domestic industry, from the invention of the stocking frame to the application of steam power to framework knitting in the 1840s. This period ends with a comprehensive survey of the industry published in 1845 as part of a report of a commission of inquiry into the condition of the framework knitters. The second period covers the initial growth of the power-based factory system, up to the publication of the first census of production in 1907. This was a period of increasing concern about the welfare of employees, especially children, in an age when production could be increased by making machines work all hours of the day and night. The government statistics in that period were compiled mainly to inform discussion of this issue. The third period is the turbulent one that included two world wars and, between them, a boom period followed by a slump. The fourth period is that from the end of the second world war to the present day, during which rapid post war growth has been accompanied by rampant inflation, followed by recession and some recent recovery.

Framework Knitting

The early growth of the hosiery industry may be traced from estimates of numbers of stocking frames in different parts of the country assembled in the well-known books of Blackner (1815), Henson (1831) and Felkin (1867). Blackner and Henson were both framework knitters, while Felkin began his career in hosiery and became a lace manufacturer. Felkin also provided data for government enquiries in 1833 and 1845, which included details of the numbers of different types of frame (in work or temporarily idle), the thread used and the products, and also estimates of the total numbers of people employed. The latter, averaging rather more than two per frame are clearly rough estimates. This is understandable in view of the domestic nature of the trade, since the framework knitter would involve his wife and children to varying extents. Fig. 1 shows the numbers of frames within the British Isles and within the Midland Counties and illustrates the tendency for the industry to become localised in these counties.

Advent Of The Factory System

The statistical sources that cover the period of initial growth of the power-based hosiery factories arise from the need to comply with the provisions of the various Acts of Parliament concerning factories and workshops. The statistics in these documents, summarised in Fig. 2 give the numbers of people and knitting frames associated with the factory system even though some of these people and machines were employed in domestic environments. They do not, however, take account of the work done by independent framework knitters and their families, who still existed in considerable numbers. This is clear when one compares Felkin's estimate of 150,000 people involved in the hosiery trade in 1866 with the official government figure of 6,580 which is the total employed under the Workshop and Factory Acts in 1867/8.

A large reduction between 1871 and 1907 in the number of hand frames operated under the factory system is responsible for the levelling-off in the total number of factory frames (hand plus power-operated) after 1871. There was an associated levelling-off of males employed in factories, since the majority of machines were operated by men. However, power frames had a much higher productivity than hand frames, so ancillary employment was generated for many more women as cutters, seamers and makers-up.

Although no published estimates of the total number of people employed in the hosiery trade have been found for dates after 1866, the decennial censuses of population from 1841 onwards provide some guidance. Fig. 3 shows the total employed in England and Wales or in Great Britain, and also the numbers of males employed, according to the censuses. It also shows the corresponding numbers for the counties of Derbyshire, Leicestershire and Nottinghamshire, taken together. (From 1921, there are two sets of census figures: the industry tables showing those involved in hosiery manufacture, and the occupation tables giving the numbers of machine knitters and 'tenters' — machine attendants.

It is the former tables that continue the single set of

Fig. 1. Number of frames before the introduction of power frames.

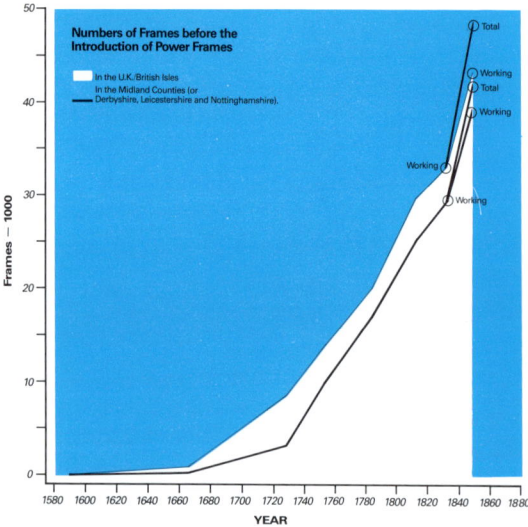

Fig. 2. Growth of the hosiery factory industry, 1862-1907.

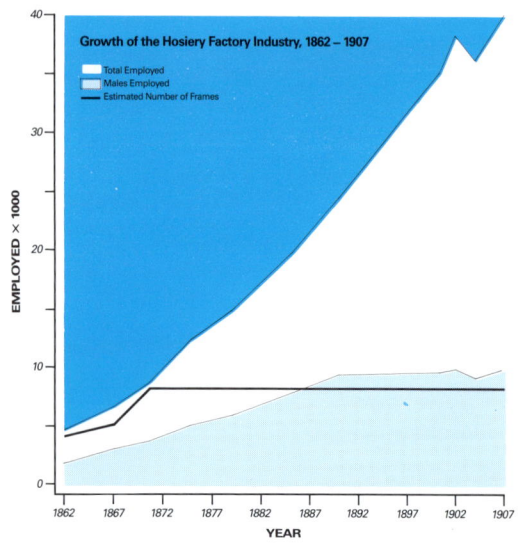

Fig. 3. Census of population, industry tables, 1841-1971. Numbers employed in the hosiery manufacturing industry.

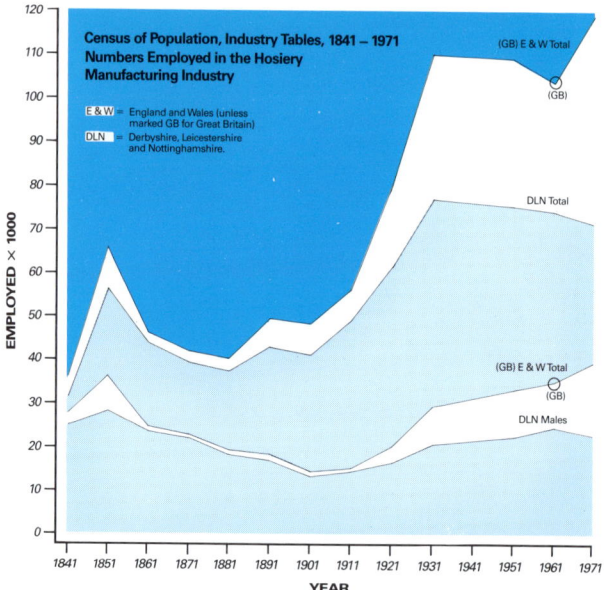

tables up to 1921 and which are illustrated in Fig. 3. These census figures still fall far short of the total involved in the industry as estimated by Felkin; e.g. from 1861 to 1871, the census total falls from about 46,000 to about 42,000 yet Felkin's estimate, quoted above, suggests an involvement of about 150,000 in 1866. Examination of the source about to be discussed shows that this must be because the census figures probably include little or none of the extensive part-time domestic employment that had always been a feature of the industry.

The only complete data for the early years of the transition from domestic to factory production are for Nottinghamshire, which appear in the factory returns in Miscellaneous Statistics for 1866. They represent only about 40 per cent of the industry, but they are probably representative and are certainly revealing when compared with a survey of frames in 1844:

	1844	1866
Domestic frames/ framework knitters	16,382	15,250
Domestic units/workshops	4,621	4,700
Factory machine operatives	0	3,700
Factories	0	31
Total employed (UK)	c.100,000	c.150,000

Clearly the traditional domestic industry was resilient to competition from industry over this period and changed mainly by shifting further from narrow to wide frames. The apparent peak in employment suggested by the 1851 census figures (Fig. 3) is probably an inconsistency in the groupings of occupations from census to census (which, in any case, only recorded a third of the people in the industry) rather than a genuine boom. If so, depression did not seriously affect the domestic industry until the late 1860s.

The decline in the numbers employed in the second half of the nineteenth century according to the census of population returns, shown in Fig. 3, contrasts with the rising numbers of those employed under the Workshop and Factory Acts shown in Fig. 2. Insofar as the decline is genuine, it must represent the depression of the domestic industry at a later stage of mechanisation. A close-up view of this effect, showing that it was by no means uniform, may be obtained by examining the detailed enumerators' returns. The numbers of framework knitters and stockingers for four representative Nottinghamshire villages are shown in the following table:

Fig. 4. Employment, numbers and distribution of factories and output this century; and the effects of the two world wars.

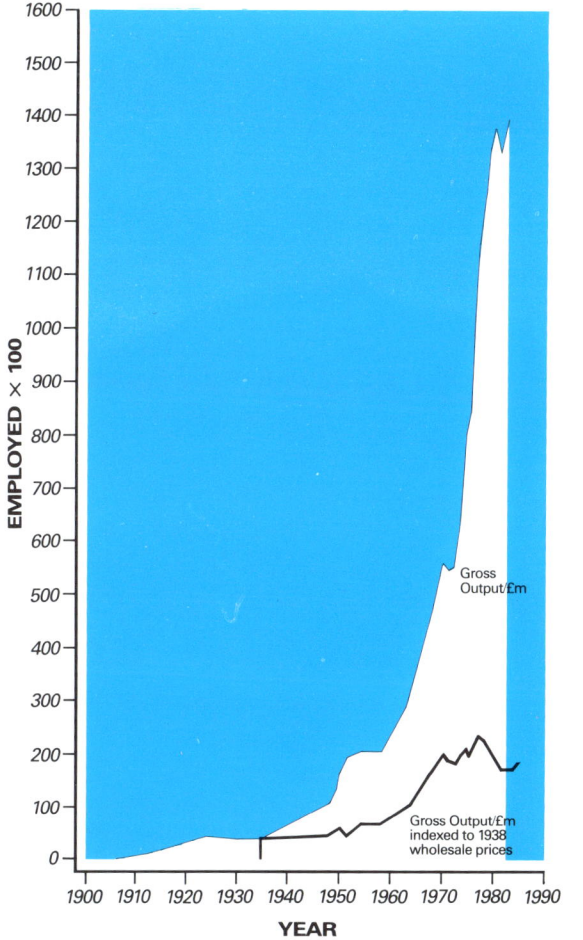
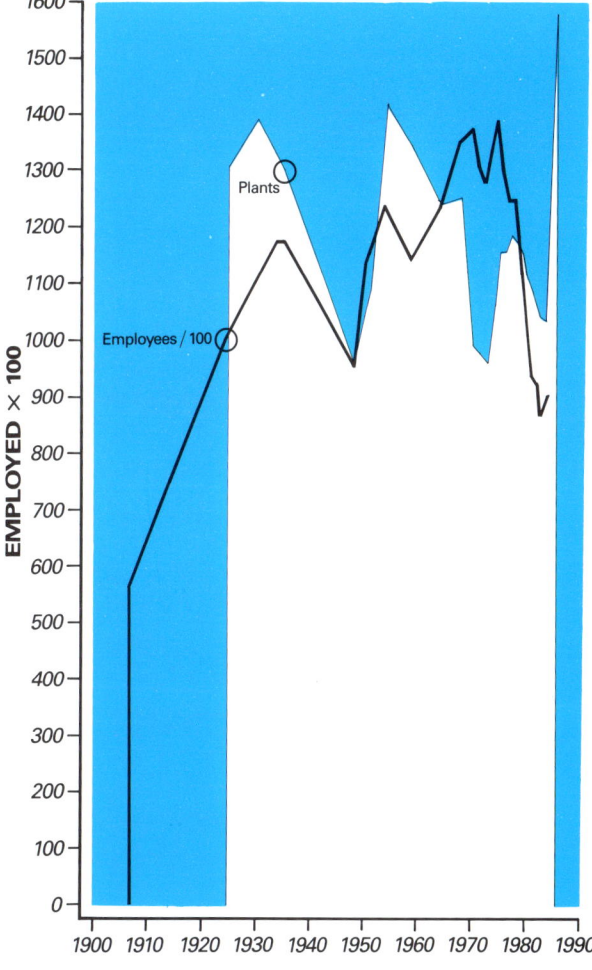

	(Frames)				
	1844	1851	1861	1871	1881
Beeston	275	188	111	81	47
Bingham	58	50	26	14	3
Ruddington	343	360	345	399	340
Sutton Bonnington	110	02	68	72	58

The marked decline in numbers in Beeston was due to the attractions of the growing lace trade and, later, of other industries. An even greater decline in Bingham was caused mainly by people leaving the village to seek work in Nottingham and larger industrial villages. Ruddington maintained its numbers because it was the main centre, outside Nottingham and Leicester, of the wide stocking frame. This was several times more productive than the original narrow frame but was opposed by the Luddite tradition in much of the manufacturing region. Sutton Bonnington suffered from its proximity to Loughborough, where the major innovators of the factory system, Cartwright & Warner and Paget, operated. (William Cotton worked for Cartwright & Warner, while the other early mechanised system of production was introduced by Arthur Paget, a member of an old family of Leicester and Loughborough hosiers and bankers).

Fig. 3 shows the almost complete localisation of the hosiery industry in the East Midlands from 1861 to 1881 (about 95 per cent), and the increasing role of women. An even greater increase in the proportion of women is shown when only the factory-based industry is considered, as in Fig. 2. By 1907, the totals of men and women employed in the industry according to the census of population (Fig. 3) were very similar to the numbers reached by that date shown in Fig. 2. This indicates that most of the hosiery workers must by then have been on factory payrolls, either as production workers or as domestic ancillaries. On this measure, the transition to the factory system took over two generations (60 years), from the late 1840s to the Edwardian era.

The Early Twentieth Century

From 1907, much more information about British industry has been collected and reported in the censuses of production. The most important items of information from this source have been summarised in Fig. 4.

The problem about counting the number of hosiery firms is that government statisticians kept changing the definitions. The data on small firms were automatically included in the 1907 and 1924 censuses of production but for 1912 only firms employing 5 or more people were involved in the complete survey and others were asked to state only the average numbers of people employed. From 1930, separate data are given in the censuses of production for small firms, now defined as those employing less than 10 (and from 1958, less than 25). However, from 1954, estimates are given in the census reports for the whole industry, including small firms, and it is these data that have been plotted. From 1970 onwards, the census of production

Ruddington Museum, the best-preserved framework knitting complex. The cottages (centre) were built in the early 1820s, the flanking workshops in the 1850s, a period that also saw the building of the earliest hosiery factories in the area.

A glove finger stocking frame at the Wigston Framework Knitting Museum. The machine and other types of specialised wide frames, proved resilient to factory production.

information has been published as a *Business Monitor* series, in some of which warp knitting figures have been quoted separately. They have been added into the totals.

Figs. 3 and 4 show that the first world war did not interrupt the growth of the hosiery trade. The shortage of male employees no doubt had less influence on this industry than on most in view of the characteristic high female employment. The aftermath of the war, however, saw a significant change in the distribution of the industry. The peacetime resurgence was brought about mainly in the south of England. This was partly based on the powerful pull of London as the principal market, including the revitalisation of women's hose, but it was also due to a wave of new entrepreneurs, some of them migrants from the Continent. Their firms included Klinger Manufacturing of Edmonton who, as early as 1926, were said to employ 3,000 producing art-silk hosiery (many more than any firm in the East Midlands), Kayser Bondor at Baldock and Ballito at St. Albans and Pasolds (Ladybird Knitwear) at Langley near Slough. The result of the redistribution of the industry was that the concentration in the East Midlands dropped from the peak of 95 per cent in 1861 to about 70 per cent in 1931.

Recent Times

The second world war, by contrast with the first, did cause an interruption in the development of the hosiery industry, as shown in Figs. 3 and 4. There was no decennial census in 1941 because of the war but comparison of those for 1931 and 1951 shows a small decline in the total numbers employed in hosiery, even though there was a small increase in the number of male employees. The acute shortage of labour after the war was mainly responsible for a further dispersion of the industry. Firms were compelled to open branch factories in rural and mining areas, where there was still a surplus of female labour. There were also government controls on building which aimed at inducing manufacturers to invest in new plants in areas where the old staple industries, such as coal mining, cotton manufacture and ship building had been concentrated.

In economic terms, it may be seen from Fig. 4 that there had been a hiatus in the growth of the British hosiery industry from about the time of the great depression in the late 1920s and early 1930s up to about the end of the second world war. The gross output fell between 1924 and 1930, and the numbers of firms and plants fell between 1930 and 1935. The post-war dispersion, referred to above, caused a temporary small increase in the number of plants but by 1971 this had fallen back to its 1948 level. This contraction was first met by the closing of outlying branch factories, thus temporarily restoring some of the traditional concentration in the East Midlands. The anomaly of an apparently escalating growth of gross output from the end of the second world war up to 1980 is seen, on closer examination, to be mainly due to inflation. If a cumulative hosiery goods wholesale price index is compiled on the basis of 1939 = 100, and this is used to scale down the gross output to 1938 values, then a much smaller growth is found and this virtually came to an end in 1970.

By 1971, the concentration of the industry in the East Midlands had fallen again, to about 60 per cent, and the number of employees in the whole country had almost reached its post-war peak of about 140,000 in 1974. After that, there was a steady decline in employment to a little over 100,000 by 1983. However, there are indications from the last points on each graph in Fig. 4 that the industry thereafter started to grow again. Finally, it is remarkable that, in spite of its varying fortunes, the East Midlands has shown remarkable tenacity in retaining the major part of the British hosiery industry for over 250 years.

The knitting room at Ruddington Framework Knitters Museum, Nottingham. This is typical of surviving workshops set up towards the end of the last century.

A framework knitter's workshop at Gunthorpe, typical of hundreds in Nottinghamshire, Leicestershire and Derbyshire last century. This was the kind of small enterprise which gradually disappeared with the advent of the factory system.

A Fashion History Of Knitting

By Terry Brackenbury

FASHION IS A term with a wide meaning; some interpret it narrowly and use it to define the work of the twentieth century couturiers and named designers and, prior to this century, the clothes worn by the Lords and Ladies associated with the Court. In this article fashion is used in its widest sense, to describe the ambient fashion of the period whilst admitting all the variations due to social class, occupation, status, wealth and personality.

The Tudor Period

In the history of knitting, technology and fashion have been inseparable partners and undoubtedly each has influenced the other throughout. Whether William Lee's invention was the result of obvious pressures due to the fashion of the period or not, it was undoubtedly fortuitous in that it occurred towards the beginning of a 250 year period in which men's fashion was dominated by the wearing of knitted hose with breeches. This fashion started in Europe in the reign of Henry VIII but had evolved from the dominant dress of the Renaissance period over the previous century. This fashion could be best described as close fitting tights of cut woven fabric, made from wool or silk, or possibly from linen, hemp and leather. Knitting is not mentioned in contemporary accounts of this period but could well have featured as an obvious way of obtaining a close fit.

Such garments were illustrated in the fifteenth and sixteenth century paintings of the Italian Masters. Paollo Uccello in the "Miracle of the Sacrament" 1468 in the Palazzo Ducale Urbino, depicts contemporary male figures in tights, some with contrasting colour legs. Such tights were worn with long sleeved short jackets, waisted and ending at slightly above crotch level. A painting by Antonio Pollainolo of "Tobias and the Angel" in the Pinacoteca, Turin, shows more elaborate dress forms with Tobias depicted in a tunic, not waisted, that descends lower than the crotch and, along with the tights, *hosen* are worn on the lower legs. The date of this painting is possibly about 1480. The paintings show the movement of fashion through transitional stages so that by the early sixteenth century the skirt of the jacket or tunic was transformed into breeches and, by the reign of Henry VIII the breeches were worn with knitted "trousers" or "close hose". Often the breeches of this period included a "cod-piece" which was regarded as vulgar by the critics of fashion which, even then, were numerous.

The stockings of early sixteenth century England were hand knitted of worsted yarn, varying in quality with price and worn according to social status. Silk hose were not recorded until 1550 when Sir Thomas Gresham presented a pair to Edward VI. Such silk hose were knitted in Spain and possibly France very laboriously on knitting pins made of fine wire. The royal wardrobe accounts of the Tudor period show they were at first very expensive. By the reign of Elizabeth I trunk breeches for men worn with hose of silk or worsted were standard dress over a wide level of society. At the Court level of society all of the clothes became richly embellished with gold and silver and much lace. Clothes became very much an exhibition of the wealth and status of the wearer.

The word hose or *hosen* was originally used to describe both the breeches and the over-socks of the earlier periods. At an intermediate stage cut-fabric

'The decapitation of Saints Cosmas and Damian' by Angelico (1470). Similar fifteenth and sixteenth century paintings by Italian masters are notable for their depiction of the fashions of the day. Contemporary male figures wear tights, some with contrasting colour legs.

stockings were actually attached to the breeches and the combined garment was called hose. During Elizabeth's reign the term stabilised into the knitted portion of the dress that we would recognise today. The term "nether stockes" was also used to describe the knitted article. In a contemporary account the Puritan writer Philip Stubbs in his book *The Anatomy of Abuses* describes them in disparaging words: "And to such impudent insolency and shameful outrage it is now grown, that every one almost, though very poor, having scarcely forty shillings wages by the year, will not stick to have two or three pairs of these silk nether stockes, or else of the finest yarn that can be got, though the price of them be a royal, or twenty shillings, or more commonly it is; for how can they be less, when, as the very knitting of them is worth a noble, or a royal, and some much more. The time hath been when one might hath clothed all his body well from top to toe for less than a pair of these nether stockes will cost".

Other articles were hand knitted in the fifteenth and sixteenth centuries besides men's hose. Ladies wore hose and socks, less ornamental than the male version but netheless containing decorations, clox that could be exposed by a flash of the ankle. Woollen caps were worn by men, a fashion dating back to the fourteenth century. William Felkin, in his chapter on hand knitting, gives a good account of the evidence, including protective laws to support this. Other knitted articles included "knitted petticotes", knitted gloves and "knitted slieves", which were attached to dresses.

The Stocking Frame

The introduction of the knitting frame did not destroy this breadth of hand knitting. All of the evidence suggests that the early framework knitters concentrated solely on hose and socks until the diversification of the eighteenth century. It is said that Elizabeth's first silk stockings were knitted in England but undoubtedly the very best quality came from Spain, richly encrusted with gold and silver threads. Her enmity of, and long war with, Spain undoubtedly affected her rejection of Lee's original patent and her entreaty to produce fine silk stockings.

After the death of Elizabeth I and the growth of the framework industry in the later seventeenth century, the fashion for men continued to be stockings of varying lengths worn with breeches. Knee-length boots were worn on some occasions and, almost always, when riding. Boot socks were worn

Front view of a knitted frock coat dated around 1780 which is in the National Trust collection at Blickling Hall, Norfolk.

Rear view of the same coat. 18th century garments of this type were generally worn with breeches and below-the-knee hose.

on these occasions to protect the costlier finer hose. These garments gradually became the products of the frame.

Fashion was intimately involved in the "Great Rebellion" as the two sides were as much contrasted by what they wore as by their political creeds. The Parliamentarians were characterised by sober and, indeed, sombre dress in browns, grey and black, the Royalists more flamboyant in Cavalier attire. Fortunately for the early framework knitters, both sides wore hose. The Parliamentarians wore plain unornamented hose and the Royalists heavily embroiderd and worked hose. The sober dress persisted among the clergy, writers and Protestant intellectuals well after the Restoration (1660). Such dress was part of the Puritan Revolution and would have been worn by Milton, Bacon, Bunyan and Dr. Johnson. During the whole of the seventeenth century women's dress hid the legs, but ladies wore hose and sometimes socks to the benefit of the hosiery industry. At the Restoration, a dramatic expansion of trade and commerce took place and Britain secured its foothold in America, India and Africa. Overseas markets and domestic prosperity benefited the knitting industry amongst others and rapid expansion took place.

Innovation On The Stocking Frame

In the eighteenth century this expansion continued and was accompanied by an outburst of innovative activity concentrated in the Nottingham area. This innovation was largely aimed at increasing the design

Sporting activities in the late 19th century led to previously-hidden garments being revealed and to knitted garments being designed specifically for individual sports. The birth of knitwear as we know it today came from fencing tops like these, featured in Harpers Bazaar, 1889. (©Dover Pictorial Archive series).

scope of the frame and diversifying the products. Garments of all descriptions including gloves, waistcoats, breeches, coats and lace pieces were produced. In spite of this range there were no garments knitted on frames that could now be recognised as knitwear.

The century started with fashion being influenced by the already contrasting styles of Restoration and Puritan. These styles eventually merged to a dress for men consisting of jackets, high waisted at the front, with tails at the rear. Such jackets were usually double breasted but at various times were worn with the lapels, comprising the length of the front of the jacket, turned back and buttoned down. This was eventually stylised into a dress form whereby the lapels were incapable of fastening and were heavily encrusted with embroidery and jewels. Such jackets have influenced military dress to the present day. The jackets were worn with breeches of a more tight fitting profile than previously with hose commencing below the knee. Shoes were worn and on the upper body shirts and waistcoat. The shirts were often embellished with lace at collar and cuff.

All elements of the above clothing were knitted although very few examples of garments other than hose have survived. The Platt Museum, Manchester has an outstanding waistcoat made of knitted silk fabric in which the pattern is generated by carefully placed stripes of space dyed yarn. Blickling Hall, Norfolk, an exceptional building in the possession of the National Trust, has in its costume collection, a man's jacket and trousers knitted in plain worsted fabric dyed grey with a possible date of 1780. Such garments are very rare and no collated records of the whereabouts of such garments exist. Women's garments were also knitted and mention is often made of dress fabrics. None, to the best of my knowledge, have been identified.

Of major importance to knitted goods was the introduction of cotton into Nottingham about 1730, at first as a luxury fibre. Demand for hose made from cotton was high. But the feature of the introduction that was to have a major influence on events in Nottingham in particular was the combination of loop transfer techniques and cotton yarn to produce point lace pieces. Such pieces were profitable to produce as they could be made much cheaper than the hand twisted pillow laces. The demand for cotton yarn in the Nottingham area persuaded first Hargreaves and then Arkwright to establish their first ventures in the town.

The fashion demand for lace also encouraged Nottingham mechanics to search for ways of making true twist lace mechanically. John Heathcoat's patents of the early 1800s resulted in and established a new and wealthy industry in Nottingham and its surrounds as well as in Tiverton to where John Heathcoat emigrated.

During the first century of framework knitting,

although the industry responded to the demands of fashion, only one fabric was produced, "plain" fabric. In the eighteenth century ingenious Nottingham framework knitters produced variations of structure and patterning including rib fabric and warp knitting. The machine remained essentially the same however and was modified with attachments. The structures were both to satisfy existing fashion demands and to suggest new fashions.

The French Wars And Victorian Years

The nineteenth century was welcomed in with war, first the French Revolutionary War followed closely by the Napoleonic War. There was also a revolution in fashion which, associated with the general depression of trade during the conflicts, was to spell disaster for the framework knitters. The fashion change was that men began wearing trousers, and breeches with hose ceased to be generally worn after 1810. This particularly hit the luxury trades knitting silk and cotton. Contemporary accounts and some modern historians associate the problems that produced Luddite activities to production methods, making shoddy goods, short cuts etc. Fashion is rarely mentioned as a major contributory factor.

On the positive side the Napoleonic War resulted

Knitwear was extremely popular in the 1920s and as this hand-knitting pattern shows, design was remarkably advanced. This lace panelled cross-front jumper came from BB Wools.

in a provisioning task of Herculean scale. Wool socks, wool hose, sailor's warp-knitted tunics and increasingly underwear was required to equip the huge armies fighting in Europe. It is conventional to point to the fact that Leicester with its concentration on woollen goods production largely avoided the Luddite activities. For a short period from 1790 to 1820 ladies' skirt lengths rose approximately from the ankle to slightly above, resulting in increased patterning being applied to ladies' hose. The length dropped again and remained long for the remainder of the nineteenth century.

The nineteenth century saw increasingly an obsession with underwear. Ladies began to wear drawers for the first time. Men wore shirts (vests) of knitted construction some of which were as heavy as winter sweaters. Jane Rapley has written a lucid account of this development which was to lay the foundations of the outerwear of the twentieth century. On the technological front the last century saw the introduction of the rotary frame in France followed by Cotton's Patent in England, enabling hose to be produced semi-automatically. Later in the nineteenth century sporting activities, swimming, cycling, running, team sports etc became increasingly popular and were accompanied by appropriate knitted garments usually in heavy two coloured stripes. On the June 1889 cover of *Harper's Bazaar* is a picture of a group of young ladies at a fencing club. The key figure is wearing a striped set-in sleeved, hip length tight fitting jumper with white shirt collar. The jumper is close fitting and is worn with neckerchief, ankle length full skirt and a loose scarf tied to hang from waist to lower hip.

In the last 20 years of the last century knitwear emerged as definable garments worn as a general part of the fashion of the day. Ladies and children began wearing jumpers and cardigans and later knitted skirts, dresses, coats and shawls. The production of such articles was intimately connected with the invention of the latch needle and the development of needle selection devices. This recognition of knitwear as a fashion article was accompanied by the widespread popularisation of hand knitting as a hobby made possible by the writing of knitting instructions in popular magazines. By the Edwardian era knitwear was part of everyone's wardrobe where it has remained to the present day. Pauline Stevenson has collected together in her book on Edwardian fashion advertisements of the early 1900s with examples of "cotton, wool and cotton/wool hose including cashmere hose at 1s 3¾d a pair".

The hose are illustrated and there is a great emphasis on vertical stripes in black with another colour. Other brand leaders began to advertise in women's periodicals at this time. Thus in 1902 "Two Steeples" were advertising vests and knickers for children, "Night Comfort" sleeping suits, ladies nightdresses in knitted cotton, pure wool "Jersey" suits for boys "Wash and Wear", and ladies' combinations in wool and cotton and girls' knit suits in all wool unshrinkable!

Our Own Time

The twentieth century has seen knitwear established as a part of general fashion throughout all of the style changes that have taken place. Knitted hose and subsequently tights have featured in every department of ladies' fashion from the turn of the century. Knitting including warp knitting is the established means of making underwear for both sexes. This century has also seen inroads made by knitting into the province normally held by woven fabrics. The popularity of jersey fabrics, however, has fluctuated widely being governed very much by macro-fashion trends.

If we were to stand back and look at twentieth century fashion and describe it in general terms, we could say that in spite of macro-variations it has been remarkably static. Men, throughout the past 90 years, have worn trousers, jackets, hovering about hip length, shirts, ties, half-hose and an extra layer coat in inclement weather. Hats for men have varied very little although the popularity of actually wearing them has fluctuated considerably. Women's dress has also varied little in its basic components, but more widely in the detail of macro-fashion than men's clothing. Dresses, skirts, blouses, jackets, coats, jumpers, cardigans, stockings have been constant features of women's clothing in this century. The twentieth century has also seen the periodic borrowing by women of men's fashion.

The most remarkable thing about the past hundred years has been the rise of the couturier accompanied by the opposite phenomenon of the ready-to-wear industry. Both are related in that they make use of predictive designing to supply the demands of various sections of the population. Prior to this clothes were produced in a much more interactive consultation with the ultimate customer and the customer directly decided the trends in fashion. This is a very simplistic view of the process as would be the description of the present process as being prescriptive, the imposition of the views of the few on the many. Any designer who designs what the ultimate customer does not want is doomed. It is a common misconception that fashion is dictated by the present day designers, but in truth nothing has changed and designers merely perceive demand before it occurs.

Fashion Trends

In spite of the continued growth of the knitting industry and the wearing of knitted articles throughout this century, the knitting industry has not always been treated kindly by fashion. The changes in fashion detail and form that take place from time to time result in more or less demand for particular knitted articles. On at least two occasions this century whole industries have been annihilated by changes in fashion. The first was the destruction of the fully-fashioned hose industry in the late 50's and early 60's by the change from seamed stockings to the bare-legged look. The second was the ruin of the double jersey industry in the early 70's by the move away from textured polyester towards natural fibre looks.

The last quarter century has been characterised by two prominent factors. Firstly the rise of variable fashion where, at any one time, differing social groups will adopt radically different dress from the mainstream of fashion. Secondly knitwear has had an almost continuous rise in popularity and a place in mainstream fashion. It could be argued that the first phenomenon has been with us for centuries and has already been alluded to in the Restoration period, but the phenomenon is now entrenched and "Street Fashion" sometimes influences mainstream fashion in the long term. The second phenomenon is mostly connected with the apparent increase in leisure activity in the Western world. Even if the activity is only sitting and watching TV people feel the need to

Designed by Armani in 1980, this sweater was the forerunner of the hugely popular padded shoulder look which ran through most of the 1980s in knitwear and dresswear.

British, and in particular London, designers in the 1980s regained some of the fashion supremacy of the 60s. Typical are these knitwear designs by Body Map from 1980.

change their clothing to more relaxing forms; mostly these include knitted articles. This has been accompanied by an increased participation in sporting activity, squash, tennis, running, jogging or other activities. Most of these activities involve a "uniform", almost always knitted, to provide freedom of movement. Some of these uniforms have spilled over into general fashion and people wear sports tee-shirts, track suits, jogging suits in situations other than those for which they are intended.

From all reports knitwear is, at the time of writing, passing through one of its troughs. We can only hope that this will not be of long duration. A major factor in this peak and trough cycle is that knitwear and knitted articles are mostly regarded as accessories in the fashion industry. Couture designers and named designers do not, on the whole, design knitwear. Knitwear design tends to be the province of the specialist, and so is underestimated or under-used by the designers of "Fashion" because they do not understand it. In spite of knitwear being a dominant feature of fashion throughout the 20th century, in McDowell's *Directory of Twentieth Century Fashion,* one would scarcely know it existed. This lavishly illustrated book hardly has any examples of knitwear of the present century although it is at the peak of its development.

It would be churlish not to mention some designers that have specialised and have been influential in raising the concept of knitwear in fashion, including Mary Farrin, Kay Cosserat, Sarah Dallas, Bridget Foley, Vanessa Keegan, Sandy Black, Julia Pine, Patricia Roberts, with profound apologies to the many others I have omitted and to the many designers whose professional skills are hidden behind brand names.

Let us hope that the next 400 years of knitted fashions is as challenging and varied as the last.

FURTHER READING
Jane Rapley
Pauline Stevenson

Marketing And Distribution: How Today's System Evolved

By Stanley Chapman

THOUGH MARKETING has necessarily played a key role in the development of the hosiery and knitwear industry, it is the aspect about which we know least. Manufacturers themselves have traditionally been very secretive and in any event concentrated their minds largely on production while wholesalers and retailers have revealed as little as possible about their sources. Nevertheless this sector has seen as much change as any other, and the dramatic developments this century provide a fascinating story.

First we must survey the features of change over several centuries from the early domestic system of production to the present time. This will provide not only the context but a fuller appreciation of the magnitude of change in our own times. The history of distribution is most easily represented in a diagram identifying the five stages of growth from the sixteenth to the twentieth century (Fig. 1). At each period except the first the heavy box shows the strongest element in the chain, the one that initiated the production sequence. The longer boxes bringing together two elements show where and when there was a close association between two of the elements such as between manufacturers and merchants in the early Industrial Revolution.

HISTORICAL SYSTEMS

(1) The Blackwell Hall Period

The rise of the domestic system of manufacturing in the later Middle Ages saw provincial organisers focusing on the various London markets, including the cloth market at Blackwell Hall and hosiery in Wood Street. These markets served not only the population of the capital but, increasingly, provincial shopkeepers and dealers who came to London twice a year to buy their stocks. This is the system so strikingly portrayed, at a mature period of its development, by Daniel Defoe in his *Tour through . . . Great Britain* (1724-26).

So far as we are aware, there was no particular dominant party in the distributive chain; indeed the system recalls that of the constitutional system of checks and balances (King-Parliament-Judiciary) in which eighteenth century Britain rejoiced. However, London was undoubtedly the fulcrum of the system and London merchants much the richest and most numerous in the land, while provincial manufacturers were clearly satellites.

(2) The Early Industrial Revolution

The second half of the eighteenth century saw not only the dramatic rise of the factory system in cotton in the north of England, but with it the rapid emergence of a class of successful mill owners who became merchants. For more than half a century (c1760-1815), the northern manufacturer-merchants set the pace, though Leeds and Manchester did not supersede the capital as centres of the textile trade much before the end of the century. The hosiery industry came late to the factory system and scarcely participated in this development.

(3) The Morrison (Cheap Warehousing) Period, c1820-1865

The commercial tribulations of the Napoleonic War and post-war depression ruined or enervated many of the first generation of northern producers, and the post-war depression saw calamitous overproduction and tumbling prices. In this climate, a group of opportunist London wholesale drapers led by James Morrison (Fore Street Warehouse Co.) siezed the initiative, establishing a new style of low-margin high-turnover warehouse. The northern manufacturers never regained the marketing initiative, but a handful of Manchester warehousemen imitated the London system.

(4) The Heydey Of The Great Wholesalers c1865-1940

Ultimately the most successful of the great warehousing concerns were Cooks of St. Pauls and I & R Morley in London and John Rylands & Co, in Manchester. In the second half of the nineteenth century these and other successful firms increased their grip on the trade by integrating backwards into manufacturing, buying up factories during periods of depression in trade, I & R Morley owned nine factories, seven of them making hosiery and knitwear. The wholesalers generally succeeded in keeping the small manufacturers and retailers well apart, despite challenges from a few early 'up-

Origins and growth 33

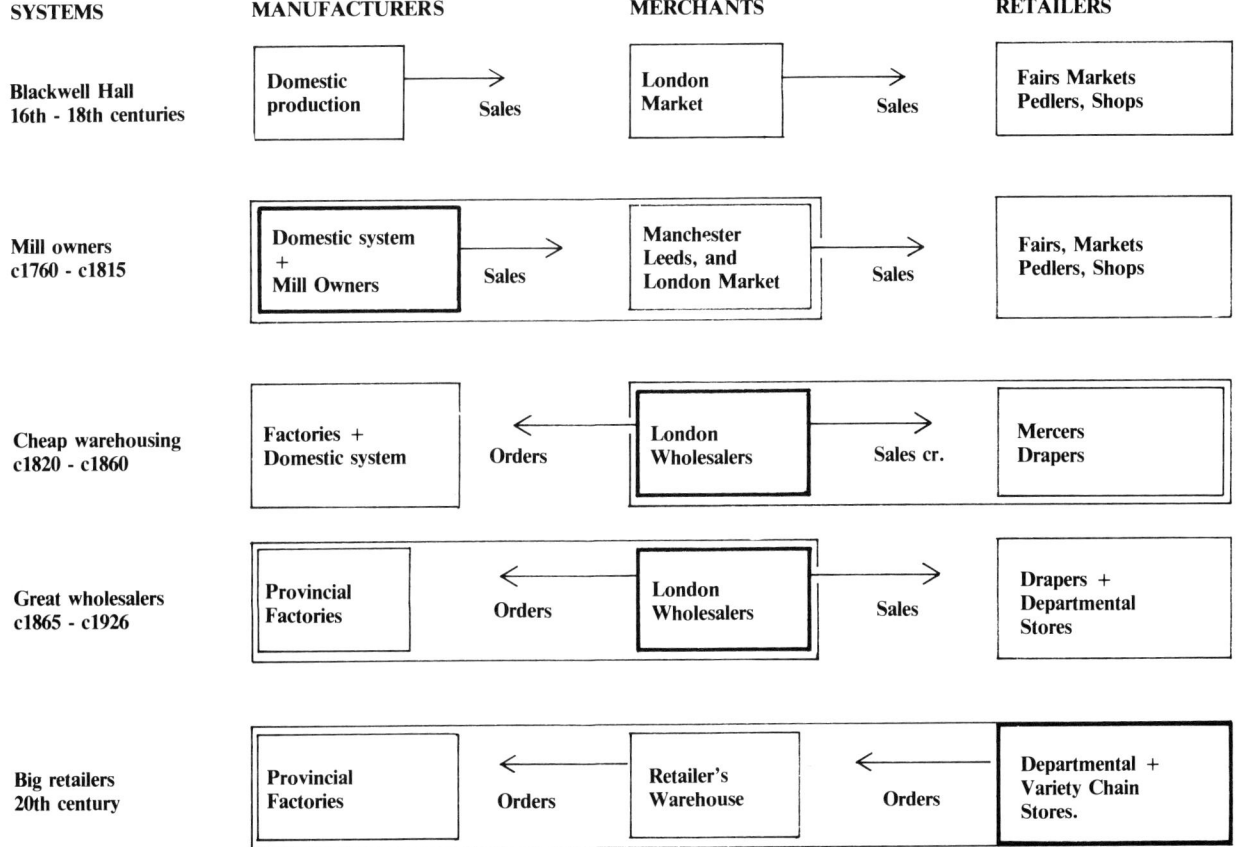

Key: the heavy box shows the strongest element in the chain at each period.

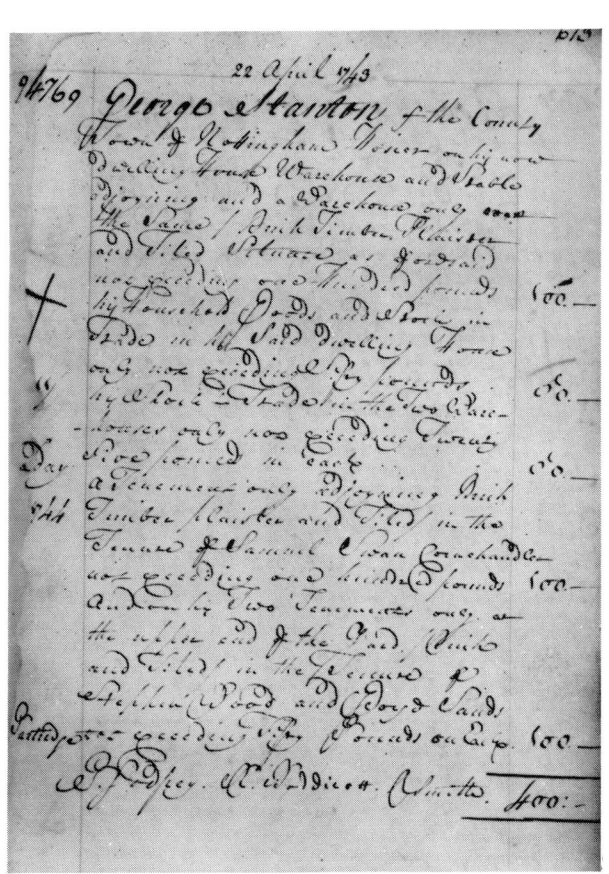

Sun Fire Office insurance policy of George Stanton, Nottingham merchant hosier, April 1743. His premises consisted of his 'dwelling house', warehouse and stable adjoining (£100) and he had stock worth £50 in his house and the same amount in the warehouse. He also owned an adjacent tenement and two cottages in the yard, all of which represented a substantial business at the time.

market' producers like Wolsey and Lyle & Scott who tried to sell their brands direct to retailers.

(5) The Big Retailers Period 1926 To Date

Growth in the scale of retailing and much improving communications evidently offered the possibility of direct links between manufacturers and the great stores from at least the end of the last century. Several departmental and variety chain stores are known to have dealt directly with their respective producers but it was not until Marks & Spencer took the initiative in the 1920s that the warehousemen's control was openly challenged and their control very gradually superseded.

At the height of their power at the end of last century and early years of this, the great 'home trade' houses of London, Manchester and Glasgow were truly kings of the trade, handling 90 per cent of hosiery and knitwear produced in the UK. They stood between a thousand or so small hosiery and knitwear manufacturers on the one side and 30,000 -

34 *Origins and growth*

Samuel Morley, MP (1809-1886), who built up I & R Morley into much the biggest hosiery warehousing and manufacturing firm of the last century. This illustration first appeared in Vanity Fair of 15 June 1872.

50,000 small retailers (variously estimated) on the other. The capital of the greatest wholesalers was enormous by the standards of the day. In 1920 Cookes of St. Paul's, the largest firm, topped £3 million, while Rylands and Morleys were more than half that sum and Arthurs of Glasgow was over £1 million. Few merchant banks in the City could show this kind of capital while there were scarcely any hosiery manufacturers with capitals above £100,000 at the period.

Morleys were the strongest wholesaler in hosiery and knitwear, their turnover being about ten per cent of the whole trade around the turn of the century. Threatened by direct connections between a few major manufacturers and departmental stores, the wholesalers formed a militant organisation called the Wholesale Trade Association to intimidate the many small manufacturers and persuade the drapers that they could provide the only good service to retailers. In the 1930s the W.T.A. struck Corah off their list of recognised suppliers and issued dire warnings to the chain stores not to deal directly with the manufacturers.

I & R Morley's warehouse in Wood Street, London soon after it was rebuilt in 1854. For generations, Wood Street was the centre of the hosiery and 'Manchester Goods' trade of Britain and was packed with scores of large and small warehouses. The whole area was destroyed in the blitz in 1940 and textiles never returned.

To maintain their supplies, Marks & Spencer appointed a secret agent in Leicester (Leslie Hinmer of Turk Smith Ltd), who negotiated coded deals with important W.T.A.-recognised firms such as Wolsey, Pool Lorrimer and Tabberer and Foister, Clay & Ward. By 1946 the wholesalers were taking about 50 per cent of the hosiery and knitwear produced in Britain.

The erosion of W.T.A. power was renewed after World War II. Lord Hollendon of I & R Morley, the chairman of the W.T.A was not blind to the subterfuge but could not find evidence to 'convict' the offending Leicester manufacturers. It is a fascinating story, as enigmatic as any MI5 drama, but no Peter Wright has come forward to tell all, notwithstanding that the most famous wholesalers have now all disappeared, gobbled up by Courtaulds in the late 1960s.

Rise Of The Chain Stores

The long domination of the great warehouses helps to explain several of the features of the system that superceded that of the leadership of the chain stores,

Cooke, Son & Co's warehouse in St Paul's Churchyard, c. 1900, the largest in London at the time. Cooke's always had a hosiery department, as many other general warehousemen did.

and particularly of Marks & Spencer. As Marks & Spencer and the chain stores cast in the same mould won a sequence of battles against the W.T.A. a leadership vacuum was created at the centre of the system. A few enterprising hosiery and knitwear manufacturers succeeded in creating an independent identity by branding and advertising, probably the most successful of these was Wolsey of Leicester, which ran a highly successful advertising campaign for 'unshrinkable' men's underwear from the turn of the century.

Selling direct to retail: Wolsey's advertising in 1901.

"WOLSEY" Trimmed Combination.

Wolsey was in fact the brand name of Robert Walker & Sons, who in 1920 united with W. Tyler Sons & Co. (Leicester hosiery manufacturers), Boswell Brown (a London wholesale house) and J. & W. Bastard (two West Riding spinning mills) to form a £2 million combine. But there was little in the industry to compare with this scale of enterprise; even the other well known brand names of the period were operating on a much more modest scale. The vast majority of manufacturers remained small and dependent on bigger concerns, whether yarn suppliers, wholesalers, chain stores, or departmental stores.

Israel Seiff identified the hosiery industry's leadership problem as early as 1947 when he gave evidence to the Hosiery Working Party that looked into the needs of post-war reconstruction. According to the formal record of his evidence, Seiff:

> deplored the lack of research in the industry and said that Marks & Spencer were proposing to get out complete specifications from raw material stage onwards with a view to achieving continuity of production right through. Thus the names of suitable spinners who make the count of yarn etc, to produce the optimum quality for a particular knitting machine and garment might be suggested to the manufacturers . . . It was really the job of the retailer to decide what colours, sizes and styles were needed but for the manufacturer to decide on the technical questions of production. In fact however Marks & Spencer had had to extend into this field.

During the war Simon Marks and Israel Seiff had sat on various technical committees which brought together teams of scientists to work out the specifications for the 'utility' schemes and they now introduced and refined this approach in their own laboratory. They began with a handful of scientists working in a Nissen hut near Baker Street head offices under the leadership of Dr. Paul Rosin (of PLUTO fame) and Dr. Eric Kann from Heidelberg.

Some of the technology and organisation that Marks & Spencer's scientists and production engineering department promoted during the following 30 years are still familar in the industry. For several years after the war they sponsored the adoption of Wildt Mellor Bromley's RTR8 knitting machines. From the 1960s Marks & Spencer worked with Dubied to develop new types of garments and stitches; the Arran stitch, which was in vogue for about 20 years (1966-86) was perhaps the most striking success. In the late 1960s Bentley Engineering sought Marks & Spencer's support before introducing a machine to knit stockings and tights without leaving a seam in the toe.

It has been suggested (by the *Financial Times,* no less) that Marks & Spencer were the original moving

Michael Marks' original stall opened on Leeds market in 1884 (top). Above, 1941 and number 21 Seven Sisters Road, Holloway was acquired by M & S from the London Penny Bazaar Company. Above right, purpose-built fascia for the opening of 120/122 Fishergate in Preston on 26 July, 1929. Right, Marks and Spencer's flagship store on London's Oxford Street at Marble Arch with 136,000 square feet of selling space.

force behind the 'double jersey boom' of the late 1960s and early 1970s. More recently the chain store has been reported to have been active in promoting Gerber computerised cutting machines.

Marks & Spencer had 60 or 70 suppliers of hosiery and knitwear by the 1970s. Bigger suppliers had an entrée to the Marks & Spencer boardroom while small firms with a promising new idea could be lifted to undreamed-of prosperity by Baker Street's encouragement and an increasing flow of orders. The major manufacturers kept sales representatives active at Baker Street several days a week, catching every shift in the wind of consumer demand, but small firms were more vulnerable to volatile movements of fashion and could be left with unsold stocks. The old family leadership of M&S were emotional people and most loyal to those who served them well, so that early suppliers like Corah and Marathon always had to be looked after.

Inter-war innovators like Djanoglys (N.M.C.), Kayser Bonder (John Goodenday), the Prevezer brothers (Derby & Midland Mills) and Jersey Kapwood (Dessau and Kaplovitch) enjoyed particular favour, though no supplier was ever allowed to fall below Marks & Spencer's exacting requirements. Innovators like Brentford Nylons (Kaye Metrebian) could quickly become major producers for the St. Michael label. It is easy to show that the manufacturers who were well geared into the Marks & Spencer system were in general more prosperous over the long period than those who remained dependent on the wholesalers or supplied their own branded goods direct to retail. Until the 1980s the chain store sector was growing fastest and main suppliers benefited accordingly.

Marks & Spencer's support of the industry was not limited to the manufacturing process. The chain store always stopped short of backward integration but actively pursued a policy of maintaining a 'flexible' (competitive) industry, especially during the 1960s when Courtaulds, Coats Paton and the Dawson Group seemed intent on gobbling up every independent manufacturer. Kearton wanted to take over Corah at one time but Marks & Spencer rebuffed him and generally encouraged good family businesses to remain independent; perhaps that is why Courtaulds' acquisitions included so many 'lame ducks'. However, Marks & Spencer were not above promoting a merger themselves when they saw that the steam had gone out of a supplier firm. This is not to suggest that the chain store's ideas were uniformly successful; their endeavour to promote new life at Bentleys (as early as 1967-68) came to nothing and that to arrest the decline of Corah in the early 1970s ultimately proved discouraging for Baker Street executives.

It is not too much to suggest that Marks & Spencer have exercised a kind of benevolent leadership over that section of the industry that supplied it, for one hears many other ways in which their influence was exercised. From the 1930s Marks & Spencer directors or chief executives held annual strategy reviews with main suppliers so as to indicate their plans for two or three years ahead and help the producer with his capital investment plan. Capital could be lent to help purchase the required machinery. Good ideas were taken round from one supplier to the next so as to diffuse 'best practice'. Help might be offered with senior appointments if a manufacturer ran into trouble.

Current Developments

It is of course well known that Marks & Spencer's traditional policy has been modified since Lord Rayner took the helm. The 'long runs' on which the major suppliers prospered for years have come to an end and some of the old paternalism has gone. The old emotional ties with suppliers are evaporating with more emphasis on performance. A system of devolution at Baker Street compels the managers of all departments to show a respectable profit. There is greater emphasis on flexibility to meet the challenge of the design-centred retailers that have been relatively more successful in the 1980s.

Nevertheless, much of the Marks & Spencer tradition remains, including the intimate connection with the hosiery and knitwear industry. When *The Times* asked Lord Rayner if the nature of his company was changing he answered: "I hope not . . . I am totally committed to the traditions that have been created". When Richard Greenbury was appointed chief executive earlier this year (1988) he said: "Simon Marks and Israel Seiff set down the principles of this business and we never forget them" and one of the traditions he most admires is the 'famous' special relationship with his suppliers. It is fair to say that Marks & Spencer are not only imitated by numerous competitors, but that they have set the pace and style of the post-war distribution system in British textiles. It remains to see what they can do for Europe and the USA, and whether the new fashion stores and textile conglomerates will set a different pace.

FURTHER READING
F. M. Thomas, *I & R Morley: A Record of a Hundred Years (1900).*
Goronwy Rees, *St. Michael. A History of Marks & Spencer (1969).*
K. K. Tse, *Marks & Spencer. Anatomy of Britain's most efficiently managed company (1985) esp. Part II.*
Eric Pasold, *Ladybird, Ladybird. A Story of Private Enterprise (1977).*
This subject is the least well documented of those covered in this commemorative book.

Three Centuries Of Knitting In Scotland

By Clifford Gulvin

SCOTLAND IS JUSTLY famed for its high-quality woollen textiles, and her high-class knitwear has become a by-word for its luxury 'feel', pastel colouring, and enterprising design and styling, only made possible by the industry's firm attachment to the purest of raw materials, in particular lamb's wool and that most aristocratic of fibres, cashmere. This emphasis upon quality arose at an early stage in the evolution of the industry giving rise to a highly skilled labour force, selective markets both at home and abroad, and until recently, a form of business organisation based on small or medium-sized 'family' firms rooted in the local community.

Although formerly widely dispersed in lowland Scotland, mechanical knitting became concentrated largely in the Border counties, especially at Hawick and Dumfries, and in the West of Scotland south of the Clyde, including Glasgow itself. These regions developed their own specialisms; the Borders became wedded to high-grade fully fashioned (that is body-shaped) garments fully wrought on flat frames and dyed in the wool or yarn. The West of Scotland section became important only after 1900 and concentrated on medium-quality products for the mass market made from 'tubular' hosiery which was then 'cut-and-sewn' into a garment away from the frame and dyed 'in the piece'. Latterly this distinction between the 'cut-ups' of the West and the 'fully fashioned' garments of the Borders has been reduced; considerable quantities of albeit cheaper 'fashioned' garments are now produced in the western region too.

Origins

Scottish framework knitting, however, seems to have originated at Haddington, near Edinburgh during the 1680s, almost a century before it appeared in the Border counties. Narrow frames and workers were brought secretly from London by the merchant founders of the New Mills Woollen Manufactory who were given financial encouragement by the Scottish Parliament to begin the manufacture of fine cloth and hosiery to try to emulate English success in this sector. The venture was a commercial failure well before the Act of Union sealed its fate, but frameknitting lingered on in Scotland sufficiently for a Master Hosiery Society in Glasgow to be given a Charter of Incorporation in 1756.

The introduction of commercial knitting into the Borders dates from 1771 when the chief magistrate of Hawick, John Hardie, brought four narrow frames from Glasgow, set up in business in the town and trained local workmen to the frame. In the following twenty years frameknitting slowly spread to other Border settlements, helped by English settlers who already knew the trade. Initially coarse worsted hose were made for local consumption but by the 1780s lamb's wool stockings were beginning to oust the cheaper variety. A combination of rising incomes and the exigencies of the French wars led to a growth in demand for woollen hose so that by 1815 Hawick

Stocking frame being worked in the Hawick firm of J. Laing and Son around 1911. (Picture courtesy Hawick Museum).

itself boasted 500 stocking frames. That year also saw the founding of the enterprise now known as Pringle of Scotland.

By 1815 a total of about 1,500 frames were working in Scotland from Dumfries and Hawick in the south to Montrose and Arbroath in the north, with considerable numbers in Glasgow and Edinburgh. By the 1840s, however, 80 per cent of Scotland's frames were located in the Borders, 60 per cent of which were in Hawick itself, the other significant centre being Dumfries. By then the dominance of fully-fashioned garments was already evident with only two hundred of Scotland's 2,500 frames at work on 'spurious' goods, that is the tubular, cut & sew' products more associated with the East Midlands of England.

Scottish Advantages

We may suggest several reasons why frameknitting mainly took root in the Border counties. Ample supplies of improved Cheviot wool existed locally; swift-flowing rivers and streams provided power for the emerging yarn-spinning mills using the new spinning technology, on whom many small cloth and knitting firms came to rely for their supplies of yarn; labour was relatively cheap in this marginal agricultural area which was shedding some labour as sheep farming was extended and enclosures took place; large urban markets were to hand at Glasgow, Edinburgh, Carlisle and Newcastle; Hawick and Dumfries were served by improving communications, firstly road, later rail. These factors helped give the region a comparative advantage over other centres which accordingly concentrated on other forms of activity to which they were more suited.

The funding of a knitting industry in Scotland at the time of the 'Industrial Revolution' did not mean the rapid establishment of a factory system. For much of the 19th century the organisation of the knitting industry resembled pre-industrial forms as much as 'factory' ones. It is perhaps best described as a semi-domestic form of organisation. Woollen yarn was progressively spun in water and steam-driven mills owned by an emerging capitalist class, who distributed the yarn to stockingmakers who worked often at some distance from their employer in 'frame-shops'. Here children were used to wind the yarn, often for their own father, while women and older children worked at home doing the seaming and 'trimming' (making button holes, sewing on buttons etc.). They were paid from the wages of the frameknitter.

A working group in the Peter Scott factory ('The Tabernacle') in 1904. By this time several companies had installed factory hand knitting machines (as opposed to handframes) which were used primarily to knit men's seaters and cardigans to imitate the chunky garments being hand knitted in Shetland and Fairisle at that time. Demand for women's knitwear built up during the 1920s.

The Scottish Framework Knitter

Because of the heavy physical exertion and concentration required on the handframe, the stockingmakers worked irregularly, much to the annoyance of employers seeking to increase output. It was rare for much work to be done on Mondays, and during the rest of the week frequent breaks were taken to read newspapers, drink, or go fishing. This informal rhythm of work resulted in furious activity on Thursdays and Fridays to meet the deadline of the 'count' on Saturday mornings when completed work would be paid for at the master's warehouse and fresh yarn would be distributed. The frameknitters were renowned for their stubborn independence and were frequently accused of indiscipline and drunkenness.

However the frame was a pre-industrial implement which could hardly be operated at the same level of intensity as mechanised factory equipment. The tension between employers' expectations of their workforce and that of the stockingers themselves largely resulted from the technological lag between spinning and knitting. Moreover the frameknitter saw himself not so much as an employee as a petty master who made garments to sell to his merchant-capitalist, cum yarn-spinner. Well into the second half of the 19th century he had to work out his own knitting instructions from the size and guage information he was given, and work up the garment to the correct shape and style. He was responsible for hiring labour for winding and seaming etc, which was not always found within his own family. The payment made to him for making stockings or underwear was referred to as a price not a wage.

However over time this 'independence' became somewhat illusory; it became rare for a frameknitter to own his equipment and if he retained for some time control over the process of production, he very soon lost control of what was produced and its subsequent disposal to the customer. Nonetheless the fancy nature of Scottish products, together with a relatively small and concentrated workforce, combined to give the Scottish frameknitter a bargaining power which was denied to most of his English counterparts. He never fell victim to the notorious 'bag-hosier', the scourge of the English knitting districts.

After 1800 it became progressively difficult for small hosiers to retain their independent status as the yarn producers could readily impose their will via their control over raw materials, yarn supplies and dyeing facilities. But while the handframe reigned supreme it was still possible for men with only a small capital to set up in business on their own account. Lyle & Scott, for example, was founded by two men with only £500 each in 1874; Innes Henderson, better known by its later name of Braemar, was started with £1,000 in 1868. The founder of Peter Scott & Co. (in 1872) was a twenty year old handframe knitter. The origins of Wm. Lockie & Co. are similar.

Advent of the Factory System

It was the advent of powered knitting machines which transformed hosiery into an industry in the modern sense. The first steam-powered frames were installed in the Borders in the 1850s but power knitting spread only slowly before Cottons Patent frames took control of the process in the 1880s and 1890s. For long, steam frames were regarded in Scotland as unsuited to the fancy wool trade if not for silk, and manufacturers clung to the handframe which had undergone no fundamental change since its original invention. It was still possible to set up in business with handframes in the 1870s and Lyle & Scott was only one of several Hawick firms which delayed introducing steam frames till the 1890s. Once adopted, however, the modern knitwear factory, often a highly integrated organisation, was made possible, with the production process now centralised.

Manufacturers, however, had long sought to concentrate the stockingmakers on mill premises, or in their own 'shops' to facilitate managerial control over working practices and quality of production. This had met with only limited success and irregular work practices in knitting continued to be a thorn in the side of the employers, who were themselves stuck fast in traditional practises such as making deductions from stockingmakers' wages for the use of machinery, and refusing to take responsibility for seaming and trimming.

Although fancy hose continued to be produced, from the 1850s Scottish knitwear became increasingly associated with woollen under-garments ranging from vests, shirts and pants to ladies combinations and body belts (usually known as cholera belts).

Hawick stocking maker at work in the early part of this century. Note the glass globe which was used to focus light on the needle bed and fabric.

400th Anniversary of the Knitting Industry

1589-1989

Knitting International
Formerly The Hosiery Trade Journal

LEADING TECHNICAL/MANAGEMENT JOURNAL FOR HOSIERY, UNDERWEAR, KNITWEAR AND KNITTED FABRIC MANUFACTURERS

国际针织（中文版）
Knitting International (Chinese edition)

TECNICA DEL PUNTO

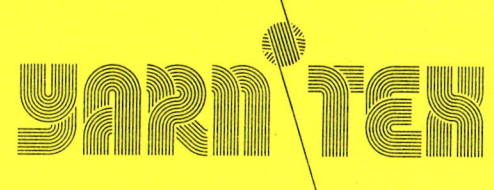

Knitting News

INTERNATIONAL KNITTING BOOKSHOP

A World-Wide Service To A World-Wide Industry

FERRY PICKERING PUBLISHERS, EASTERN BOULEVARD, LEICESTER LE2 7BN, ENGLAND
TELEPHONE (0533) 548271. FAX (0533) 470194. TELEX 341088

SCOTTISH COLLEGE OF TEXTILES
(A Central Institution of Higher Education)

SCOT is a College:

★ Which has an international reputation for producing Honours Graduates and Diplomates in Textile Design, Chemistry, Textiles and Clothing Studies.

★ Which has diversified successfully into Accounting, Computing and Business Studies Courses.

★ Which has extensive research facilities, with a wide ranging programme of projects sponsored by Government and Industry.

★ Which has various Post-graduate Courses to MPhil/PhD level.

★ Which has plentiful accommodation on and off campus in a thriving Borders town which is easily accessible to main centres of population.

For further details apply to Dept M1/88. The Scottish College of Textiles, Netherdale, Galashiels, Selkirkshire TD1 3HF. Tel 0896-3351. Fax 0896-58965.

Ruddington Framework Knitters' Museum

CHAPEL STREET, RUDDINGTON, NOTTINGHAM NG11 6HE

We welcome visitors...

The Museum consists of a group of 1829 purpose-built cottages and workshops—including *working* machinery—which have been restored to illustrate the living and working conditions of 19th century framework knitters.

Opening times for 1989...

**Tuesday, Wednesday, Thursday, Friday, April—October 10.00a.m.—4.00p.m.
All Bank Holiday Mondays, or by appointment throughout the year.**

Enquiries: Phone (0602) 846914.

Admission...

Adults £1.50. Children 75p. Concessionary Family Rates to Museums Association Passport Holders.

The Textile Institute

ANNUAL WORLD CONFERENCE 1989

TEXTILES: FASHIONING THE FUTURE
MATERIALS · METHODS · MARKETS

NOTTINGHAM · UK · 16/20 OCTOBER 1989
(in conjunction with the William Lee Quartercentenary Celebrations)

The Textile Institute, which operates under a Royal Charter, is the international society for those professionally committed to the design, manufacture, use, understanding or marketing of textiles or any end product derived from fibres.

- *Qualifications to enhance the professional standing of members.*
- *Contact through its groups, sections and conferences.*
- *Publications, including the monthly 'Textile Horizons', learned journals, proceedings, 'International Textile Calendar' and 'Textile Terms and Definitions'.*
- *Information on all aspects of the textile industry, research and educations.*

The Institute welcomes applications from individuals for membership with or without qualifications and from companies and organisations for Patron Membership.

Enquiries about membership, publications and conferences to:

The Textile Institute
International Headquarters
10 Blackfriars Street
MANCHESTER M3 5DR
UK
Telephone: 061-834 8457
Telex: 668297
Telefax: 061-835 3087

*P*ARTNER WITH THE KNITTING INDUSTRY

ICI (UK) Fibres, Hornbeam Park, Hookstone Road, Harrogate, North Yorkshire HG2 8QN. Telephone (0) 423 872821
ICI Fibres is a business of ICI Chemicals & Polymers Ltd., a member of the ICI Group

Leavers and Raschel Lace Manufacturers

BELPER STREET WORKS . ILKESTON DE7 5FJ
DERBY . ENGLAND

TELEPHONE (0602) 325031 . FAX (0602) 440590 . TELEX 378318 CLUNY G

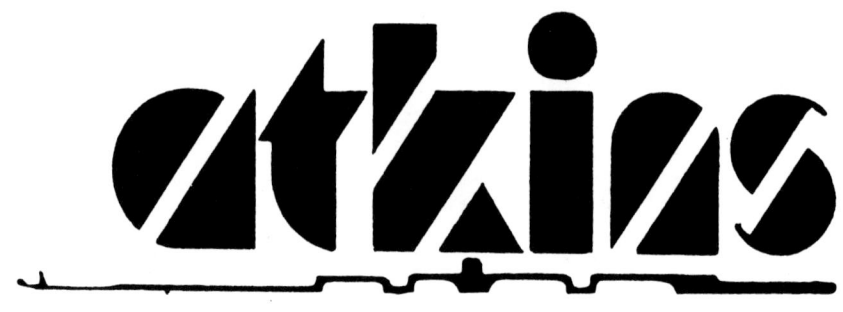

of Hinckley Ltd

MANUFACTURERS OF QUALITY HOSIERY SINCE 1722

ATKINS OF HINCKLEY LTD.
P.O. BOX 3, BOND STREET, HINCKLEY, LEICESTERSHIRE LE10 1QX

Telephone (0455) 251300   Facsimile (0455) 251369   Telex 341826

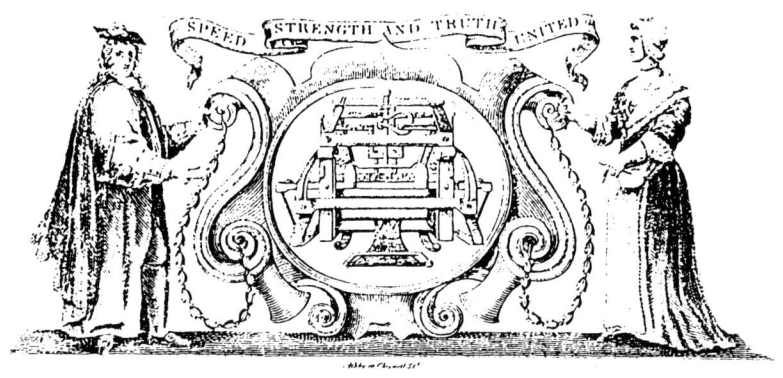

THE WORSHIPFUL COMPANY OF
FRAMEWORK KNITTERS
CELEBRATE 400 YEARS OF INNOVATION AND PROGRESS.

William Lee's invention of the knitting machine in 1589 began the evolution of the entire knitting industry in the UK and later throughout the world and in 1657 it led to the incorporation of the Framework Knitters Livery Company.

THE INSTALLATION DINNER
Wednesday 19 April 1989

The first of the Livery Company's two principal events to mark this historic year will be the Installation Dinner at the Plaisters Hall, London Wall.

This superb Hall provides a lovely setting for such a festive occasion and this year tickets will be available to all members of the Livery, their Ladies and Guests.

A senior member of the Government will be the Guest of Honour and many leading figures are expected to attend.

CELEBRATION BANQUET
London's Guildhall, Wednesday 11 October 1989

The Celebration Banquet, to be held in the truly magnificent setting of London's Guildhall, will also be open to all members of the Livery, their Ladies and Guests.

The evening will be enhanced by much City pageantry, the Orchestra of the Scots Guards, Trumpeters and complemented by a memorable menu.

An invitation has been extended to the Royal Family and the Company are hopeful that they will be honoured by a Royal presence but will not receive a decision from Buckingham Palace until nearer the day.

Leading figures from the City, industry, commerce and the professions are expected to attend and friendships with other Livery Companies will be renewed through invitations to the Masters and their Ladies of many other Guilds.

From the proceeds of these functions a charitable donation will be made to the Framework Knitters Cottage Homes in Oadby which provide sheltered accommodation for retired members of the industry.

Application forms for tickets for both functions will be sent out in good time and it is hoped that a large proportion of the Livery will be able to attend and make 1989 a year long to be remembered.

Members are urged to note these dates in their diaries.

G. H. HURT & SON LTD

MANUFACTURERS FINE LACEY KNITTED SHAWLS, WRAPS, SCARVES, ETC.

65 High Road, Chilwell, Nottingham NG9 4AJ, England
Telephone (0602) 254080

CHILWELL HANDFRAME KNITTERS C1912.

no linking

With the new CMS selectanit, you can produce exceptional styling features, such as pockets that are knitted as an integral part of the fabric and that can incorporate special surface effects, jacquard motifs and even pocket flaps.

Please ask for our very comprehensive leaflet. It gives a lot of detailed information on all the advantages of the new CMS Generation.

STOLL
selectanit · Strickmaschinen · Systeme

H. Stoll GmbH & Co. · Postfach 25 44 · D-7410 Reutlingen 1 · Telefon (0 71 21) 3 13-0 · Telex 7 29 808 · Fax (0 71 21) 3 13-1 10
Smitex Limited · 57, Craven Street, Leicester, LE 14BX · Tel. (05 33) 53 82 96 · Telex 3 4 370 · Fax (05 33) 53 82 19

1589
WILLIAM LEE
The first knitting frame

1989
KENNEDY WAGSTAFF
The first for knitting machines

SHIMA SEIKI MFG LTD. Japan, Electronic Glove, Flat Knitting Machinery & Design Systems
TEXTIMA EXPORT-IMPORT, German Democratic Republic,
Malimo Stitchbonding, Liropol Terry Knitting, Carpet Looms, Dyeing & Finishing Machinery
IRMAC SpA, Italy, Single Cylinder Sock Machines
G. MARCHISIO & CO., Italy, Single, Double Jersey, Interlock & Rib Knitting Machinery
BEFAMA BIELSKO-BIALA, Poland, Non Woven Cards . F. JOFRE PLANET, Spain, Purl & Plain Strappers
PRINCE HS, Hat & Scarf Knitting Machinery . ROMSIT, Romania, Baret Machines
CHRISTOPH LIEBERS GmbH, W. Germany, Knitting Elements . CONDOR S.A.S., Italy, Needles & Knitting Elements

KENNEDY WAGSTAFF
EST 1832   LTD.

Incorporating R & M Knitting & Machinery Ltd.
153 PARKER DRIVE . LEICESTER LE4 0JP . ENGLAND
Tel (0533) 354321 . Fax (0533) 366447 . Telex 341214
Cables Prince Leicester

MONK DUBIED COTTON

Three historic names in the manufacture of straight and flat bar knitting machines applaud this important anniversary of innovation in the field of knitting technology.

As trustees of our heritage we shall continue in the spirit and tradition of William Lee to further the development of manipulation of the knitted stitch.

S. A. MONK-WILLIAM COTTON (SALES & SERVICE) LTD.
Sutton-in-Ashfield and Loughborough, England.
MONK-DUBIED S.A., Couvet, Switzerland.
MONK-DUBIED S.A., (Nadelfabrik), Rheineck, Switzerland.
MONK-DUBIED S.A., Paris, France.
MONK-DUBIED LTD., Leicester, England.
MONK-DUBIED, New York, U.S.A.

A STORY OF SUCCESS BASED ON INNOVATION

COUTURE MARKETING LIMITED, STATION ROAD, STONEY STANTON, LEICESTER LE9 6LU.
TELEPHONE (045 527) 2322 TELEX 341756 FACSIMILE (045 527) 4395

Vernon Cooper Ltd

CIRCULAR AND FLAT BED KNITTING MACHINE SPECIALISTS

 **USED AND RECONDITIONED MACHINES**
INSTALLATIONS AND GUARANTEE
SPARES - SERVICE - CONSULTATION

 **NEW MAYER + CIE CIRCULAR KNITTING MACHINES**
ACCESSORIES - CYLINDERS - DIALS
YARN FEEDING DEVICES

VERNON COOPER LTD.
47 WENLOCK WAY
TROON INDUSTRIAL AREA
LEICESTER LE4 7HU

Telephone (0533) 764141
Fax (0533) 740860 - Telex 34369

Established fo 50 years!

Glen Alva LTD.

Registered Office:
HALLPARK MILLS, WHINS ROAD, ALLOA, SCOTLAND FK10 3PL.
Phone Alloa (0259) 723024. Fax (0259) 218644. Telex 779561 suntex g.

Sales and Marketing Office:
ADVANCED BUSINESS CENTRE,
CITY HOUSE, MAID MARIAN WAY, NOTTINGHAM NG1 6BH.
Phone Nottingham (0602) 413619. Fax (0602) 413820. Telex 377844.

25 years of age next year, we are a leading manufacturer of infants' and children's knitwear.
Glen Alva Limited is a privately owned company which offers a versatile and flexible plant with the most modern knitting and making-up technology.

---

quality assurance specialists...

LABTEST is one of the world's leading international inspection and testing laboratories and is accredited by many leading international organisations and institutions.

A wide range of specialised testing facilities exists to evaluate all forms of consumer products for value in use and fitness for purpose, including:

- FLAMMABILITY: Including Nightwear (Safety) Regulations
- TOY TESTING: Toy Safety Reg. 1974 : BS 5665 and EN 71
- FIBRE CONTENT: Quantitative and Quality Analysis
- 'TOG RATING': Continental Quilts (BS 5335 : 1984)

Labtest Inspection Services UK Ltd
3 Museum Square, Leicester LE1 6UF
Telephone:(0533)553599 Telex:342714

These goods were wrought from high grade lamb's wool, Llama, Shetland and cashmere. Warmth was the main consideration, little attention being paid to colour.

A bewildering variety of goods was on offer from each firm, normally available in any quantity; ribbed kneecaps for rheumatic people and even a ribbed sock for wooden legs figured among the products available. Most were aimed at the domestic market but Innes, Henderson made silk underwear for the Harem of the Sultan of Turkey. In 1907 Robert Pringle launched "Interchangeable Part Combinations" enabling customers to "renew those parts which are subjected to the greatest wear". Hosiers endeavoured to expand sales by courting consumer loyalty through extensive advertising, branding, and direct selling to retail outlets rather than remaining 'hidden' and selling through wholesalers. Thus Lyle & Scott developed their brand name "Ellan-Ess", & Peter Scott "Pesco" goods in the 1880s and often a guarantee against shrinkage was provided — an important consideration for much-washed underwear.

Early Twentieth Century

The long-term future of Scottish knitwear, however, lay not with undergarments but with outerwear, developed from around 1900 when several companies began to manufacture sweaters and cardigans (sometimes called 'coat' sweaters) on a trial basis. These were made on factory hand-knitting machines (as opposed to handframes), in imitation of the chunky hand-knitted garments emanating from Shetland and Fair Isle. Initially menswear was predominant, an orientation which was consolidated during the First World War when the pull-off 'jumper' was found warmer and more convenient than clothes needing to be fastened. Many troops wore woollen underwear for the first time in the trenches which helped to sustain demand after the war until lighter cotton-based garments superseded the woollen variety. The inter-war period, however, witnessed a greater emphasis on outerwear and, with the special exception of Lyle & Scott who began to make Y-Fronts under licence in 1938, underwear gradually declined, at first relatively and then absolutely. By the 1960s very little was being made in Scotland.

Woollen outerwear quickly became popular with women in the more relaxed social atmosphere of the 1920s. At first 'barrel-line' dresses were in vogue, suited, as one observer put it, "to sexless, bosomless, hipless, thighless creatures" because of their straight contours. These were usually made from tubular knitting made in England but when fashion shifted around 1930 to a greater emphasis on body-hugging designs, the fully-fashioned goods of Scotland's traditional producers were strongly in demand. In Hawick it was Innes, Henderson's 'Braemar' goods which led the trail in ladieswear; interestingly Pringle was a relatively late arrival in this field. At neighbouring Dumfries ladies' outerwear was pioneered by J. D. McGeorge Ltd. and Jas. Dunwoodie Ltd., while J. & D. Robertson had, by 1932, developed a sufficiently sizeable export trade in ladies' cashmeres to challenge Braemar in the United States market. Indeed it was at this time that the present orientation towards exporting was established among Scottish producers, especially in the Border fancy trade; overseas representation was quickly established, in Braemar's case as far apart as China, India and Latin America, a spread which was by no means untypical.

It was at this time that the knitwear industry of the West of Scotland district became important. A spate of new firms sprang up in Glasgow, Irvine and other centres in the 1920s stimulated by the burgeoning ladies' trade in particular. The output of this region differed from that of the Borders in that the emphasis was placed upon medium quality plain goods made on circular frames aimed at the 'mass' market catered for by the large departmental chain stores. Although West of Scotland firms endeavoured to maintain a degree of specialisation, these garments were made up on the 'cut & sew' principle and were dyed in the piece. Though attention was paid to design and styling, they were cheaper than the fashioned products of the Borders and the rarer fibres were seldom used. Thus in Glasgow and adjacent towns a huge trade in ladies' costumes and frocks grew up while, north of the Forth, Raschel warp-knitting machinery was introduced to work up a different kind of fancy outerwear. The West of Scotland did not restrict itself to top garments; in the 1930s millions of undergarments were also fabricated on the circular frames and seamed on the overlock machines of the region.

Fully fashioned knitting was to become the mainstay of the Borders trade this century and this early 'four division' Cottons Patent frame was in J. Laing & Son's factory at Hawick in 1912. (Picture courtesy Hawick Museum).

By current standards the ladies' garments of the 1930s were comparatively plain, based on a restricted range of colours and almost entirely designed in the 'classic' round-necked style. Gradually more sophisticated designs appeared with stripes, spots and diamond shapes being incorporated, and different necklines introduced. With growing competition at home and overseas, firms had to pay more attention to design and could no longer depend on the intuition of production staff alone. Thus trained professional designers began to be hired like Otto Weisz, an Austrian refugee from Nazism, who joined Pringle in the mid-thirties and helped his company overhaul the lead gained earlier by Braemar. Pringle's success was largely founded on Weisz's 'dressmaker' range which set new standards in the industry. In similar vein, Christian Dior acted as a designer for Lyle & Scott in the 1950s.

Recent Years

Following the termination of hostilities in 1945 a huge surge of demand was experienced in Scottish knitwear which lasted, on trend, into the early 1970s. Exports became a high proportion of total output in the Borders, less so in the West of Scotland whose

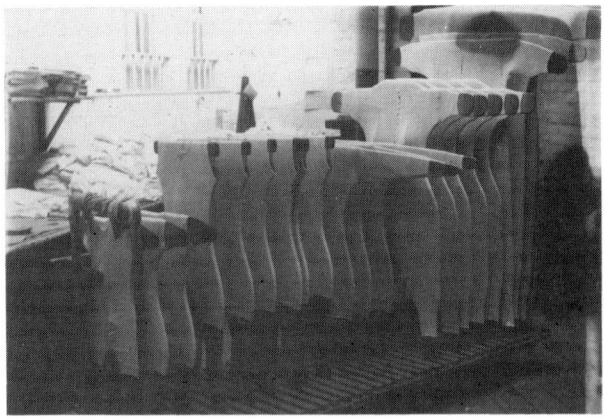

From the 1850s through into the first quarter of this century Scottish knitwear was mainly woollen under-garments, like these combinations on stretchers at a Hawick factory in 1901.

goods were aimed more at the domestic consumer. Markets for 'Hawick' goods were found in most of the higher income areas of the world, but also in some African countries. Hawick gained a reputation as the highest dollar earner per head of population in the United Kingdom, with almost 90 per cent of its output, at one time, going to the United States. By the late 1960s Scottish knitwear production had

The sewing room in Peter Scott's factory on Duke Street, Hawick in 1913. The company had been founded by a twenty year old handframe knitter in 1872 at a time when it was still possible for men with only small capital to set up on their own account. Lyle and Scott, for example, was established by two men on just £500 each in 1874. (Picture courtesy Hawick Museum).

reached £40m per year and by the early 1970s about £70m. In 1935 the figure had been £4m. Even allowing for inflation this represented an impressive degree of real growth, which, sadly, has not been maintained.

A marked feature of the Scottish knitwear industry in recent times has been business reorganisation and 'rationalisation', especially but not exclusively in the Border trade. Many of the family firms were merged or taken over in the 1960s and 1970s and some were closed completely as producing units, notably Braemar though the label was maintained. Some companies, facing rapid technological change and a pressing need to re-equip their concerns, found themselves strapped for capital and went public where they provided fair game for the predators. Sometimes it was their very success which made firms the object of take-over bids, such as Lyle & Scott's legal battle with the House of Fraser in the 1950s which went as far as the House of Lords.

The drive towards greater integration came from yarn spinners on the one hand and important retailers on the other. Thus Todd & Duncan of Kinross, a firm of fine cashmere spinners and part of what later became Dawson International, bought up several well-known Border producers of cashmere goods in order to secure guaranteed outlets for its yarns. Both Braemar and Pringle of Scotland came under the Dawson umbrella. Similarly Courtaulds, through its subsidiary Wolsey, bought over Lyle & Scott, while Jaegar acquired Renwick of Hawick. Subsequently other interests moved into knitting such as Illingworth Morris, Imperial Tobacco, the Baird Group and Tillings.

Not for the first time in its long history the knitwear trade of Scotland is currently facing strong challenges from its competitors. Its future, however, lies in maintaining that genuineness and flair that has given Scottish knitwear its exclusive niche in world markets. Today, with a turnover of about £140m per annum, the industry is keeping its head above water but hardly expanding. Wm. Lee's stocking frame, so long the basis of the industry, has long since given way to technological progress now enshrined in the latest electronic, computer-controlled frames which fill the factories of the Borders and the West. But the challenge for today's manufacturers is not dissimilar to that faced by their pioneering forebears — to keep abreast, if not ahead, of fashion and to meet the exacting standards of their sector of the high-class clothing market. The "Made in Scotland" tag must mean nothing less.

FURTHER READING
C. Gulvin, The Scottish Hosiery and Knitwear Industry Edinburgh, 1984.

Salient Features Of Knitting Technology

By Tony Nutting

NONE OF THE HISTORIANS of the hosiery and knitwear industry have been textile technologists and so they have tended to gloss over the problems of machine and fibre developments in the industry. Of course, there have been plenty of books written by textile technologists but, apart from the early years, they have concentrated intensely on one type of machine and lack any sense of historical evolution. In this short article I will try to step back from the concerns of the moment to pick out the salient features of 400 years of development. Inevitably all detail must be sacrificed in pursuit of the outstanding developments.

Lee's Stocking Frame

The evolution of Lee's stocking frame is a large subject in its own right and here it is possible only to pick out three points. The first is that recent research, notably by Peta Lewis at the Ruddington Museum, leaves no doubt that Lee's original invention was not really economically viable. It was not until lead sinkers, 'trucks' (wheels bearing the weight of the mechanism), the sley, caster-backs and front stops were added that the machine came into common use in England in the later 17th century.

The second half of the following century saw a period of refinements and additions to the stocking frame beginning with Strutt's 'Derby Rib' attachment in 1759. Some of the meshes produced in this period and knitted from the patent specifications by Miss Lewis are shown in the adjacent plates. The third point that must be made is that in the later stages of this intense period of artisan development, various products were being made on the frame that were really unsuited to it, particularly the fancy striped stockings that were made horizontally on the frame.

Nevertheless, such was the commitment of the artisan mind to the Lee frame that a certain myopia developed which made him blind to other technical possibilities. It was for this reason that warp knitting, first introduced in 1775, saw little development for more than a century, and then it was in Saxony rather than England where it was developed. Similarly, the circular knitting machine was invented in France by Decroix (1798), Aubert (1803) and Leroy (1808) but not taken up there at the time.

A naturalised Englishman called Brunel took out a British patent in 1816 but again there was little response. The invention that really created the modern circular knitting industry was Matthew Townsend's latch needle, but Leicester failed to respond and the inventor eventually migrated to America. The full development of automatic circular hose knitting machines was left to the end of the nineteenth century when Scott & Williams, Standard Bros, Hemphill & Banner and other American machine builders seriously began to exploit its possibilities. Meanwhile British interest was largely confined to the mechanisation of the motions of Lee's stocking frame, a sort of bespoke tradition that stood aloof from the cheap 'leg bags' produced by circular knitting machines.

The Early Factory Age

The main problem of mechanising the stocking frame was developing an automatic system for narrowing and widening. In 1861 Arthur Paget of Loughborough (England) was the first to produce an automatic machine with a moveable horizontal needle bar. It had some commercial success but according to contemporary sources, was difficult to set up and maintain. The machine sold well on the Continent and was later improved in Troyes and Chemnitz (Saxony). Finally in 1863 Wm. Cotton of Loughborough was granted his now famous patent for a multi-head fully-fashioned machine with a moveable needle bar with the needles in a vertical plane, much as they are on modern Cotton's Patent machines.

Elsewhere knitting machine developments followed different paths. In Germany Eisenstuck designed a flat knitting machine using latch needles and having two needle beds parallel but inclined at an angle to each other. In his British patent of 1857 he described the use of the machine to produce fashioned circular hose. In 1866 Rev. I. W. Lamb of America produced a flat knitting machine similar to the Eisenstuck model. The acceptance of the flat machine in America was slow and so Lamb came to

England and had his machine built by Coltman & Arkwright; later he sold the European rights to Edouard Dubied of Neuchatel. In 1881 Grosser obtained a patent to apply a jacquard principle to individual needle selection on flat machines for pattern production.

The industry was nevertheless slow to move into factories. Small hand operated circular machines, such as the Griswold, were in common use in the workers' homes to knit hose having a shaped heel and toe pouches. To achieve this, half of the needles were put out of action and then knitting continued on the remainder with a reciprocating action, taking one needle out of action after each knitting stroke. The pouch was then completed by reversing the process. The taking out and putting into action of each single needle had to be done by hand. In 1887 and Kelly, an Englishman, applied for a patent to perform this picking action while under power using a series of four cams. A number of improvements followed until in 1899 the American 'SS' machine succeeded in performing the operation with a single picker.

Meanwhile Leicester was striving to make up lost ground by developing an entirely new principle. A sequence of inventions which began in 1899 with the so-called links-link needle led to the double cylinder knitting machine patent of Stretton & Johnson. William Spiers and Thomas Grieve did the pioneer work in the early years of this century but the real commercial exploitation and success did not come until the launch of the Bentley 'Komet' in the 1920's. Hilscher and Schubert & Salzer of Chemnitz followed in the early 1930's. The double cylinder machine knits both plain and rib stitches and has the facility for transfer of either needles or stitches between the two cylinders.

In 1908/9 Scott & Williams of America obtained patents for a new fabric and a machine to knit it. The fabric was interlock and it derived its name from the construction of two one by one rib structures

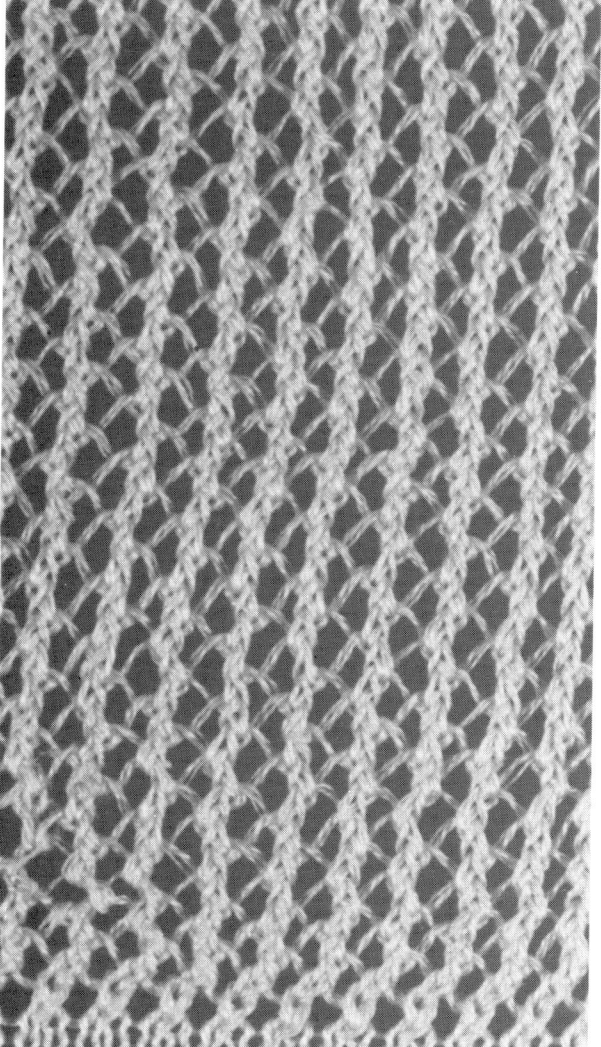

Net work made on the stocking frame by Morris and Betts of Mansfield about 1764, when their patent was registered. The technique has been reconstructed by Peta Lewis at Ruddington Museum.

Point net lace made by Thomas Taylor of Nottingham on the stocking frame in 1778. The structure photographed here has been reproduced by Peta Lewis.

interlocked together. This was the first time that a knitted structure required more than one feeder to complete it. The fabric was the forerunner of the class of fabrics later known as double jersey. In the early 1920's several British companies took out licenses to produce the fabric and Vedonis and Meridian in particular were very successful. The fabric was not really a commercial success in America until after 1945.

Developments Between The Wars

Two further developments took place to reinforce the American lead in this period. In 1915 Scott & Williams took out a patent for the automatic transfer of the welt on a circular hose machine. Until then welts had been produced on a separate machine and sewn on to legs from other machines, or on the more modern machine welts were knitted continuous with the legs and subsequently folded over and sewn down. The patent was so strong that it virtually stopped further research by both circular and fully fashioned machine builders elsewhere. The second development was from the Brinton machine company who in 1931 produced a design wheel for automatic needle selection at each feeder of a circular multi-feed large diameter machine. Until this patent patterning had been restricted to plating, reverse plating and striping on these machines. The principle involved depressing the needle out of the path of the cam to avoid lifting the needle to knit.

It has already been mentioned that Germany dominated warp knitting machine production. However, in the 1930s Sir James Morton took out patents that were to result in a revolutionary warp knitting machine. The F.N.F. machine had eccentrics in place of cams to actuate the main knitting elements and compound needles in place of bearded needles. It knitted at 1,000 cpm, twice as fast as its rivals. Commercial exploitation of the F.N.F. machine was delayed until 1945, and after some years of success it was eventually eclipsed by warp knitting machines from a resurgent German industry.

Developments Since 1945

Prior to 1939 much of the effort of knitting technologists focused on the Lee tradition of attempting to achieve by machine what could be done by hand. Later on in this same period other work was directed towards exploiting the concept of the knitting machine itself. However, from 1945 onwards some significant changes took place. Competition and innovation among the world's knitting machine manufacturers has been intense and great changes have taken place in the leadership and centres of production. Rather than itemise individual technological innovations in isolation it would be better to identify five trends which underly such changes.

Influence Of New Fibres And Yarns

After 1945 nylon progressively replaced silk and cotton in the manufacture of fully fashioned stockings. German and American machine builders, particularly the Textile Machine Works of Reading (USA), developed fast automatic fine gauge models to a peak of perfection. But when the bare leg fashion became popular in the 1950s and stimulated circular hose production the fully fashioned industry was almost annihilated. Innovation in the circular hose machine industry now became intense and the initiative was seized by Italy and Giorgio Billi in particular. He produced simple fast multi-feed machines which knitted tube hose and relied entirely upon the heat setting property of nylon to give a leg shape. In 1967 Billi showed at the ITMA exhibition an eight feed machine which went on to dominate the world markets. Textured stretch nylon yarns and later on tights — necessary because of the miniskirt

A reconstruction, by Peta Lewis at Ruddington Museum, of 'two plain net', knitted on the stocking frame with a 'spoon' tickler by Holmes and Frost about 1777.

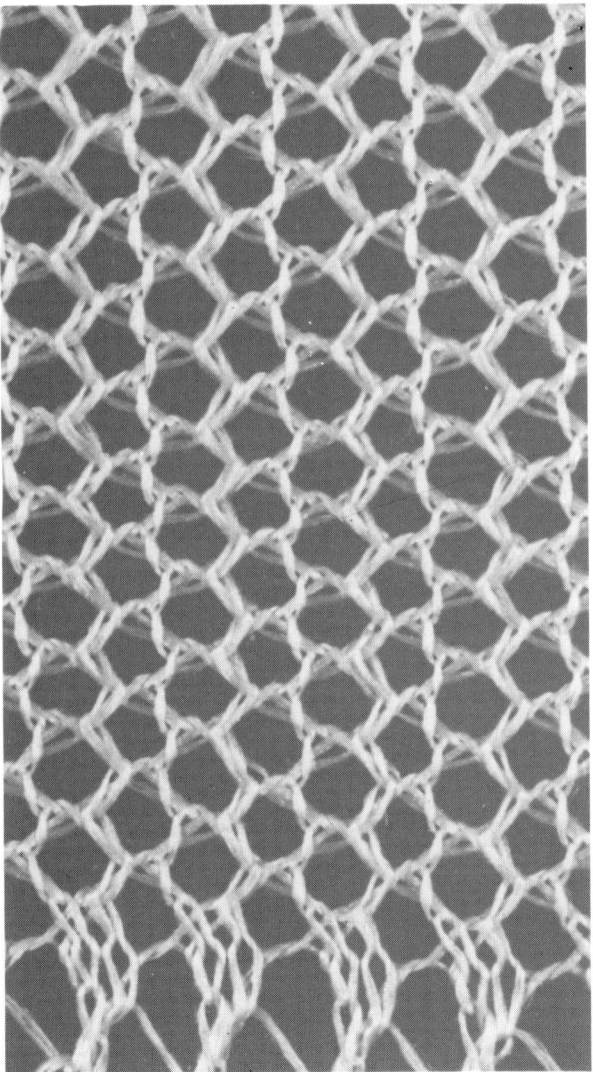

An early Cottons Patent rib frame (picture from Quilter and Chamberlain, Vol. 1, p. 233). It was in 1863 that William Cotton was granted his now-famous patent for a multi-head fully-fashioned machine with a moveable needle bar and the needles in a vertical plane.

fashion — stimulated further machine innovations such as the knitting of one piece tights including closed toes. Because of off machine developments these later developments have not been widely used. Italy is now the only country with a circular hose machine industry of any size and even that has needed substantial government support in the last few years.

Two other fibres which made a big impact on machine builders, knitters and consumers were fine count acrylic yarns such as Courtelle and Acrilan and Crimplene textured polyester from ICI. These fibres reinforced the change from woven to knitted fabrics in women's outerwear. The double jersey machine builders strove to meet a sudden surge in demand for fine gauge (18 to 28 needles per inch) and large diameter (30 inches) machines. These demands posed severe engineering problems and involved developing assembly-line techniques of manufacture and new methods of hardening and cutting the large cylinders. On these new machines the fine strong yarns could be knitted with great efficiency and low fault rates, less than one fault in ten million stitches. At the peak of the fashion the market for women's wear looked unlimited and there appeared enormous potential in men's wear, but by the mid 1970s the double jersey bubble had burst and with it went a number of well-known knitting companies and machine builders.

Electronics, Computers And CAD

All through the growth and boom years of double jersey, machine manufacturers were spending a great deal of effort on improving pattern jacquard mechanisms — this despite the fact that over 50 per cent of fabric produced was plain. Technology was imported from other industries and by about 1963 Morat had a prototype computerised electronically controlled jacquard system working. At the 1967 and 1971 ITMA exhibitions most double jersey machine manufacturers had electronic patterning systems available and linked to some form of CAD system. Although Protti were the first with a similar system on flat knitting machines, it was at the 1975 ITMA exhibition that Stoll showed the first commercially successful flat machine.

The application of electronics and computers to flat machines included needle selection for patterning, machine controls such as stitch structure, transfer, and the fine control of mechanical movements like cams by the use of stepping motors. Most classes of knitting machines now have similar systems.

Integral Garment Production

The ability to shape and produce shaped garments makes knitting unique among fabric producing methods. The current driving force behind the search for machines that can produce a nearly completed garment is the ever-increasing costs of labour to sew garment pieces together. Dr. Wignall's FCM machine uses a specially built six inch diameter double cylinder half hose model modified to produce two heel pouches opposite each other. By folding and cutting in a special way he was able to obtain a child's simple outerwear garment. Only sewing along the top of the sleeves is necessary for completion.

The Basque beret machine inspired McQueen (who has been given little credit for original ideas) in 1960 to design an electronically controlled modified flat knitting machine to knit one piece garments. In the event neither the electronics nor the machine were capable of performing the tasks asked of them. The Stereoknit from Czechoslovakia, also based on a flat machine, produces a simple outerwear garment and had a limited success in that country.

In 1966 Betts and Robinson of Courtaulds produced the first of a large number of patents all aimed at knitting garments on modified flat machines that required little subsequent sewing. Their ideas have not yet been developed by knitting machine builders and only one small facet of the work is being used, the presser foot to produce three dimensional stitch structures. The Shima Seiki automatic glove machine is at present the most successful commercial machine in this class. Until the launch of the latest machine which can knit socks and ties as well as gloves only single purpose machines have so far achieved commercial success. Many people are convinced that integral garment production is the way forward. An almost equal number firmly believe that the knitting industry lives off fashion and such machines will always be too restrictive!

Productivity

Knitting machine productivity has increased greatly over the last thirty years both by increasing machine speeds and the number of feeders. Increasing the number of feeders has been particularly noticeable on large diameter circular machines. In 1946 the standard was about one feeder per inch of diameter. This then moved up to one per inch of circumference. The number of feeders has been further increased by various methods aimed at reducing the cam length. The cam angle had been increased as much as possible and needle makers reduced the length of the latch, compound needles have been introduced by Monarch, Marchisio and Vignoni, the latter two on machines showed at the 1987 ITMA exhibition.

At the same exhibition, Mayer and Jumberca showed knitting machines in which the needle and another loop forming element make complementary vertical movements to reduce the vertical distance to achieve loop formation. The rotational speeds of large diameter machines have increased, but it is with the small diameter machines that the most startling increases have occurred. For example single feed hose machines in the 1940s had speeds of 200 rpm: now 8-feed machines rotate at 1500 rpm. This produces 9 million latch movements each 24 hour day! Theoretically research since the 1960s has studied the forces acting on needles and cams as they collide. As a result of these studies and practical trials, the non-linear cam has been introduced to bring the needle to an upward motion very gradually, but accelerate the needle rapidly after that.

Control Of Fabric Quality

The control of knitted garment weight and dimensions is as old as knitting. Circular machines, by their method of loop formation, are particularly prone to variation in quality due to changes in yarn tension and friction. As early as 1914 the American J. F. Tomkins drew attention to the importance of loop length in a fabric and its likely effect on weight and dimensions. This idea was taken up by Doyle and Munden at HATRA in 1956 and the whole idea of loop length and fabric dimensions were put on a scientific basis and produced the concept of positive feed. Yarn is fed into a knitting machine in a positive manner rather than allowing the needles to pull the yarn into the machine. The first HATRA patent was taken out in 1956 and many others followed covering most classes of knitting machines. Patents for other methods of positive feed were taken out by Rosen of IRO in 1960, and this system has dominated the large diameter machines.

Needles

Knitting needles have had only cursory mention in this article; to do justice to the needle industry at least another article would be needed. The contribution that needle makers have made to the advancement of the knitting machine cannot be overstated. Design for a purpose has been remarkable, but design for durability has been outstanding. Long live the needle makers.

Matthew Townsend, whose latch needle invention in 1847 gave birth to the modern circular knitting industry — even though Townsend had to migrate to America to find recognition.

Acknowledgement

Although the selection of salient features of knitting technology is my own, I am indebted to my friends in the industry who have discussed the topic with me. The input from Fred Carrotte, Roger Duffy, Bill Dutton, David Elson, Eric Keates, John Millington, Dennis Munden, Michael O'Brien, Frank Robinson and Jack Smirfitt has been most welcome and instructive.

FURTHER READING
Peta Lewis, 'William Lee's Stocking Frame: Technical Evolution and Economic Viability 1589 - 1750', Textile History XVII (1986) pp. 129-148.

W. Felkin, History of the Machine-Wrought Hosiery and Lace Manufacturers (1867).

J. H. Quilter and John Chamberlain, Framework Knitting and Hosiery Manufacturer, (Leicester, 1911-14) 3 vols.

Nils Modig, Hosiery Machines. Their Development, Technology and Practical Use (Bamberg 1988).

G. Willkomm, Technology of Framework Knitting, (Trans. W. T. Rowlett — F. Hewitt).

J. F. Tomkins, Science of Knitting (Wiley 1914).

Commissioners of Patents, Abridgments of Specifications to Lace-Making, Knitting, Netting, Braiding and Plaiting 1675 - 1866 (The Commissioners of Patents, 1879).

Rise And Fall Of The Knitting Machine Builders

By Paul Stibbe

IN JANUARY 1894 James Quilter of Leicester published the first number of 'The Knitter's Circular and Monthly Record'. Its frontispiece shows the famous painting of William Lee at home with his wife, his child and his knitting frame. It is a domestic scene. By contrast, the inner pages of Quilter's new journal reveal a factory based industry using plant supplied by specialist machine builders. Amongst the advertisers are G. Blackburn & Sons and Moses Mellor & Sons of Nottingham, with I. L. Berridge & Co. and H. Wildt & Co. of Leicester. Cottons of Loughborough do not feature, but J. Kiddier & Sons and Kiddier Brothers in Nottingham are both offering Cotton's Patent equipment.

In line with the knitting manufacturers who were their customers, these machine builders were private family businesses. The same pattern was to be found throughout the European knitting centres. Dubied at Neuchatel and Stoll at Reutlingen had been building flat knitting machines since the 1860s. Terrot, in Canstatt, was building circular knitting frames, in competition with Fouquet & Frauz in Rottenberg. At Chemnitz, Schubert & Salzer were already well established as builders of fully fashioned knitting machines.

The titles of these British and continental firms remind us that few of the early machine builders enjoyed limited liability. The proprietorial families were carrying considerable risks. We may speculate on their approach to the notorious instability of the capital goods market: how did they plan to match their output to the fluctuating requirements of the knitters, who in turn were subject to the vagaries of fashion?

The Machinery Market

The machine builders' dilemma is best illustrated by J. M. Clarke's principle of the accelerator. Table 1 shows why changes in the demand for a manufactured product are reflected more than proportionately in the derived demand for machinery. It assumes that in a stable market the manufacturing industry has a total stock of 1,000 machines, and that the machines have an expected life span of ten years. In Year 1, therefore, the machine builders are expected to deliver 100 machines to replace worn-out items.

In Year 2 the manufacturers anticipate a 10 per cent uplift in their market and need to increase their stock of machines to 1,100. The machine builders are required to double their output to deliver 100 new machines and a further 100 for replacement. In Year 3, if the consumer market stabilises at its new level, no machines are required for expansion, and the call-off reverts to 100 for replacement. Finally, in Year 4 the market returns to its original level, and no new machines are required at all.

So variations of only 10 per cent in the consumer market are causing the demand for machinery to double or halve (more or less, according to the durability of the machines) or to disappear altogether. This is an over-simplified picture, of course. Nevertheless the accelerator shows why machine builders seem slow to rise to the occasion in good times; and how, in bad times, they are the first to catch a cold. The sudden changes from a sellers' to a buyers' market are all too familiar.

Engineers Or Merchants?

To some extent the effects of the accelerator are mitigated by the existence of an international market. But for most knitting machine builders one of the greatest safeguards has been to offer a wide range of alternative lines. This was sometimes achieved by trading in the complementary range of another builder. Looking back to Quilter's publication of

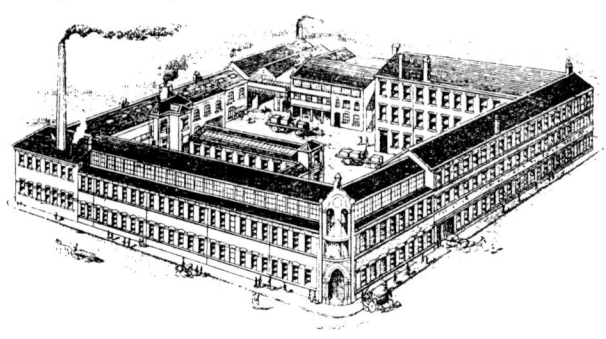

The Atlas works of G. Blackburn and Sons, Nottingham. The factory was typical of knitting machinery establishments at the start of this century.

TABLE 1 DERIVED DEMAND FOR MACHINERY

	Manufacturers' stock of machines	Machines required for replacement	Machines required for expansion	Total demand for machines
Year 1	1,000	100	0	100
Year 2	1,100	100	100	200
Year 3	1,100	100	0	100
Year 4	1,000	0	0	0

1894 we find that Blackburn was advertising Scott's circular hose machine, imported from the USA. Wildt offered Terrot circular machines from Germany, and Stibbe was announcing a new model manufactured by Dubied in Switzerland.

The expansion of circular knitting in the first three decades of this century was largely taken up by American builders, who exported through the established European channels. This enabled Blackburn, who represented Scott & Williams, to offer circular hose machines (Models B5 and K7) as well as models for rib and interlock fabrics. Stibbe's Maxim circular hose machines were actually built by the Hemphill Company in Pawtucket, and the range of circular fabric and garment length machines offered by Stibbe was built by Wildman in Norristown.

Schubert & Salzer in Germany, and the Textile Machine Works in Pennsylvania built circular hosiery machines to complement their fully fashioned hosiery machines. This way they survived the frequent changes of fashion between the two kinds of stocking. And latterly, Dubied, by tradition a builder of flat machines, entered the double jersey machine market with the successful Weveknit range.

The mergers which took place in the '50s and '60s can also be seen as protective measures against the accelerator. Stibbe extended its range of circular fabric machines by acquiring the Berridge models

Plain rib and underwear machines designed and built by G. Stibbe & Co of Leicester around 1924. They are shown here installed in a factory in Derby.

and entered the fully fashioned market through S. A. Monk. On a larger scale, the Bentley Group was formed and became the biggest knitting machinery supplier in the world.

Emergence Of The Bentley Group

Bentley's original interest lay in circular half-hose machinery, which was mainly a British development.

In 1900 two Leicester men, Stretton and Johnson, supported by William Spiers and Thomas Grieve, had invented a machine in which double-ended needles were transferable between two superimposed cylinders, using the German links-links principle. Rib tops could now be knitted on the same machine as the rest of the sock.

The advanced Komet machine, launched by Bentley, soon became a world leader. Competition was minimal. But Bentley's rapidly expanding business was entirely dependent on the demand for machinery derived from sales of men's and children's socks. For their own protection, therefore, and believing it would benefit the whole industry, Percy Bentley and his son, William set out to form a group comprising builders of every kind of knitting machine. In such a group — which included Grieve, Wildt, Cotton, Blackburn and Mellor Bromley, as well as Bentley itself — the accelerator effect should have been balanced out.

Integration of these diverse components proved difficult. Personnel within the Bentley Group still talked about the Wildt side and the Mellor Bromley side of the business, even after Wildt-Mellor Bromley was concentrated into one factory. However, as Bentley became part of Sir Charles Clore's Sears Holdings, more resources than hitherto were applied to research and development. Informal talks took place between some of the non-Bentley builders, with a view to sharing the cost of joint development projects, but these usually broke down on the question of sovereignty.

Innovators Or Copyists?

A powerful way of combating the accelerator would be to invent and build an entirely new machine. Theoretically, this should have the effect of reducing the life span of existing machinery through

A scene in a typical hosiery knitting room in the 1920s with banks of belt driven machines and men and women working alongside each other. This particular room in a Hinckley factory houses a plant of Maxim machines installed by Stibbe around 1924.

obsolesence, raising the replacement demand, and giving the inventor and his backers a head start over the competition. In practice it has seldom happened that way.

Research and development programmes in the knitting machine industry have been largely confined to improvements, rather than real innovation. Knitting in finer gauges has become possible. Machine productivity has risen with higher running speeds and more feeding points. Quicker pattern change and automatic stitch transfer have been introduced. Electronics have been applied to stopmotions and detectors and, more importantly, to needle selection. There have been no commercially successful innovations in stitch formation since Townsend invented the latch needle in 1847. New man-made fibres and yarns are here to stay, but nothing radically new in knitted structures has appeared since interlock (1908).

Established machine builders have been slow to take up inventions offered to them by outsiders or newcomers. The medium sized family firms, once typical of the industry, were always cautious about deploying the profits which they ploughed back in good years; pursuing a Corn in Egypt policy, they tended to amass liquid reserves as a bulwark against the lean years of deceleration. They were disinclined to speculate in long term ventures. Production requirements remained paramount.

Alongside this vested interest in the current technology there is the big unsolved marketing problem. Who decides what garments the ultimate customer is going to buy over the counter? And who carries the risk of developing a new product and the machinery to make it? The machine builder, the manufacturer, the retailer, or the designer?

From Interlock To Double Jersey

The only great innovation in knitting within living

A line of Wright linkers in an American factory about 1924. Interestingly, the hosiery machines behind the linkers, while still belt driven like their UK counterparts, took their drive off a shaft running at floor level, not suspended from the ceiling.

memory, interlock, would not have survived without the support of two British underwear manufacturers. The first patent for interlock fabric was granted to the Americans, Scott & Williams in 1908. The Scott Williams interlock machine was patented in the following year. George Spencer (Vedonis) and J. B. Lewis (Meridian) recognised its potential long before the initial technical problems were resolved; they obtained their licences to manufacture in 1910. In 1925, when the patents were due to expire, the development expenses had still hardly been met. An extension to 1930 was granted. Since then, many of the industry's fortunes and misfortunes have been attributable to interlock.

By an important coincidence, the British government's introduction of import duties in 1932 occurred only two years after the expiry of the Scott & Williams interlock patents. Blackburn and Stibbe found the prospects for American-built machinery severely dented, and Stibbe was embarassed by its lack of engineering capacity. Ironically, too, interlock had made little headway in the American market, whereas underwear manufacturers in Europe were keen to emulate the success of Vedonis and Meridian.

So the development of interlock machinery was taken up by builders on this side of the Atlantic, most notably by Mellor Bromley. Eric Pasold describes a visit to the new Mellor Bromley factory at Leicester in 1933:

> "The visit proved an eye opener for us. We had not expected such a large, modern, and clearly very efficient engineering concern, which compared favourably with any we had seen in Germany. The machines they made inspired confidence . . . "

It is significant that in 1933 Pasold took German engineering as his criterion. The highest reputation for Cotton's Patent machinery had passed, long since, from the eponymous firm in Loughborough to German firms such as Schubert & Salzer, whose expertise spread to the Textile Machine Works in Pennsylvania. The established centres for V-bed and flat machines were Reutlingen in Germany and Neuchatel in Switzerland. Wildt was renowned for the garment length machines which it built in Leicester, but other well known circular machines from Leicester and Nottingham were, in fact, built in the USA. British supremacy — confined to double cylinder machines and interlock — was to prove short lived.

Figures assembled in 1939 show the leading British knitting machine builders in order of payroll size, with Mellor Bromley well ahead:

Mellor Bromley	640
Stibbe	493
Wildt	465
Bentley	445
Cotton	300
Blackburn	253
Berridge	170
	2,766

Thirty years later, the payroll figures of the same firms, now formed into two groups, were:

Bentley Group	9,000
Stibbe Group	2,550
	11,550

Given that the labour content of knitting machine building had not changed, the payroll is a fairly accurate indicator of growth. In the immediate post-war years there had been a large replacement demand for all types of machinery. This was followed by a boom in seamfree hose. The fully fashioned machine builders recovered from this reverse by developing their models for classical twin sets and cardigans.

However, the major cause of continued expansion in the 1960s was the growing use of knitted polyester fabrics in place of traditional woven materials. Interlock, originally used for cotton underwear, now emerged as an outerwear fabric with the appropriate name of *Double Jersey*. Double jersey machines, like interlock machines, were developed by European

The Dubied Wevenit. Although Dubied was more associated with the building of flat knitting machines, the Wevenit was introduced in response to the double jersey boom and proved to be among the most successful of all machines of that type.

builders: in England, by Wildt-Mellor Bromley, Stibbe, and Kirkland; on the continent by Dubied, Morat, Mayer, Terrot, Fouquet and Lebocey.

Eclipse Of The British And American Machine Builders

An ominous trend accompanied the last phase of the machine builders' remarkable growth. Contrary to traditional wisdom, they narrowed their range instead of extending it. Gradually they put more eggs into fewer baskets, becoming more vulnerable to the accelerator than ever before. After the seamfree boom, for instance, Stibbe opted out of hosiery machinery in the face of new competition from Italy; its circular machine programmes now concentrated on rib, interlock and double jersey models.

Meanwhile garment manufacturers, following the dictates of the retail chains, demanded high volume, single purpose machines. Cut-and-sewn garments were the rage. The new generation of circular knitting machines was designed for high output. Versatility took second place. By 1970, twin-sets and cardigans were no longer being worn, and the demand for fully fashioned machines was negligible. Bentley-Cotton and Stibbe-Monk were both suffering the consequences.

On the other hand, the stock of double jersey machines in the UK alone increased from 1,100 in 1962 to 2,500 in 1970. The order books of the circular machine builders' were filled for three years ahead. Many of the knitters now belonged to the fibre producers, who had moved in to secure their outlets. Figures published in the *Financial Times* showed that sales of knitted fabrics increased from £5 million in 1954 to £55 million in 1968. The market share of knitted fabrics (as opposed to woven) had risen from 28 per cent in 1955 to 42 per cent in 1965. The projection for 1975 was 66 per cent. Would the machine builders deliver on time?

With the Bentley Group owned by Sears Holdings, the City spotlight fell briefly upon Stibbe. The *Financial Times* (28th April, 1971) quoted Stibbe's claim that it was increasing its output of circular machines by 45 cent in the current year, and would double it again by 1975. Famous last words! By 1975 Stibbe was in the hands of the Receiver, and several other builders were in dire straits. During the ensuing years, Sears Holdings has withdrawn its support from Bentley and parts of the group were subject to management buyouts. In 1988, thirteen years on,

The Dubied plant at Neuchatel. Dating back to 1867, the original part of the factory can be seen on the right of the picture.

Bentley itself followed Stibbe into receivership. From Switzerland came news that Dubied — one of the oldest and most respected machine builders — had been rescued from its financial difficulties.

One bright exception to a gloomy picture is the successful development of new circular hose machines by Italian builders. The achievements of Matec (Giorgio Billi), Lonati, Santoni and Samo can be illustrated by their combined record in the American market. From a zero start in 1960, the stock of Italian-built machines in the United States reached 6,698 (9 per cent of the total) by 1969. The Italians' position continued to improve dramatically in spite of a general downturn. Between 1969 and 1985 the total stock of women's circular hose machines in the USA fell more than a third, but the number of Italian machines in US mills rose to two-thirds of the total, and is still rising.

Otherwise, from an historical standpoint, the Golden Age of the knitting machine builders seems but a brief episode. Happily there are moves afoot to revive the industry in ways more appropriate to the needs of today. I wish them success.

REFERENCES AND SOURCES
J. M. Clark, Business Acceleration and the Law of Demand, *Journal of Political Economy, March 1917.*
Ralph Innes, The rise and fall of a knitting machine giant, *Knitting Technique, Vol. 10 (1988) No. 3.*
Eric W. Pasold, Ladybird, Ladybird, *(Manchester University Press, 1977).*
The Kempton Records, Leicestershire Records Office.
Financial Times, 28 April, 1971.
Survey & Analysis of Circular Hosiery Machinery in the United States, *Speizman Industries Inc, Charlotte, NC, 1969, 1972, 1975, 1980.*

400 Years Of Domestic Machine Knitting

By Kathleen Kinder

IF ONE TAKES "domestic" to mean "worked in the home", then modern domestic machine knitting can trace its ancestry directly back to the Lee invention of 1589. Moreover in the 17th century, framework knitting tended to be very much a family affair. Framework knitters within 20 miles of the City of London were commanded to bind their children to be apprentices to the trade for 7 years. The real concern was to see that none of the framework knitters' skills was communicated to foreigners and to fellow countrymen who might be competitors. The framework knitters did their best to ensure that none of their discoveries and inventions was carried overseas. Since no instructions were in document form, the restrictions were placed on people and on their movements. Clause 24 in the London Framework Knitters Charter 1664 reads:

"The invention being purely English . . . no person, whether freeman or foreginer, denizen or alien, shall presume to carry, or cause to be carried any frames used for making silk stockings or used in framework knitting beyond the seas upon any pretence whatsoever".

If the modern industrial knitter regards Clause 24 as a bitter irony as he/she ponders the future of the British industry in the face of relentless overseas competition, then the modern domestic knitter also marvels at how 200 years after publication, Clause 24 and its prohibition were completely ignored and forgotten as redundant frames and their manuals were shipped out to Japan. No one gave a thought in the 1870s and after, to the fact that the technology of yesterday could shape the technology of tomorrow in the hands and minds of the innovative and skilful. Had the prohibitions of the framework knitters charter been observed, the history of the domestic knitting machine in the 20th century could have been very different.

Even in the frameshops of the 18th century, a family atmosphere often prevailed in the relationship between the master hosier and his knitters. After all, these concerns were very small and cannot even be described as manufactories in the grandiose and awful Victorian manner. Henson tells the delightful tale of Charles Villiers, master stocking maker and reputedly the descendant of the Duke of Buckingham, favourite of James I and Charles I. Charles Villiers appears to have inherited the inordinate vanity of his illustrious predecessor.

He was the possessor of a pair of shapely legs but was unhappy that the stockings he and his knitters produced did his limbs scant justice. Accordingly around 1750 Villiers worked out a pattern which must certainly be the first recorded machine knitted pattern, and gave his knitters written instructions on how to improve the narrowing (shaping) of their stockings. Henson said that Villiers did this in spite of its seeming "vainly ludicrous and puerile". The suggestion is that information was passed by word of mouth or by observing others, and that no self-respecting knitter ought to have it written down. Significantly, these workmen could read and as I have noted in my new book for Batsford "Hand and Machine Knitting: international pattern design", this marks a step forward in the progress towards written communication. Helen Bonney, writing in SlipKnot the magazine of the Knitting and Crochet Guild, June 1988, has argued very convincingly that Villiers wrote his pattern in the form of a jingle, so that his knitters could memorise the instructions without looking too often at the card. Charles Villiers and his knitters would be much more at home amongst the pattern-swapping members of a modern domestic machine knitting club than amongst the monitors of the latest computerised factory.

The view that the knitting machine could be adapted for ladies' work in the home was put forward by Felkin in his History of the Machine-Wrought Hosiery and Lace Manufacturers 1867. On p508 we read:

"A small domestic knitting frame was contributed by a mechanician name Backenheim to the Cologne Exhibition a few years ago. It was highly spoken of. It had 84 needles and the machine was said to weigh not more than 14-15lbs and might be adapted to any table for ladies work. It is said to produce 10,000 to 35,000 loops per hour and be worked with great facility. Whether it is a mere modification of the old stocking frame, or of the circular knitting machine, or an entirely new arrangement is not known".

It is very tempting to suggest that the machine described by Felkin was a predecessor of the Griswold circular sock machine. Certainly circular sock machines were immensely popular as domestic machines in the last quarter of the 19th century, though small hand-powered V beds were used increasingly in domestic concerns from the 1880s onwards once the sportsboom got underway and people began to wear sweaters and jerseys as fashionable casual wear.

Family Knitter

An advertisement for the Lamb V bed machine in the New Zealand Chronicle June 10th, 1886 gives evidence of the domestic industry in the 19th century. The advert is similar to others in my collection from the UK and USA most of which were aimed at women in the home and which appeared in newspapers as well as in women's publications. "It (i.e. the Lamb machine) is now the standard machine for manufacturing and the only family knitter that fits the bill".

There are two misconceptions about Victorian hand and domestic machine knitting which need to be dealt with straightaway. First, historians of handknitting have actively encouraged the view that drawing room handknitting was merely to while away leisure hours usefully. In 1851, the year of the Great Exhibition, out of a population of about 6 million women over 20, one half had no place in non-domestic industry, and stayed at home as wives and daughters. If they remained as spinsters or became widows, they had to depend on private means or on the goodwill of relatives for support. By the last quarter of the 19th century, the problem of the distressed gentlewoman was acute and how handknit historians can close their eyes to the increasingly bitter references in needlework manuals and women's publications really has me puzzled! In an 1871 issue of 'The English Woman's Magazine', we read an answer to a correspondent:

"We grieve that it is not in our power to assist you. Needlework is a drug in the work market and even the most successful workers earn little. Thousands of letters such as yours are received by us yearly and we are obliged to own our inability to solve the problem of employment for women".

In my collection, I have all the issues of Mrs. Leach's Fancy Workbasket for 1886. Mrs. Leach gives no less than 15 addresses for work societies to which distressed gentlewomen can appeal for help, to find a market for their needlecraft. Her comment is biting and surprisingly feminist:

"It is sad that amongst all the branches of employment that the benefactors of our race profess to have opened out to women, we can still find so few roads open to those who are really gentlewomen both by birth and education, and who yet are forced to seek some means of earning or least augmenting their income".

The second misconception which is current, is that the domestic knitting machine had no place in the Victorian drawing room needlecraft and that when a machine knitted piece is identified as Victorian it must have been produced in an industrial environment. That is simply not true. Members of the Knitting and Crochet Guild, many of whom are expert in all three member crafts, are combing the pages of Victorian manuals and are coming up with all kinds of exciting discoveries. Here is a quotation from the Girls Own Paper 18.8.1883, contributed by Margaret Deshmane to SlipKnot, June, 1986, and we see that the term "gentlewoman" could include those whose family had made it into the middle class and who therefore had a status to maintain. Mrs. Leach was too snobbish by half!

"We sympathise much with you in your various troubles and are glad to find you so self-reliant and brave. With regard to the knitting machine, we think you would find it answered if you could always be sure of getting work for it. This you should enquire about before expending the money".

The Bishop of Leicester has very kindly sent to me two photocopied pages of Mrs. E. Lewis's book "Wools and how to use them" 1884. The conclusion is devoted to the knitting machine.

"It is an admirable invention, perfectly satisfactory in every way, but its present high price prevents its being adopted in ordinary households.

"It is very generally used in large institutions; it has already found its way into some English homes, and a case was brought under my notice quite recently of a lady who made a large sum of money towards building a church from the profits of her knitting machine".

It seems then that the knitting clubs who today run many events in aid of various good causes have an honourable precedent and what is so interesting

Victorian domestic V-bed machine circa 1890 which appears to be closely related to its factory counterpart but without the iron support frame. (Picture courtesy the Museum of North Country Life, Settle, North Yorkshire).

about this machine knitting lady of 1884 is that she does not appear to be in the least bit "distressed" and could use her machine to help others. Mrs. Lewis concludes:

"If we ever do find ourselves the happy possessor of this delightful invention we shall find our knowledge, skill and experience more valuable every day". Mrs. Lewis gives us one reason why machine knit stitch patterns and garment recipes were confined to the manufacturers instruction manuals and their follow up volumes. The fact that machine knit material, except for adverts, was absent from ordinary needlecraft publications, has given rise to the view that there was no domestic industry to speak of. Mrs. Lewis believes that the machines did not do any "fancy work". They did, but not the handknit kind she recognised. The implication is that machine knitters could copy handknit patterns by handtooling. Indeed machine manuals contained instructions for the hand-working of lace and single bed tuck stitches at the machine. Lace in particular was easy to produce and after all it was one of the most popular handknit stitches done in the Victorian drawing room. It is often very difficult to say whether a 19th century piece had been machine knitted in a domestic or an industrial environment and we can now understand why.

Mrs. Lewis also thinks that the knitting machine could be used by "the better class of servants', but declares prophetically that "in the next generation, it will be considered quite as much a necessity as the sewing machine is now".

Indeed she didn't have to wait till the next generation. The Education Acts of 1870 and after spawned an entirely new needlecraft manual, that for teachers in elementary schools who were required to teach needlework and that included handknitting (the latter to Standard V). In Elizabeth Rosevear's Needlework, Knitting, Cutting Out (Macmillan 1893), we read: "Sewing and knitting machines cannot be disregarded, because they are in more general use than a few years ago".

Certainly education from the companies selling machines played an important part in the dissemination of machine knitting skills from the 1870s onwards. Some years ago, two letters from the archives of Jaeger (William Spence Huntly Ltd) were kindly sent to me via Knitting International. These letters showed that Miss Harrison herself was employed by her family firm as a tutor of domestic knitting machines in 1878. From another Harrison manual c1890, we learn that Miss Warren, who was blind, could teach anyone similarly handicapped, how to use a knitting machine. I can think of advertisements for domestic knitting machines nearer our own time which made similar claims to those of Miss Warren!

By the end of the 19th century there were signs that the domestic knitting machine could enhance the status of women and not diminish it. There is an interesting account by J. W. Harrison of the firm of that name, of the domestic hosiery industry in England and Scotland, and of its extension in Ireland in the Journal of Agriculture III no. 2, 1903 (kindly sent by the Ulster Folk Museum).

"A large number of people in the rural centres of Durham, Northumberland, Yorkshire and Lancashire, carry on this industry in their homes with often only a single machine".

The Irish proved just as quick at learning the knitting machine as their English and Scots counterparts. The writer quotes the example of a 16 year old girl, whose father bought her a machine at the Cork exhibition of 1902. Eventually the girl proved so successful that she had 4 machines and provided work for 6 or 7 girls in her area. It seems that the modern craft fair had its antecedents in 1902:

"There is also another system of pushing sales in vogue which requires a little more time and attention, viz, attending the country fairs or markets in the villages or towns within a certain radius of their homes. They carry a portable stall whereon their goods are displayed along with one or two wicker or cane skits in which their stock is carried".

Rewarding Dividend

If the study of Victorian needlecraft literature and manuals is paying a rewarding dividend in the search for our domestic machine knitting heritage, then the study of items in our museum collections is even more rewarding. There must be thousands of knitted items stored away in museum warehouses which rarely go on public view. Keepers of textiles and their assistants are trained to do their jobs. A few handknit. None I've met machine knit. Most knitted items in collections are labelled as handknitting, though I've come across several museums which have considerable machine knit collections c1920 and which suggest that the first knitted "fashion" was both machine knitted and cut and sew — a suggestion which does not please some of my 'handknit-only' friends. Recently, my husband (a Passap knitter) and I went to York Castle Museum to photograph some Victorian handknitting. A tiny pence jug was put out for us. It was unmistakably machine-knitted in the opinion of both of us. (1 × 1 rib, and racked half cardigan stitch for the full part of the jug and stitched up rather badly on the seam). The discovery caused the greatest excitement amongst the staff. No one had ever heard of a machine knitted pence jug before. In my mind, this discovery has given an entirely different slant to Victorian machine knitting. Someone a hundred years ago must actually have used a machine for *fun!*

Many people think that the emergence of the Japanese and their subsequent domination of the domestic machine knitting industry is a 20th century story. Not so. In the Knitters Circular and Monthly

Record June 1895, published in Leicester and the ancestor of "Knitting International" no less, we are told that the first knitting machines were taken to Japan from England and then from other countries as well. In the Osaka region in 1895 the machines "were of hand power and operated in private houses, from one to five being found in a house".

The view that "the Japanese have copied all, thus deteriorating it", would certainly not be valid now. As far as the domestic knitting crafts (hand and machine) are concerned, the Japanese are leaders of innovation. The revival of popular knitting, its continuing growth, the development of a personalised approach and the dissemination of design ideas internationally, all could depend on the acceptance of the Japanese system.

In 1924, according to Japanese authorities, a lady, Masako Hagiwara "invented the first handknitting machine for the home". This seems an extraordinary claim when one considers previous developments in the West, but the Hagiwara device was completely different from its predecessors in Europe and America. It appears to have been a simple, straight bar frame similar to the one which, it is believed, William Lee made in the 1580s as prototype for the stocking frame, and similar to the primitive Passap D frame of 1939. Certainly, the Hagiwara machine was based on a concept of home machine knitting which owed very little to the Victorian hand machine. The Japanese saw from the very beginning that knitting machines had to be light and easy to use. They had to be attractive in appearance and occupy a space in the modern home no larger than that required by an ironing board. The machines should pack up and store easily. Most important of all, the Japanese were the first to see the home knitting machine as the creator of exclusive knitted fashion, a view which handknitters later developed for their own special kind of knitwear. There is no doubt that the modern Japanese machine can trace its ancestry back to the Hagiwara device, but nevertheless in the development towards greater sophistication Japanese technology has drawn heavily on European tradition and expertise.

The European-made domestic machines which made their appearance in the 1950s heralded the start of the modern era both in machine and in literature. The writers of the period were however somewhat patronising in their address to the "housewives" who would machine knit "useful and warm" garments for the family. When the Japanese push-button Brother and Knitmaster machines first made their appearance in the 1960s, followed by the punchcard and electronic machines of the 1970s and 1980s, a comparison was immediately drawn between their and similar products from European firms, products which were much closer to their industrial counterparts. Moreover, machine knitters who today use both European and Japanese machines recognise a difference in attitude to the operator. The Japanese positively encourage individual creativity and have developed a liberal, imaginative approach to the teaching of personalised design. Though the European tradition is well ahead of current British handknit practice, which appears to be in a state of confusion, the firms involved do not regard the knitters as being capable of understanding the whole design to pattern process from start to finish. The move towards computerisation is being closely monitored by leading machine knit writers and teachers, and incidentally, there is no rush, only a steady trickle towards the electronic machines. The punchcard machines look set to hold their popularity for some considerable time to come. The excitement that is being generated is concerned less with the novelty of new machines and more with plumbing the riches provided by the existing ones. The domestic machine knitting industry is described as "buoyant" by those expert at scanning profits, losses, and it looks as if it will continue to grow slowly but steadily and it is being recognised that its growth and health depend less on spectacular style operations like those that promote handknitting at the present moment, and more on expanding and deepening its teaching base in clubs and classes (especially the ones sponsored by City and Guilds) and through its quite remarkable private and professional publishing tradition.

Finally, mention must be made of the significant contribution made to the British knitwear economy by firms using domestic, mainly Japanese machines. In this respect, we think not only of small designer enterprises, but of much larger operations employing considerable numbers of outworkers. We also pay tribute to promotional organisations which provide a market place and advisory services to individual knitter designers. The most representative of all these functions and the most impressive in terms of organisation and production is the knitwear industry of the Shetland Isles.

ACKNOWLEDGEMENTS AND FURTHER READING
History of the Framework Knitters — Gravenor Henson. Edited, Stanley Chapman, David & Charles, 1970.
Alexandra Rowlands, Colchester.
The Knitting & Crochet Guild (SlipKnot), 3 Gale Drive, Lightwater, Surrey GV18 5TX. Tel. 0276 71124.
Shirley Smith, Auckland, New Zealand.
Victorian Fancywork. Markrich and Kiewe. Pitman 1975.
Knitting International (October 1978 and December 1978).
Knitting Pattern Dafting by Charts — Okamoto Pub. Co. Japan. 1976.

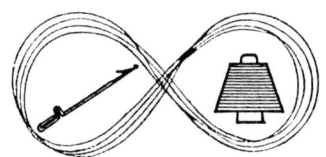

THE DIRECTORS OF TEXTURED JERSEY P.L.C. ARE BOTH HAPPY AND PROUD TO BE ASSOCIATED WITH THE WILLIAM LEE 400th ANNIVERSARY COMMEMORATIVE VOLUME.

TEXTURED JERSEY P.L.C.—ENGINEERS WAY—WEMBLEY—MIDDLESEX HA9 0PD
Telephone 01-903 3621—Telefax 01-902 2299—Telex 263780

BASF United Kingdom Limited

suppliers of

System Products for the Textile Industry

are delighted to be associated with the

WILLIAM LEE QUATERCENTENARY

Textile Division

BASF

Marks & Spencer is proud to support the William Lee Quatercentenary.

W. K. LOWE & Company

A DIVISION OF KENNETH LOWE (HOLDINGS) LIMITED

Manufacturers of

Jersey Fabrics &

Ladies' Outerwear including

Dresses & Fashion Separates

for leading chain stores

& their customers.

ALBERT ROAD. BOLLINGTON. MACCLESFIELD. CHESHIRE SK10 5HS
TEL: BOLLINGTON (0625) 74825. FAX: (0625) 72943. TELEX: 668656

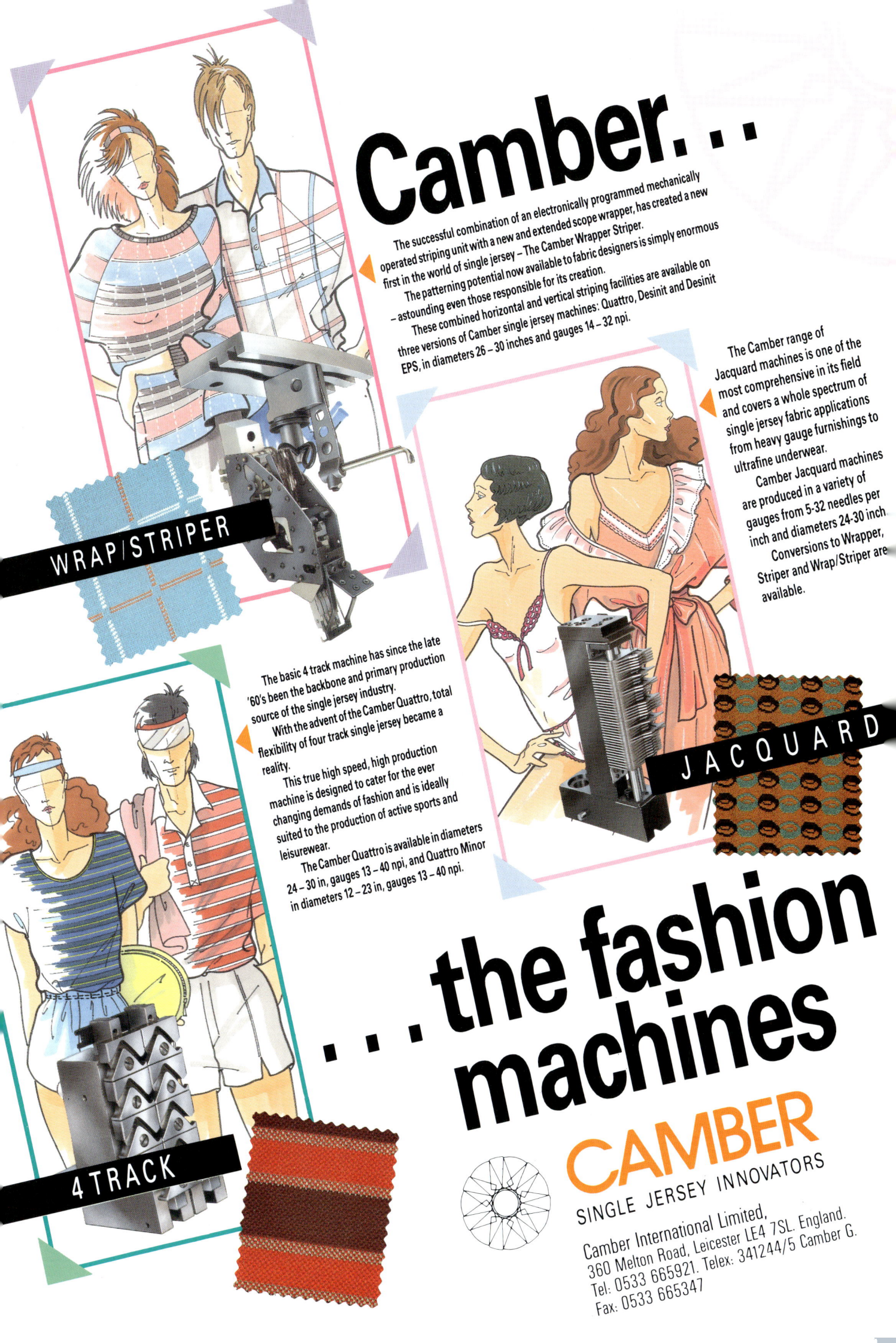

GEDLING BOROUGH COUNCIL, NOTTINGHAM.

WILLIAM LEE

RESIDENT OF CALVERTON
IN THE BOROUGH OF GEDLING.

The Borough Council congratulates the knitting industry and offers continued support.

SERVICES OFFERED BY
THE BOROUGH COUNCIL INCLUDE

1589   1989

BUSINESS SUPPORT

Managed workshops   Business Directory

Land Inquiries   Sponsored business courses

and

LEISURE

Indoor Bowls Target Golf Dry Ski Slope Swimming

Racket Sports Keep Fit Gymnastics Football Cricket

Childrens Parties Theatre

Conference & Exhibition Facilities

Country Parks

LEISURE. TEL. 0602 670067. BUSINESS SUPPORT. QUATERCENTENARY

PROFITEX The Business Consultancy with a difference.

PROFIT from our EXperience!

DESIGN — SOURCING & SELLING — MARKETING AND CORPORATE IDENTITY
EXECUTIVE SEARCH — INCENTITIVE PAYMENT SYSTEMS
QUALITY ASSURANCE — TRAINING.

PROFITEX LTD., ONE, THE DALE, WIRKSWORTH, DERBY DE4 4EJ, ENGLAND.
TELEPHONE (062) 982 4949. FAX (062) 982 4773.

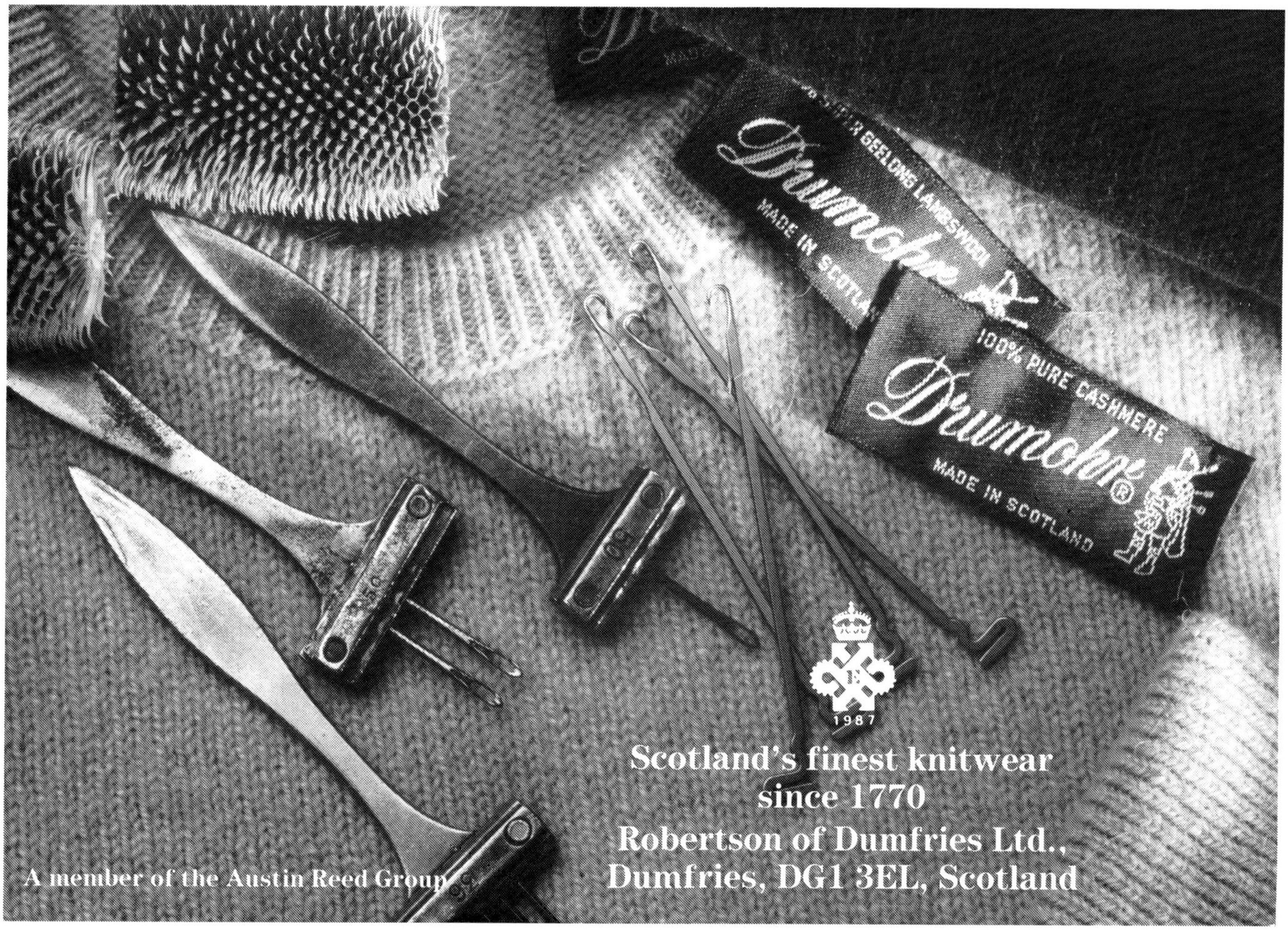

Scotland's finest knitwear
since 1770
Robertson of Dumfries Ltd.,
Dumfries, DG1 3EL, Scotland

A member of the Austin Reed Group

Having decided on quality its...

The consumer chooses hosiery in varying qualities, quantities and styles. This diversity is reflected in the constant demands placed upon the manufacturer.

If he is to maintain almost impossible schedules, whilst absorbing the latest refinements, using maximum capacity from high speed machines, including compound needle applications, he has no choice.

He will have to rely on the staying qualities drawn from time proven research and development into latch needle technology.

In choosing quality, Exeltor gives you a decided advantage.

...Advantage Exeltor

EXELTOR
Your partners in progress

CANADA	U.S.A.	ITALY	UNITED KINGDOM	AUSTRIA
Exeltor Inc., Bedford, Quebec, Canada. J0J 1A0 Telex: 055-61009 Tel: (514) 248-4343 Telefax: (514) 248-4441	Exeltor Corp., Suite 404, Friendship Centre, Greensboro, N.C. 27419 U.S.A. Tel: (919) 292-8800 Telefax: (919) 855 5844	Exeltor Canada S.p.A. Via S. Giovanna d'Arco 3, 20124 Milano, Italy. Telex: 312238 Tel: (2) 67 09 266 Telefax: (2) 69 09 269	Exeltor Ltd., Bodmin Road, Wyken, Coventry, U.K. Telex: 51-312408 Tel: (0203) 617181 Telefax: (0203) 612468	Exeltor G.m.b.H. Kaerntnerring 2A, A-1010 Vienna, Austria. Telex: 131139 (EXTOR A) Tel: (1) 505 28 37 (1) 505 28 47 Telefax: (1) 650 90 20

Industry Leaders Reflect On The World Of Knitting

Lord Young
Secretary of State,
Department of Trade
and Industry

I AM VERY PLEASED to contribute to this publication commemorating a very early and highly significant example of British enterprise. The knitting industry with its many facets has an important place in the history of economic activity in the UK. By harnessing the genius of British invention, as exemplified by William Lee in 1589 and continued through the years, the development of one of today's major industries has been made possible.

The knitting industry, like all others, has developed in meeting the needs of the consumer, adapting to changes in the requirements of the market and responding to competition. In the future, as in the past, there will be uncertainty; this is inherent in the activity of wealth creation. There must be a determination to maintain competitiveness by keeping unit costs low, by training and good management, by paying proper attention to the importance of good design, quality and marketing and by enterprise.

The William Lee Quatercentenary is a timely opportunity for firms in the industry to take stock, to assess where they are now, and to plan ahead for the future. In this context the relationship between business and the education system at all levels is crucial. The Government's Enterprise and Education Initiative is designed to build links to strengthen the relationship. Employers and teachers alike are concerned to see that young people leave school with a full range of attitudes and skill that they will need for the outside world and prepare them for the world of work.

One of the main objectives of the Enterprise and Education Initiative is to ensure that every young person leaving school has at least two weeks' work experience. We need the knitting industry to play its part to the full helping children to develop enterprising attitudes.

Then, of course, there is the completion of the single European market in 1992. This is the greatest challenge and offers the greatest opportunities since we joined the European Community in 1973. A market of 320 million consumers, more than equal to the size of the US and Japan together, offers tremendous opportunities as well as challenges. The coming of the single European market will strengthen the already well developed integration of the knitwear trade in the economy of the European Community.

In 1987, 69 per cent by value of UK's exports of knitwear went to other Member States of the European Community. In turn they accounted for 46 per cent of our imports. Inevitably our EC competitors will be turning their attention to the opportunities the single market offers them. It is for all UK firms to ensure that we gain the edge. I am pleased to learn that the knitting industry is taking an active interest in the implications of the single market. Now indeed is the time for individual firms to be planning their action strategy for the 1990's. The Government is ready to help with information and advice.

The UK knitwear industry has come far since William Lee developed his stocking frame; I wish it every success for the future.

Lord Rayner
Chairman,
Marks and Spencer plc

OVER THE LAST sixty years Marks and Spencer has developed close working partnerships with British knitwear, underwear, hosiery and jersey fabric manufacturers, who continue to serve us well.

Although the company is developing as an international business, we remain committed to our British suppliers and look to them to play a part in supplying our new outlets in Europe and North America.

Merchandise of high quality and good value is in demand throughout the developed world. There are tastes and lifestyles common to all the affluent countries and fashion is becoming universal. The potential to develop international trade has never been stronger.

In the last ten years, the knitting industry has faced considerable difficulties yet it has invested substantially in technology, design capability and management. It is now well equipped to compete internationally while retaining the flexibility needed to respond to the requirements of a demanding market place.

Competition will become tougher as trading opportunities open up. The industry understandably seeks reasonable control of imports but this will not be enough. The way to make progress lies in improving competitiveness. We need to be open to international fashion trends and alert to technical developments in centres of excellence around the world.

The words "Made in Britain" still command a great deal of respect. It is necessary to market the quality that British goods represent — the traditional British standards of fabric, fit, colour, styling, reliability in performance and the honouring of delivery times. The challenge is to ensure the right niche for British garments in the international market place and to promote them in those countries where there is as yet an unsatisfied demand.

There have been many technical and marketing advances since William Lee invented the knitting frame and further strides will be made in the future. There is no reason why the British knitting industry cannot remain in the forefront of these developments.

progress. But innovation cannot be achieved without research — and today the costs of research are rocketing. To reward those costs, we must seek wider markets and often the only market wide enough is the global one.

This is why my company strongly supports the creation of a single European market. To be world competitive, we must have a home base comparable in scale to those of the other main trading blocks. This is the true relevance of 1992. It should enable Europe to regain its proper position in the world's industrial league table. We must make sure that the legislation emanating from Brussels is clearly focused on that goal. We need the right kind of legislation — and not too much of it. 1992 should be about opportunities, not headaches.

In the knitting industry there will be many new business opportunities not only in such traditional areas as classic Scottish knitwear and quality ladies' tights and the new sports and leisurewear shirts in "high-tech" high-performance fabrics.

The knitting industry has weathered many storms in the past because of its versatility and flexibility. I am confident that these qualities will take it forward into the next century to maintain a robust and dynamic business. This confidence is evidenced by the major investments in research and technology that are being made at our own ICI Fibres, which now develops and sells knitting yarns worldwide for end uses ranging from fine hosiery to swimwear and from socks to "high-tech" sports shirts.

If William Lee were to reappear in the '90s, I believe he would see an industry driven from an open European base, using the unique innovative powers that we Europeans possess, to assume a strong presence on the worldwide stage.

From what I understand of Lee, I think he would be happy to see so many people within the knitting industry having the opportunity to prosper.

Denys Henderson
Chairman, ICI plc

I WONDER WHAT William Lee would say today if he could see the enormous global industry which has grown from the knitting machine he invented. Innovation, then as now, is the key to industrial

Sir Christopher Hogg
*Chairman and
Chief Executive,
Courtaulds plc*

I AM DELIGHTED to have the opportunity of contributing to this commemorative book, as William Lee's invention of 1589 was the foundation of the hosiery industry of which some of the oldest companies still prosper today within the Courtaulds Group.

The stocking frame was one of the most

Programme Of Celebrations

April 28	"Leicester Presents" A Pageant of Knitting History and Fashion Spectacular presented by Leicester Textile Society.	Bardon Hall, Coalville, Leicestershire
April	Launch of Design Council Design Competition sponsored by Marks & Spencer plc.	The Design Council, Haymarket, London.
May 6	Ruddington Framework Knitters' Museum. Opening of the Parker Room, an exhibition of 100 years history of the Parker family.	Chapel Street, Ruddington, Nottinghamshire.
May 29	Opening of the Wigston Framework Knitting Museum.	42/44 Bushloe End, Wigston, Leicestershire.
June 12-15	Interknit International Knitting and Hosiery Machinery Exhibition.	National Exhibition Centre, Birmingham.
June 17 & 18	Ruddington — A Pageant illustrating a Framework Knitters' Village of 1850.	Ruddington, Nottinghamshire.
June 18	Annual Livery Service of the Worshipful Company of Framework Knitters.	Leicester Cathedral
June 24	Two weeks of celebration events commence at Calverton, William Lee's birthplace and the village where the stocking frame was invented. Events include: Special Historical Display, Guided Walk, Flower Festival, Cricket Match, Historical Lecture, Street Market, Pig Roast and Barn Dance.	Calverton, Nottinghamshire.

July-September

July	Leicestershire Museums launch a comprehensive exhibition of 400 Years of Knitting. Museum of Technology, Leicester. To run until December.	Museum of Technology, Pumping Station, Corporation Rd, Leicester.
July 7-9	Conference "The History of Framework Knitting and the Hosiery and Knitwear Industries". Organised by the University of Nottingham in association with the Pasold Research Fund and the William Lee Quatercentenary Committee.	Hugh Stewart Hall, University of Nottingham
Sept	The Meeting Ground Theatre Company sponsored by Nottinghamshire County Council are to perform a musical to be called "Luddites" in co-operation with the Nottingham Playhouse.	To Be Announced.

October-December

Oct 11	The Worshipful Company of Framework Knitters' Celebration Banquet.	The Guildhall, London
Oct 16-20	Annual World Conference of the Textile Institute. "Textiles: Fashioning the Future".	Albert Hall, Nottingham
Oct 17	Royal Fashion Spectacular, with Presentation of Quatercentenary Year Design Awards.	Royal Concert Hall, Nottingham
Oct 20	Conference of International Federation of Knitting Technologists.	Leicester Polytechnic
Nov 24	Closing Event and Valedictory Address.	City Rooms, Leicester

LOOKING FOR QUALITY AND RELIABILITY AT SOURCE?

  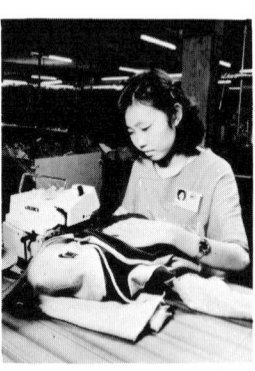 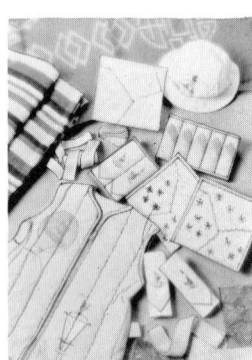

SOUTEX
- Cotton Yarn
- Polyester Yarn
- Polyester Sewing Thread Yarn

KNITEX
- Knitted fabric
- Dyeing & Finishing
- Printing

BANDARTEX
- Contract manufacture of garments

ESPEETEX
- General trading in textile related goods

If you see your requirements here, talk to us soon.

With our wholly-owned subsidiaries — SOUTEX, KNITEX, BANDARTEX, ESPEETEX — the SPTI Group, a pioneer of the textile industry in Malaysia, with an experienced workforce of over 2000, is a leading vertically-integrated textile mill in Asean.

Our reputation for quality and reliability is your assurance.

LOOK NO FURTHER!

SOUTH PACIFIC TEXTILE INDUSTRIES BERHAD
583, 3rd Milestone, Jalan Kluang, 83000 Batu Pahat,
Johor, Malaysia. Tel: 07-442433
Telex: SOUPAC MA 60708 Fax: 07-410288

KUALA LUMPUR OFFICE:
17.4 Menara Kewangan, Jalan Sultan Ismail
50250 Kuala Lumpur, Malaysia.
Tel: 03-2305490 Telex: SOUTEX MA 30640 Fax: 03-2305498

SINGAPORE OFFICE:
20 Peck Seah Street, Unit #02-00, Singapore 0207,
Tel: 02-2259393
Telex: BANTEX RS55258 Fax: 02-2259292

at Du Pont
each day, fresh ideas come to life

Through research and high technology, Du Pont brings added value to the daily life of people around the world.

Four centuries ago it was the fresh ideas of William Lee that revolutionised knitting, but look how the 1939 introduction of nylon changed the world!

Then came Orlon* acrylic, Dacron* polyester and Lycra* elastane. Today, fresh ideas with Lycra are making fashions perform better, fit better — from hosiery and innerwear to swimwear and outerwear. Advances that benefit both knitter and consumer.

Each day, fresh ideas based on the chemical, biological and physical sciences come to life at Du Pont.

**Du Pont (UK) Limited
94 Regent Road
Leicester LE17JD**

*Du Pont's registered trademark

Yarns for all Seasons.

Expertly dyed to customer shades.

SUN-RAY SPINNERS & DYERS LTD.

Head Office/England Sales Office
Friday Street, Leicester LE1 3BT.
Telephone (0533) 515161. Telex 342602.

Scotland Sales Office/A. Y. Agencies
Millbank, Cargill Avenue, Maybole KA19 8AD.
Telephone (0655) 83041. Telex 776108.

Spinning Mill/Schappe UK Ltd.
Rackery Lane, Llay, Wrexham, Clwyd LL12 0PF.
Telephone (0978) 832124. Telex 617097.

Serving the Industry Nationwide..

THE KNITTING INDUSTRIES' FEDERATION

The **KIF** is the "Voice of the Industry" with:—
- political representation into Whitehall, Westminster, and Brussels.
- full participation in Mailleurop, the NEDO Knitting Sector Group, the Triple Alliance and the CBI.
- liaison with the local, trade and national media.
- a comprehensive industrial Industrial Relations Service, including the negotiation of the National Agreement.
- representation at Industrial Tribunals; Health and Safety Services (interpretation of employment legislation) etc.
- statistics on production, imports, exports and employment etc.

Hatra

The Industries' Technical and Management Centre offering:—
- a wide range of management consultancy, including "World best" Company Performance Databanks.
- collective research dedicated to enhancing international competitiveness.
- unparalleled technical information services.
- investigational and routine testing.
- Quality Management, Business Forecasting and industrial engineering.

Is your Company supporting and benefiting from these vital activities? If not, further details are available from the Company Secretary on 0602 621081, or by writing to the following address.

**THE KNITTING INDUSTRIES' CENTRE
7 GREGORY BOULEVARD, NOTTINGHAM NG7 6NB**

Are you helping to pay for the very bomb that could blow you out of existence?

In 1987 the flow of knitted imports into the UK increased by 23% to £1.13 billion.

It's a similar story throughout the EEC. Key growth areas in this scenario were countries such as China, Turkey, Mexico and South Korea.

It is estimated that almost ½ million jobs in the European garment industry, 80,000 of them in the UK, are at risk now as a result of this import activity, most of it heavily subsidised in one way or another.

United, European garment manufacturers and European yarn manufacturers can fight this rising tide by design and technological skills. Alternatively, garment manufacturers can continue to buy subsidised yarn from non-European countries, and contribute generously to the financing of the garment imports which so threaten them.

Isn't it time to talk to Burnleys?

Colourful. Competitive. And closer to home

BURNLEYS
A GREAT EUROPEAN SPINNER

Knitted Clothing Imports to UK

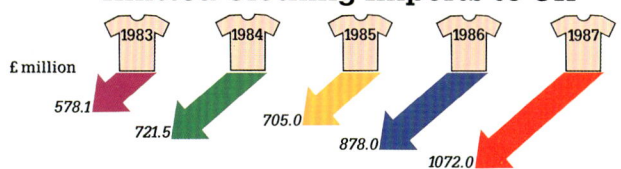

Man made fibre yarn imports into UK

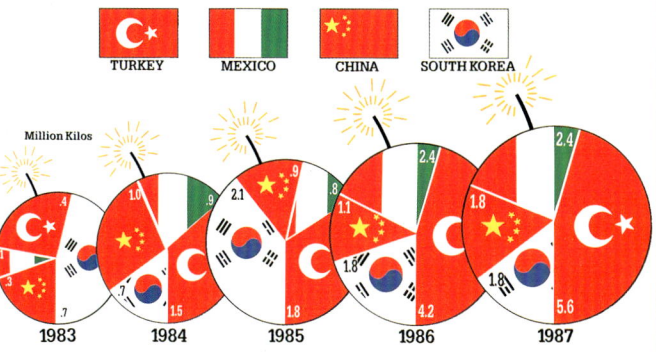

Are you going to help their garment imports achieve the same pattern?

SHIMATRONIC
NEW TECHNOLOGY

TOTAL KNIT

Shima Seiki's new technology has created a compact carriage that is lighter, shorter and cleaner. This reduces repeat loss at the end of the stroke and minimized the total machine size making for efficient floor utilization.

In addition, the new technology offers ergonomic designs for greater operational ease, super high-

SHIMATRONIC® Knitran System

Introducing the world's first 5-cam computerized flat knitting machine. With its extremely narrow carriage width, this model is amazingly compact. The result is reduced repeating loss and improved productivity.

SEK235FF
Five System Computerized Jacquard Flat Knitting Machine

Developed along with exclusive hardware and software based on the Micro SDS, the Micro SDS (PGM) is a multi-purpose system that allows pattern making, grading and marking of knitted cloth. In particular, the Shimatronic original "Figure input" system forms patterns by inputting dimensions for fast and accurate patterning.

PGM
PATTERN/GRADING/MARKING

The Micro SDS uses innovative "KnitCAD" software the world's first automated control program for patterns used with SHIMATRONIC computerized flat knitting machines. With "KnitCAD" a complicated program requiring 3 to 4 days or one week can be processed within a short space of time.

micro SDS
SHIMATRONIC DESIGN SYSTEM

ING SYSTEMS

speed operation, and improved performance and external appearance. For the exterior, Shima Seiki selected a simple and elegant design so the unit blends right in when placed next to existing plant. As always, Shima Seiki has designed with the user in mind.

SHIMATRONIC®
Knitran System

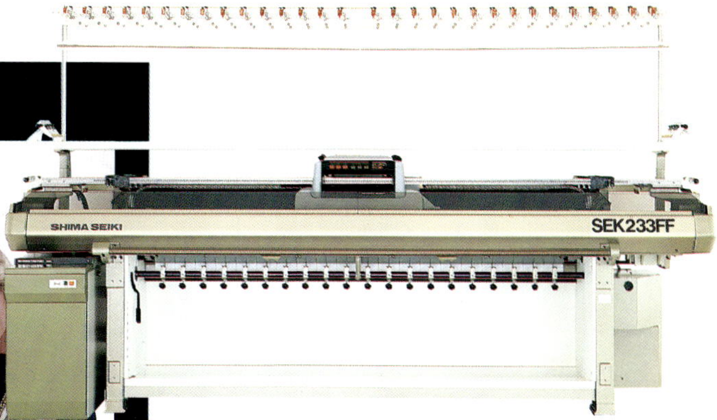

Combined operational ease and productivity. This machine uses two Knitran (knit and transfer) systems with a knit only cam system between them making for versatility and high production.

SEK233FF
Three System Computerized Jacquard Flat Knitting Machine

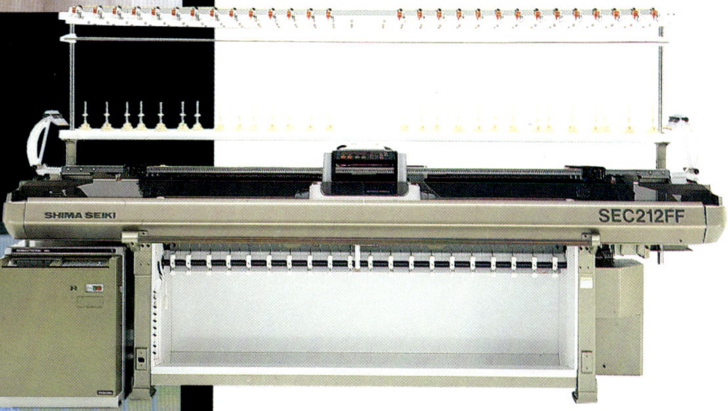

Shima Seiki's policy of continued new technology has made this machine by refining our most popular SEC 202 FF. It looks better and has higher production as well.

SEC212FF
Double System Computerized Jacquard Flat Knitting Machine

TOTAL KNITTING SYSTEMS
SHIMA SEIKI

SHIMA SEIKI MFG., LTD.
85 Sakata, Wakayama, Japan
Telephone (0734) 71-0511   Fax (0734) 71-1670
Telex 5542-243
Cable address SHIMA SEIKI Wakayama Japan

SHIMA SEIKI EUROPE LTD.
Michigan Drive, Tongwell,
Milton Keynes,
Buckinghamshire MK15 8HP.
Telephone (0908) 210888.
Fax (0908) 210777.
Telex 82330 Shima G.

- Kennedy Wagstaff Ltd., England ●Arbitex S/A, Spain ●International Trading Bureau, Greece ●Orsi Macchine Tessile SPA, Italy
- Terrot France S.A., France, Austria, West Germany and Benelux ●Textrima OY, Finland ●Chemby Marketing Ltd., New Zealand
- Overseas Export-Import Ltd., Israel ●Ramsay McDonald Group Industries Pty. Ltd., Australia.

DEREK TINEY LIMITED

Distributors of machinery to the knitting industry at home and abroad since 1963.

Texma House Kingsley Street Knighton Fields Leicester LE2 6DL
Telephone Leicester (0533) 702311 Telex 34477 Fax 0533 700305 England

BENSON TURNER

SPINNERS & DYERS

High-Tec Yarns in:	**Delivered in your shades with:**
HIGH BULK ACRYLICS	QUICK RESPONSE
WOOL RICH BLENDS	QUALITY
SPECIALITY YARNS	SERVICE

Head Office:
STATION MILLS . WYKE . BRADFORD BD12 8LA
Telephone: (0274) 601122 . Fax: (0274) 691170 . Telex: 517683 BENTUR G

THE POWER IN THE LAND

What this country needs is a power source that's plentiful, economical and environmentally safe.

And that's exactly what we have in the new face of British Coal – a dynamic, hi-tech industry with a sharp competitive edge in the market place.

Power that lasts

There are enough coal reserves in this country to last for hundreds of years.

And our coal industry has never been in better shape.

Coal production costs are the lowest in Western Europe. Productivity has rocketed 21% in a year. Coal is low in price and high in availability – a pattern British Coal is confident can be maintained well into the 21st century.

We have the technology

British Coal leads the world in both mining and combustion technology. That means companies using coal enjoy the world's most advanced equipment – in design, automatic control and environmental safeguards.

British through and through

Virtually all our mining equipment and boiler plant is designed and made in Britain. Every year British Coal spends more than £1000 million with British suppliers and over £38 million on research and development. We are part of British industry, we invest in British industry and we work for British industry.

A wide portfolio of help

British Coal offers every kind of coal to every type of industry. We help produce everything from chemicals to cars, tomatoes to tarmac, pints of beer to pintas of milk. And every one of our customers has the backing of our free technical service and countrywide support through the Coal Distribution Trade.

Make your move now

If your organisation needs a source of energy with a price that's not at the mercy of the dollar or international juggling, do what so many other leading companies have done. Make the move to British Coal. Ring Marketing Department (Industrial Branch) on 01-235 2020.

British COAL

 *Spinning fine wools and cashmere in Scotland and England for customers throughout the world.*

Patons RTN Limited

BLACK ROCK MILLS, LINTHWAITE, WEST YORKSHIRE HD7 5NT, GREAT BRITAIN.
Telephone (0484) 842233. Fax (0484) 844553. Telex 51262 RTNHUD G.

DERWENT MILLS, MATLOCK, DERBYSHIRE DE4 3FR, GREAT BRITAIN.
Telephone (0629) 3263. Fax (0629) 580241. Telex 377575 PATONS G.

LORNSHILL FACTORY, TULLIBODY ROAD, ALLOA, CLACKMANNANSHIRE FK10 2EZ, SCOTLAND.
Telephone (0259) 721472.

 A member of Coats Viyella Plc.

SANDOZ – PARTNERS IN TECHNOLOGICAL DEVELOPMENT

HIGH QUALITY PRODUCTS FOR THE PROFESSIONALS.

DYERS AND CHEMICALS TO MEET THE HIGH DEMANDS OF TODAY IN FASHION, PHYSICAL FORM AND FASTNESS.

SUPPORTING THE "LEE QUATERCENTENARY CELEBRATIONS"

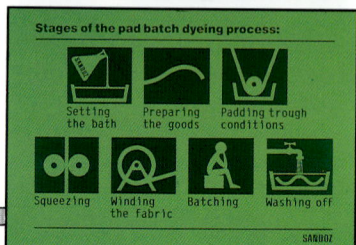

SANDOZ CHEMICALS A Division of Sandoz Products Ltd.
Calverley Lane, Horsforth, Leeds LS18 4RD. Tel: 0532 584646. Fax: 0532 390063. Telex: 557114. Sandoz Leeds.
Mandervell Road, Oadby Ind. Est., Leicester LE2 5LQ. Tel: 0533 714131. Fax: 0533 710876.

Village That Saw The Birth Of The Knitting Frame

By Chris Peck

IT WOULD SEEM that the settlement known as Calverton was established sometime about the sixth century AD. The name, which was likely to have been given soon after the place was occupied, contains the Anglo-Saxon element 'ton' (an enclosure or village) and can be interpreted as "calves' farm". However, evidence of settlement in earlier times survives in the form of earthworks from the Iron Age and Roman Period on nearby hill-tops. During the Saxon era there was a general migration from hill-top settlements to new sites in valleys and thus Calverton was probably founded on its present site. Brecks or clearings would have been made around the settlement and cultivated, giving it a chance to become an established and stable community in the forest.

The Domesday Book records that before the Norman Conquest of 1066 Ulvric the Saxon had a manor at Calverton which was given to a Norman — Roger of Poitou. There was also some Thane land which had been held by Alvric, a Saxon, and, after the Conquest, was obtained by William Peverill, Lord of Nottingham Castle. The Archbishop of York also held land at Calverton and there was a church and a priest. During the medieval period Calverton appears to have been a relatively important place. It was within the area of the Royal Forest of Sherwood and was one of four places where Forest Courts were held. These courts were concerned with the management of the forest and cases of trespass by people and animals.

By the sixteenth century much of the forest in Calverton was in the form of heathland, which was used for sheep pasture. Sheep-farming became such an exclusive business that other forms of agriculture suffered and many areas of arable land were converted into pasture.

According to Henson's *History of the Framework Knitters (1831),* the long-staple wool of Sherwood Forest sheep was particularly suitable for worsted and knitting. The 'barren forest ground' compelled the poor peasantry to welcome any alternative source of income.

It was at Calverton that William Lee first conceived the idea of imitating the action of a pair of knitting needles on a machine and thus began the industry which now ranges world-wide. However, it was not until the early eighteenth century that the hosiery industry began to thrive in the area. The system in use was that of "domestic outworkers", by which stockingers worked in their own homes, but they probably owned neither the machines nor the materials used on the machines. In the early stages

Dovey's workshop in Calverton, the largest of the old framework knitting shops in the village. Silk stockings were made here right through to the second world war.

South Terrace, Main Street, a group of stockingers' cottages in Calverton after restoration. (Picture courtesy Calverton Preservation Society).

machines were simply placed in a room of an existing cottage — such as the living room. But as more machines came into use there must have been an increasing number of cottages in which one room was used exclusively for making the knitted garments and spinning the necessary yarn. In 1844 there were 128 knitters' workshops in the village.

Inadequate

Soon it must have been realised that the small windows of the cottages then existing were inadequate for a workshop. Thus, as the industry expanded, houses were built or adapted to accommodate the frames in the best possible position, with long, wide windows. A number of these cottages still exist along the Main Street in blocks usually consisting of three or four dwellings.

The hosiery industry based on the domestic system survived generally until near the end of the nineteenth century. Groups of knitting machines were also worked in small workshops during the nineteenth century, which at first were hand-operated as were those in the cottages. In the latter part of the Victorian period steam-power operation of machines came into use which allowed larger factories to be built. Examples of both types of buildings still exist in Calverton. Hand machines were operated in a factory on Main Street, near the junction with Georges Lane, until 1956. This two-storey building has the characteristic elongated windows, similar to those of the stockingers' cottages. A factory using power-machines was built, also on Main Street, about 1890 and is still in use at the present time, using modern machines which incorporate the same essential features that William Lee introduced 400 years ago.

During the second half of the nineteenth century and until the 1920's there was a decline of about one third in the population of Calverton to just over 1,000 people. This decline was probably the result both of the concentration of the hosiery industry into the factories and of the changing nature of agriculture. By 1951 there were 1,300 people living in Calverton, the increase due to some extent to the establishment of a coal-mine, which began production in 1952. During the 1950's a large number of houses were built for colliery workers and their families, many of whom had moved from declining mining areas in other parts of the country.

By 1961 the number of people living in the village was more than four times that of ten years earlier. During the last 25 years the growth of population has continued but at a slower rate as Calverton has become a "dormitory" village for people who work in other places, particularly Nottingham.

A number of commemorative events are taking place in Calverton during 1989, most of them at the end of June and the beginning of July. The main celebrations begin on **Saturday June 24th** with a Flower Festival at St. Wilfrid's Church. During the afternoon there will be a Garden Trail when a number of local gardens will be open to the public. In the evening the Calverton Orchestra will be giving a concert in St. Wilfrid's Church. The Flower Festival continues on **Sunday June 25th** when there will also be a cricket match between Calverton and Ruddington cricket clubs.

The Flower Festival concludes on **Monday June 26th** and is followed during the evening by a Memorial Service, when a plaque or stained-glass window will be unveiled in memory of William Lee. The service will be conducted by the Vicar of Calverton, the Rev. Roy Catchpole, with the Rt. Rev. Richard Rutt, Bishop of Leicester and Rev. T. O. Hoyle, former Vicar of Calverton, also taking part. The evening ends with a buffet supper organised by the Calverton Preservation Society.

On the evening of **Tuesday June 27th** a Public Lecture organised by the Calverton Branch of the Workers' Educational Association (WEA) will be given by Dr. S. Chapman (Nottingham University) about William Lee and the history of the framework knitting industry. The lecture will take place at the Methodist Church Schoolroom.

Celebration Revue

A Celebration Revue will be presented by the Calverton Theatre Group on the evenings of **Wednesday, Thursday and Friday June 28-30th.** The events on **Saturday July 1st** will begin with a Street Market and Pig Roast, when part of Main street near the church will be closed to traffic. There will be a variety of stalls, street entertainers, musical

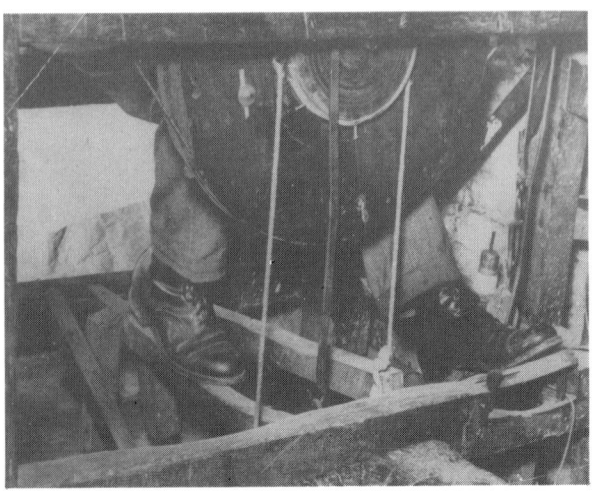

What computers and micro-electronics do today, hands and feet did yesterday. (Picture courtesy Calverton Preservation Society).

performances and other displays and attractions. The day will be rounded off with a Barn Dance during the evening.

In addition to these events Guided Walks, led by members of the Calverton Preservation Society, will take place on **Sunday June 11th and 18th.** The Calverton Folk Museum, featuring a special William Lee exhibition, will open on the last Sunday afternoon of each month starting in February and at other times by appointment. (Phone Notts. 652836).

A special display is also planned at Calverton Library from mid-June until mid-July.

Apart from all these events, a Lace Competition for children is being supported by the Lace Hall, Nottingham, a postcard of three views of Calverton is available and a book about Calverton's past history and anecdotes is to be published.

For more details about any of the events mentioned phone either Nottingham 654555 or Nottingham 654843.

Some UK Museums And Places Of Knitting Interest

Compiled by Doreen Beardall

RUDDINGTON

RUDDINGTON FRAMEWORK Knitters' Museum is an independent working museum housed in restored early 19th century framework knitters' cottages and workshops. The frameshop contains an extensive collection of hand frames in working condition. The cottages have been reconstructed to 1850 and 1900 dates respectively. Other features are a collection of circular sock machines, two exhibition rooms, a lecture room with video and a shop and reception area.

Opening Hours: The museum is open Tues, Wed, Thurs, and Friday from April to October and between 10am-4pm or by appointment throughout the year. Tel. (0602) 846914.

Special 1989 Events programme: **March.** Launch of raffle for double size pure silk and lace bedspread made in the museum workshop by Peta Lewis. **April.** April 1 "Coming of Age" open day and celebration (1971-1989). Launch of Ruddington Framework Knitters' Heritage Trail 12.00 (local trail only). **May.** May 6 Opening of the "Parker Room". Exhibition of 100 years of the Parkers of Chapel Street (sponsored by British Gypsum plc). Publication of "Hanah's Pantry". One hundred years of cooking in a hosier's cottage. Publication of "The History of Chapel Street and the Parker Family" by Dorothy Shrimpton. **June.** June 16 and 17. A Pageant. "Ruddington — A Framework Knitters Village of 1850". **July.** July 15 and 16 "Flowers, Knitting and Lace". A Festival of Flowers with knitting and lace as the theme, arranged by The South Notts. Flower Group in conjunction with the Friends of the Ruddington Framework Knitters Museum. **September.** September 16 Ruddington Framework Knitters' Museum 18th agm. Open day and showing of video films of the knitting industry of the past.

Peta Lewis working one of the stocking frames in Ruddington Framework Knitters' Museum. The museum preserves and demonstrates the traditional skills, living and working conditions of the 400 year old industry.

G. H. HURT & SON

Handframe shawlmakers, of 65 High Road, Chilwell, Nottingham NG9 4AJ. Opening hours April -September (holidays excepted). Mon, Tues, Wed. 7-9pm, Fri 2.30-6pm, Sat 9-4.30pm. Tel. (0602) 254080.

CALVERTON

Birthplace of Wm Lee and the Nottinghamshire village where the stocking frame was conceived and developed. (See features and display details with special article on Calverton). Opening hours (February 1989 onwards) last Sunday in every month 2pm-5pm. Other times by appointment. Tel. (0602) 652836.

THE LACE HALL, NOTTINGHAM

Nottingham lace is famous worldwide and the Lace Hall at the heart of the Lace Market tells the story of how the City invented and developed machine made lace, originally from the stocking frame. Working lace machines, bobbin lace demonstration, period setting, lace today video and auditorium show, talking figures. Lace and exhibition shops, coffee shop. Opening hours 10.30-5.30 every day including weekends, except Christmas Day and Boxing Day. Admission charge for entrance to the Story of Nottingham Lace. Tel. (0602) 484221.

HAWICK MUSEUM

Situated at Wilton Lodge Park, Hawick, Roxburgh. The Knitwear Room features displays showing the history of the internationally renowned knitwear industry of the Scottish Borders. Opening hours: April -September, Mon-Sat 10-12noon and 1-5pm. Sun 2-5pm. October - March, Mon-Friday 1-4pm, Sundays 2-4pm. Tel. (0450) 73457.

WIGSTON FRAMEWORK KNITTING MUSEUM

Number 42/44 Bushloe End, Wigston, Leicestershire is a master hosier's house with a two storey Victorian frameshop in the garden. The house dates from about 1700 and shows signs of various alterations. At the rear in a cobbled yard with water pump a two storey workshop extension has been added to the back of the house. The garden shows traces of the foundations of early frame shops. Nothing too unusual for this part of Leicestershire with its long tradition of worsted knitting.

Wigston in 1845 had some 550 hand knitting frames and out of a population of 2,000 well over a half were involved in the hosiery trade.

Wigston Framework Knitting Museum, a unique complex which became accessible only in 1986 and contains a number of machines which are some 150 years old.

The significance lies in the fact that the property has remained unaltered for 40 years. With the death of Mr. E. Carter the last master hosier in the early 1950s the workshop was locked and left. Inside on the ground floor were eight hand frames for making gloves, mitts and fancy rib tops for golf hose, together with all the moulds, tools and artifacts associated with each machine. On the upper floor was a "Griswold Graveyard". Stepping into the workshop is like stepping back into history. The machines are about 150 years old and were last in use in the 1920s. Even at that time they were relics from a past age.

This time capsule was known about and indeed was described and photographed by David Smith in his book 'Industrial Archaeology of the East Midlands', 1965, but it remained inaccessible until 1986.

With the death of Grace Carter, the property became available. A Trust was set up to buy 42/44 Bushloe End, the intention being to repair and restore the building and then open it as a museum. Raising the £51,000 to purchase the property proved impossible. Fortunately its importance was recognised by the District Council who bought the property and rented it to the Trust at a peppercorn rent.

The estimated cost of repair and restoration is about £70,000. £20,000 has already been raised and spent (largely on repairing the Swithland slate roof) by the Trustees. A commitment to phase II means the trust has to raise £26,000 by early 1989. Support is being sought from grant making bodies and the industry. A flourishing Friends organisation of 250 members is also supporting the Trust.

To help mark the Lee 400 anniversary the Trust is determined to have the museum open to the public, irrespective of the state of restoration. Obviously the more resources, financial and materials, that can be obtained the better the museum will be. Work is being done to get two of the handframes back into operation, a twelve finger frame and a rib top frame. Several Griswolds have risen from the graveyard and are in working condition. More help is always needed. Realistically those involved are looking at a long term project that, with support, will develop over several years.

May 29th, 1989 has been set as the opening date. The intention is then to have the museum open on Sundays and Bank Holidays and for parties by private arrangement. This however, has not been finalised and official details of opening times will appear later.

It is an exciting project with tremendous appeal in Leicestershire and the East Midlands because of the long tradition of hand frame knitting in the region. It is hoped that those interested in the project will consider how they might help. That 42/44 Bushloe End has survived is fortunate. That the workshop with its original machines and tools has survived is remarkable. Those who visit and see for themselves will unfailingly be delighted and amazed.

TIVERTON MUSEUM

The Old School, St. Andrews St, Tiverton, Devon. The John Heathcoat Room has displays under the title "From Loughborough to Tiverton — Framework Knitter to Bobbin Lace Manufacturer". On view — original lace-making machine designed and built by John Heathcoat. Opening hours: From January 30 to December 24 Monday - Saturday 10.30-4.30. Open Bank Holidays. Tel. (0884) 256 295.

CASTLE GATE COSTUME MUSEUM

This Museum of Costume and Textiles at 43-51 Castle Gate, Nottingham, is open daily from 10-5pm (not Christmas Day). Admission free. Tel. (0602) 483504.

INDUSTRIAL MUSEUM, WOLLATON PARK

Industrial Museum, Courtyard Buildings, Wollaton Park, Nottingham is open: April - September daily 10-6pm, Sundays 2-6pm; October - March Thursday & Saturday 10-4.30pm. Sunday 1.30-4.30pm. Tel. (0602) 284602.

GODALMING MUSEUM

Collections illustrating the history of the town and its immediate area, including framework knitting. Opening times: Tuesday - Saturday 10-5pm. High Street, Godalming, Surrey. Tel. 04868 426510.

DERBY INDUSTRIAL MUSEUM

The museum is housed in a silk mill, originally water-powered when it was first built in 1702, although a larger and successful mill with new machinery was added in 1717-21. Here 300 people were employed on five storeys. It stood for nearly two centuries until it was badly damaged by fire in 1910 and then substantially rebuilt. The mill provided a model for subsequent textile development and preceded Richard Arkwright's first cotton mill by more than 50 years. Within the 9,000 sq. feet of display space is a gallery introducing the textile industries — handframe knitting and narrow tape weaving with a new gallery planned. Opening hours: Tuesday - Friday 10-5pm, Saturday 10-4.45pm. Closed Sundays, Mondays and Bank Holidays. The Silk Mill, off Full Street, Derby. Tel. Derby 293111 ext 740.

ARKWRIGHT'S CROMFORD MILL

Restored original mill built by Richard Arkwright in 1771. He invented a cotton spinning frame and his mill was the first successful water-powered cotton spinning mill. Arkwright was the thirteenth son of a Preston tailor who amassed a large personal fortune and was knighted in 1786.

Opening hours: Summer. Easter - last weekend in October, Mon-Fri 10-4.30pm, Sat, Sun and Bank Holidays 11-5pm. Winter: Last weekend in October -Easter. Wed-Fri 10-3.30pm, Sat-Sun 11-3.30pm. Close Mon, Tues and Bank Holidays.

There are numerous other tourist attractions along the Derwent Valley. Included are the Ashford Bobbin Mill and John Smedley's Lea Mills, mill and factory shop. Smedley is a 200-years-old fully fashioned knitwear manufacturer.

LEICESTERSHIRE MUSEUM OF TECHNOLOGY

From July 1 - December 31 an exhibition "400th Anniversary of the Knitting Machine" at Leicestershire Museum of Technology, Corporation Rd, Off Abbey Lane, Leicester. Tel. (0533) 661330, will look at the legacy of William Lee's invention of the knitting machine in a variety of ways:

1. Through the history of the development of the machines themselves (and some of the people involved).
2. The lives of people who operated such machines both in "cottage industry" form and in factories through the nineteenth and twentieth centuries.
3. Showing the development of the products of the machines and their importance, particularly in the East Midlands region.

The extent to which the above can be achieved will naturally depend on funding and limitations of space. Certainly the invention of the machine will have to be set in its historical context (i.e. the time of the Armada) and the story concluded with a look forward to the industry's potential as a wealth creator and employer.

The exhibition will be open at the same times as the Museum: Monday - Saturdays 10.00am-5.30pm; Sunday 2.00pm-5.30pm. Admission will be free, except on Special Event Days (these are Sundays September 17 and December 17 during the period of the exhibiton). Any additional opening times (e.g. evenings) will be announced in the local press and other media.

The museum has extensive free parking. Regretfully refreshments are not generally available, except on Special Event Days. Lunch time meals are available at local inns.

The museum is accessible by public transport from Leicester railway station and the city centre by Leicester City Bus routes 29 and 29A. It is also clearly signposted from the surrounding roads with the familiar brown "tourism" signs.

For visitors from further afield the museum is about 3 miles to the north of the city centre and is accessible from the M1/A50 exit and, more directly, from the A6 Loughborough - Leicester road.

Further enquiries regarding the exhibiton should be directed to: Mr. R. Bracegirdle, curator, at the Industrial Heritage Museum, Snibston Mine, Ashby Road, Coalville, Leics. Tel. (0530) 510851.

Quatercentenary Projects And Competitions

TECHNOLOGY COMPETITION

GRIEVE LTD, the Coalville-based needles and knitting elements maker, are the sponsors for the William Lee Technology Competition. Carrying a £7,500 prize, the competition is to create a technique or mechanism which comprises an advancement or enhancement of knitting technology. The competition is open to young people worldwide between the ages of 18 and 30.

Entries must be received by July 1st at the Knitting Centre, 7 Gregory Boulevard, Nottingham, England. Winners will be notified during the second half of September.

"As the only remaining successors in the UK to the people who supplied Lee with his needles, we felt it was important to support the Quatercentenary", says Grieve sales director Colin Commons.

The £7,500 prize money which Grieve are putting up is part of their total sponsorship of £12,000 for the Lee Quatercentenary. "We are involved as sponsors because 1989 is our centenary and it is an opportunity to combine the Quatercentary and our own celebrations in a practical way", explains Mr. Commons.

The William Lee Technology Competition is an attempt by the organising committee to re-kindle the spirit of Lee in the hope that someone in the world has an untapped original thought or concept which will be released by this competition.

Entrants are assured that full security will be guaranteed with regard to the intellectual property rights of their entries.

The chairman of this prestigious technology prize panel will be the eminent Eur. Ing. Professor Gordon Wray FRS, F.Eng, FTI, F.I.Mech.E.

HISTORY CONFERENCE

UNIVERSITY OF Nottingham in association with The Pasold Research Fund and the William Lee Quatercentenary Committee will hold a **Conference on "The History of Framework Knitting and the Hosiery and Knitwear Industries"** in the Hugh Stewart Hall, University of Nottingham on July 7-9th, 1989.

Provisional Programme

Friday 7th July: 10.30-1pm Registration; 1-2pm Luncheon; 2.15pm Welcome by Prof. D. C. Coleman, chairman of the Governors, Pasold Research Fund; 2.15-3.30pm Dr. Joan Thirsk, St. Anne's College, Oxford. "Hand Knitting and Fashion in Early Modern Europe"; 3.30-4pm Tea; 4-5.30pm Mr. Negley Harte, University College, London. "The Legend of William Lee". Chairman: Rt. Rev. Richard Rutt, Bishop of Leicester; 6-7pm Dinner; 7.30-9.30pm Visit to Ruddington Framework Knitters' Museum (coach provided).

Saturday 8th July: 8-9am Breakfast; 9.30-11am Dr. Marilyn Palmer, University of Loughborough; "The Transition from Domestic to Factory Production in the British Hosiery Industry"; 11-11.30am Coffee; 11.30-1pm Dr. Colin Heywood, University of Nottingham. "The Transition from Domestic to Factory Production in the French Hosiery Industry". Chairman: Prof. Roy Church, Univesity of East Anglia; 1-2pm Luncheon; 2.15-6.30pm Conducted tour of framework knitting villages and visit to Wigston Framework Knitters' Museum (Leicester); 7pm Conference reception; 7.30-9pm Conference dinner; 9.00pm (approx) Presentation of old films relating to the hosiery industry.

Sunday 9th July: 8-9am Breakfast; 9.30-11am Dr. Stanley Chapman, University of Nottingham. "The Vicissitudes of the Hosiery and Knitwear Industry in Britain since World War II"; 11-11.30am Coffee; 11.30-1pm Dr. Robin Ward and Dr. Roger Smith, Trent Polytechnic, Nottingham. "The Emergence of the Asian Sector of the British Hosiery and Knitwear Industry"; Chairman: Prof. Charlotte Erickson, University of Cambridge; 1-2pm Luncheon, conference disperses.

SCHOOLS ESSAY COMPETITION

TWO POINTS that are regularly raised in relation to the knitting industry are it's poor image, and the lack of suitably qualified young people that wish to make textiles their career. One avenue that has not been explored until now is what the young would do in that situation, how they would market the industry to their peer groups, and what methods they might employ that attracts the attention of those groups.

Now a Schools Essay Competition will give those in secondary education in Leicestershire and Nottinghamshire a chance to put their case. It was felt that it was most important that the younger classes should not be excluded from such a project, so it was agreed that the competition should be open to the total school, regardless of the pupils age. The competition is having a wide appeal as it's title "How to Increase Awareness of the Knitting Industry, and it's Opportunities for Career Development", can fit into many segments of the overall curriculum.

The winning school will receive a prize of £500 donated by the Derbyshire company Profitex Ltd that shares the same chairman as the William Lee Quatercentenary Committee, Andrew Winkler. The children will not only be asked to write about their ideas, but will also be encouraged to illustrate them if they feel that it would help to get their message across. There may well be some new ideas about recruitment literature, or perhaps even a video that will pose a further project for the industry itself to take up after the schools have submitted their thoughts.

WILLIAM LEE PAINTING

GEDLING BOROUGH COUNCIL — the Council which embraces Calverton, home of Lee and birthplace of the stocking frame — is sponsoring a competition for a new William Lee painting. This will call for a 20th century interpretation of William Lee and his invention in the light of historical evidence and new knowledge available since the painting of the two previous Victorian representatives. Enquiries to Jack Smirfitt, Librarian, Hatra, The Knitting Centre, Gregory Boulevard, Nottingham.

STOCKINGS FOR THE QUEEN

PRETTY POLLY LTD are arranging for the knitting and finishing of a pair of stockings which will be as nearly as possible a replica of those first knitted by William Lee on his stocking frame. On behalf of her Majesty Queen Elizabeth II these will be presented to her only daughter HRH The Princess Royal.

A gift of tights specially knitted to commemorate the Quatercentenary has been accepted by the Rt. Hon. Bernard Weatherill, Speaker of the House of Commons. A pair has also been offered to Sir Christopher Collett, the Lord Mayor of London who similarly wears tights on ceremonial occasions.

MACHINE-KNIT A TOY

WILLIAM LEE'S knitting frame was intended for persons knitting at home. Today there are thousands of women who take pleasure and pride in producing beautiful knitted garments on the domestic knitting machine, which is directly descended from Lee's original machine.

The charity to be supported by the William Lee Quatercentenary Committee is the Save The Children Fund, and with this in mind an opportunity has been created for the domestic machine knitter to be involved in the celebration in 1989.

A competition is to be launched through World of Knitting magazine, sponsored by Atkinson Designer Yarns and Jones + Brother for a machine knitted toy, with prizes to the value of £1,500.

Each competitor will be asked to pay £1 entrance fee which will go to the Save The Children Fund. The toys will be sent to the magazine whose editor Sandra Williams is very excited about the whole project. The competition will be launched in World of Knitting magazine (circulation 28,000) in April, on the front cover, and followed up in May, with a closing date at the end of July.

PUBLISHING PROJECT

The Committee is assisting a sponsored publishing project which has the aim of stimulating in young people and their teachers an awareness of the textile and clothing industry. This is to be done through the production of lively and attractive GCSE course material, published and marketed by well established educational publishers.

In the course of a wider feasibility study recently completed, the publishers, Hobsons Publishing plc of Cambridge, have consulted teachers panels. These have confirmed that the industry provides an ideal practical basis for teaching science. It is proposed that GCSE science course material be published, "Learning Science through the Textile and Clothing Industry".

Through this core curriculum subject all 14-16 year olds could be reached with the message that the textile and clothing industry is exciting and of interest to them. By creating an accurate impression of today's high-tech industry, it is hoped to increase awareness of and respect for the industry's potential as a future employer.

Impact Of Future Change On Makers Of Knitted Products

By Rodney Gunston, Kurt Salmon Associates

IN THIS PAPER, specially researched and prepared for the Wm Lee Quatercentary, Rodney Gunston, a director of Kurt Salmon Associates in the UK assesses the changes which are expected to occur in the market for knitted products. In the light of these changes amongst consumers and at retail, he analyses the ways in which manufacturers will be called upon to respond.

1. INTRODUCTION

In order to understand what the future holds for domestic manufacturers of knitted products it is essential to recognise the changes which are occurring among the final consumers and hence in the retail sector.

First a look at the demands of the consumer.

2. THE CHANGING CONSUMER

An examination of the buying motivations of consumers shows that the last five to ten years have been characterised by a rapidly expanding range of stimuli to demand including:

      more time for leisure activities
      wider range of leisure activities
      wider overseas travel opportunities
      television lifestyle models
         soap/pop/sports
      emerging royal fashion influence.

Consumers have been rapidly exposed to these and other key influences by an ever more sophisticated and influential media and communications system.

This in turn has resulted in a fragmentation of consumer demand, and patterns of demand which operate in time frames which are independent of and often in conflict with the traditional two season structure.

This results in more fashion changes which reverberate through the supply system in a less predictable manner as consumers attempt to differentiate themselves from their peers, and a more sophisticated and a more affluent consumer who is no longer prepared to accept the limitations of just two clearly defined seasons each year.

3. IMPACT ON THE RETAILER
a) Fragmentation Of Demand

In recognising these changes in terms of consumer requirement for uniqueness and differentiation, retailers have been forced to respond by widening their offer and developing merchandising systems capable of supplying the market in a multi-seasonal mode.

As these seasons or 'waves' multiply, the retailer inevitably has to offer many more new styles or variations and is thus under considerable pressure to provide from his own or his suppliers' resources an increased flow of design ideas. This flow of ideas is essential to provide a fresh look in each 'season'.

b) EPOS Application

Running in parallel with these seasonal changes has been the development of Electronic Point of Sale systems. These systems are currently in their infancy in terms of full exploitation and we expect data capture systems to become increasingly sophisticated. More importantly the retailers and their suppliers will learn how best to analyse the EPOS data for the benefit of the whole supply system and how to react to the findings. These systems will thus allow the retailer to interpret more rapidly the sales performance of each style, colour and size. With more detailed information available earlier, the retailers will then begin to re-examine the criteria by which they select their suppliers, giving progressively more emphasis to those organisations which can provide superior response.

There will be an increasing recognition that in many cases an apparently lower initial margin due to a higher supply price from a flexible domestic supplier will in fact produce a real increase in margin due to a significant reduction in markdown losses and lost sales due to stockouts.

c) Return To Variety

It is interesting to note however that in parallel with these changes in consumer demand and retail technologies, there have been other key developments which have tended to work against the required retail response.

Even in the 1970s, the ownership of UK retail outlets was uniquely concentrated in a relatively small number of companies when compared with other advanced western economies. In the 1980s this ownership has consolidated even further to the point where the consumer is beginning to react against a certain 'sameness' which has emerged in the high street.

We thus expect to see some changes occurring which will restore more variety either through a break up of existing groupings or a greater level of merchandising autonomy for individual operating companies within the large groups.

d) Danger Of Oversupply

Already there are signs that the UK is moving towards the USA position of being 'overshopped' with too many stores chasing the available volume of business. This can only lead to the emergence of even greater competition within the retail system with individual groups attempting to gain an advantage through a chosen mix of prices, service and design.

4. MANUFACTURER RESPONSE

a) Introduction

In the light of these changes at retail and amongst the consumers, some key strategic issues emerge for consideration by manufacturers. These include:

  the merchandising role of the manufacturer
  the key role of product development
  Quick Response in product supply
  new thinking on vertical integration
  the potential for later colouration

We will now examine the required response from manufacturers in each of these areas.

b) Manufacturers As Merchandisers
i) The Merchandising Role

First, as markets continue to fragment it will become increasingly difficult for retail buyers and merchandisers to recognise and interpret all the many fast changing trends in the market place. They will thus inevitably look increasingly to their suppliers for design input and for coordinated offers covering broader ranges of products. This in turn means that suppliers will have to be prepared to develop and offer such packages which are likely to include products manufactured in-house together with items sourced from sub-contractors at home and overseas. (Chart 1).

The decision by a manufacturer to buy in a product will thus be motivated not only by criteria of cost but also the need to supply products outside his normal range and to allow him access to additional design input from external sources.

ii) Problems Of Control

Where manufacturers reach the point of significant volumes of sourced merchandise they will have to recognise the need to strengthen their resources in both design and merchandising and in systems for production planning and control and quality assurance. Without such a strengthening there is considerable evidence to suggest that there can be major problems with sourcing programmes in terms of late delivery and sub-standard garments.

c) Product Development

Manufacturers will also need to be able to respond more quickly to satisfy the more sophisticated, more demanding consumer described earlier. This in turn means that suppliers of knitted products will need to sharpen up their product development capability to significantly reduce the time taken from design concept to a product ready for manufacture (or sourcing). This implies investment in both technological solutions such as Computer Aided Design and computerised control over the development process and in closer relationships with suppliers and customers.

Chart 1. Manufacturer as merchandiser.

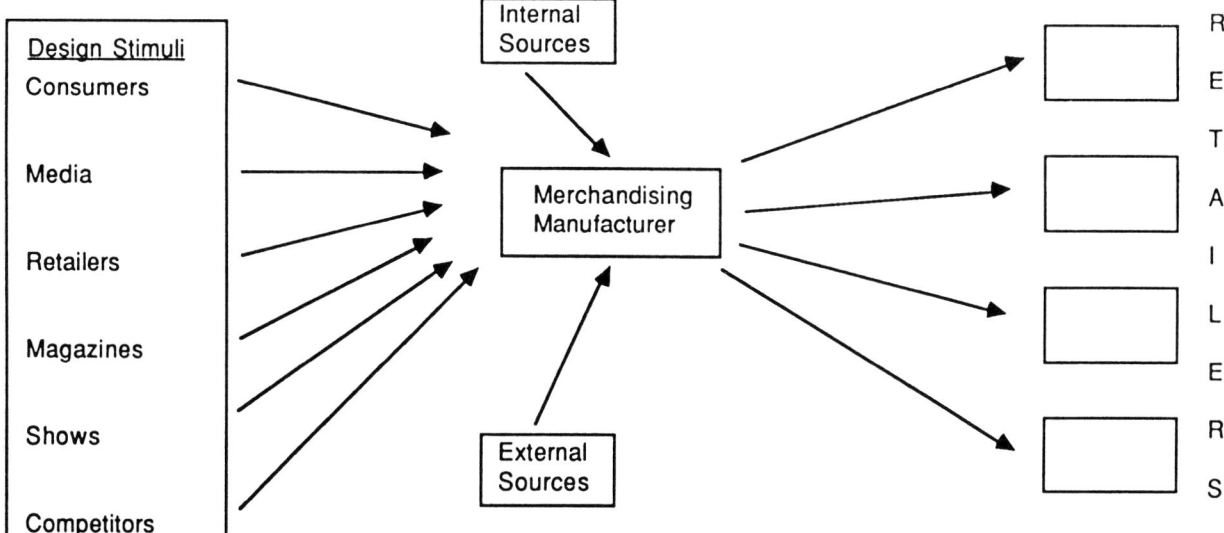

The attitude that samples are simply an irritant which get in the way of manufacturing efficiency will have to change. The control of the product development sequence will become a task for management at the highest level and employees at all levels will be called on to find ways to accommodate increased sampling activity with minimum disruption to normal production.

d) Product Supply
i) Quick Response

With retailers looking to be able to limit their exposure by ordering later, more frequently and in smaller quantities, it is clear that suppliers who operate with lower stocks of finished goods, work in progress and raw materials will be able to respond more readily to the retailer's requirement. We thus envisage that many of the successful companies of the future will shift their emphasis to achieving profitability through improved response to the retailers' needs. These improved levels of customer service have been shown to generate a higher level of sales, a reduction in *overall* unit cost and hence higher margins and profitability. Some investment and a total commitment are however required to achieve such results. The main thrust has to be towards a more *flexible manufacturing* resource.

ii) Flexible Manufacturing

As run lengths shorten and the number of styles proliferates, traditional methods of manufacturing become increasingly inappropriate. We thus see a trend towards 'modular manufacturing' where the process design is built around relatively small groups of operators making narrow ranges of products, with very low levels of inventory and fast throughput. This approach will be coupled with group based incentives, total quality responsibility within the group and inevitably increased employee involvement. This approach will in some cases lead to an increase in standard work content but a reduction in overall unit costs due to:

      lower labour turnover (lower training costs)
      fewer imperfects (better margins)
      less time spent on repairs (more volume)
      increased sales due to quicker response

Sceptics are quick to pour scorn on these concepts but there is extensive experience especially in the USA to show that the approach works. The benefits accrue to the more flexible manufacturer from two sources. First, because he is more responsive he achieves a larger share of the retailers' business with the resulting well-understood volume benefits. Secondly because retailers find that they have fewer losses due to markdowns and stockouts on merchandise sourced from the more flexible manufacturer there is room to negotiate these few extra vital percentage points of gross margin which can mean the difference between profit and loss.

iii) Supplier And Customer Links

We are already seeing electronic links between the major high street chains and their contract suppliers. This is only the start of a process which will see links between other types of retail outlet and their suppliers. (See Chart 2).

Electronic links between knitters and yarn and trim suppliers will also be developed to speed up the flow of information and merchandise between these key elements in the chain.

Chart 2. Future electronic links.

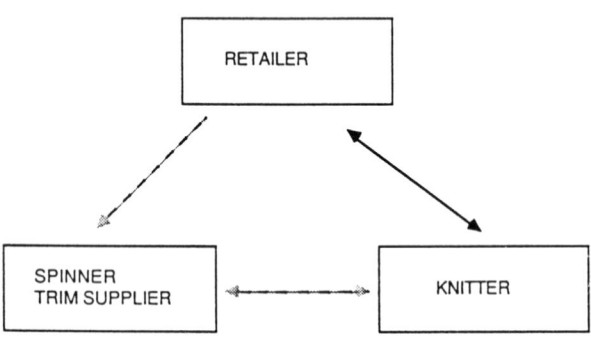

In some cases we shall even see electronic links between retailer EPOS systems and the yarn and trim suppliers, aimed at further reducing the replenishment lead times within the system.

e) Vertical Integration

In order to respond to the changes occurring at retail we also see in some cases a move towards more *vertical integration* with knitters owning and operating some of the upstream processes, especially in the areas of fabric or yarn colouration. Much historical and current evidence suggests that vertical integration is a recipe for failure but this is because the strategic thinking has usually been misguided.

Most attempts at vertical integration have been directed primarily towards capturing more of the added value within the supply system simply by linking processes and attempting to maximise the operating efficiency of each element. This strategy has led to the building in of a whole series of operating restrictions which in turn result in an unwieldy and inflexible system incapable of offering the required levels of response.

A new approach to integration is thus required with a strategy of a more integrated supply system orientated towards customer service.

The process design has to be engineered to minimise throughput time using many of the techniques we have already discussed. In addition, due to the more complex nature of a more vertical organisation, an integrated approach to production planning will also be needed. This almost certainly means using the power of the computer to balance the sometimes conflicting requirements of successive stages in the process.

With this new strategic approach, vertical integration will provide some companies with a true advantage over their non-integrated competitors.

e) Later Colouration

The colouration of fashion products is perhaps the most important factor in the consumer's final selection from the retail shelf. A subsconscious decision on price has already been made by entry into a particular type of retail outlet. The decision process at the counter or the garment rail is thus usually:

    Is the colour right?
    Do they have my size?
    Does it fit?
    How will it perform?

Since colour is the least predictable of the fashion elements in the consumer's choice it follows that a commitment to colouring should be delayed to the latest possible point in the manufacturing process to allow maximum time for response to consumer demand.

We thus see major benefits for those manufacturers who press forward with any techniques which can delay the colouring decision. Chart 3 shows why late colouring is so important in reducing forecast error, and hence markdowns and stockouts.

In some cases, technological development will be required to find new ways to achieve acceptable levels of finish and performance but the rewards for those companies which are successful are likely to be enormous. The potential benefits are thus likely to direct research and development towards solving the many technical problems associated with expanding the scope of finished garment dyeing, and to providing yarn dyed products comparable with the performance of their fibre dyed counterparts.

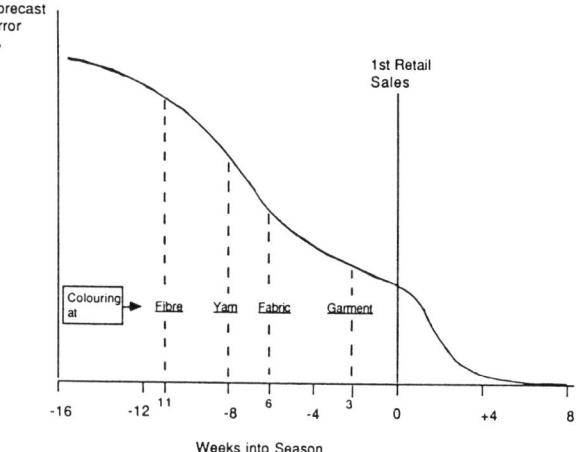

Chart 3. Colouring and forecast error.

5. CONCLUSION

If William Lee's technological breakthrough is to prosper in its next 400 years in its country of origin, then manufacturers will have to be prepared to respond to the ever changing needs of the consumer. We see every indication that consumers will continue to demand more and more variety and more frequent changes in the merchandise they are offered. This fragmentation of demand can be seen as either a THREAT or an OPPORTUNITY for the manufacturers of knitted products.

Profitable survival in any company may depend on which of these two attitudes prevail.

Future Prospects For 1992 And Beyond

By John Harrison, Knitting Industries' Federation

"Methinks I am a prophet new inspired"
King Richard II

ECONOMIC FORECASTING is always a precarious but never trivial pursuit — ask any Chancellor of the Exchequer! Predicting the future of an industrial sector such as knitting is particularly fraught. The widely diverse product range with varying degrees of intensiveness vis a vis capital and labour; the increasing dynamic cyclical vagaries of fashion and demand; a burgeoning number of suppliers, particularly in the developing countries; accelerating transportation and technology transfer, all combine into a veritable medley of uncertainty. Nevertheless, within this myriad of imponderables, certain clear signals are to be found.

Above all, the worldwide demand for hosiery and other knitted goods can confidently be expected to expand at a healthy rate for the remainder of the 1990's and beyond into the rapidly approaching 21st century. This confidence rests upon two central trends which are already self evident. Firstly, knitted goods are now firmly established as an integral part of the fashion scene in the industrialised countries. The inherent two-dimensional stretch of the knitted structure and associated ease of aftercare encourages its growing use in the production of actionwear, which abounds off the back of increased leisuretime and the body fitness hype. Secondly, living standards in many Third World countries are improving, including the standard of clothing, and this can be expected to continue and spill over into more of the increasingly populous emerging nations.

The crucial issue is "How much of this increased demand will be filled by knitters in the industrialised countries as opposed to those who are located in the newly industrialised and developing countries?". The answer to this key question is predictably unpredictable and locked in a vicissitude of unknown elements. All of them, in differing scale, will impact on the equation. Among them are the future of the GATT Multifibre Arrangement after 1991, the outcome of the Uruguay and future rounds of Multilateral Trade Negotiations, the vagaries of exchange rate movements, the impact of the Single European Market beyond 1992, the dynamism of fashion, technological evolution, demographic change and the global economic situation.

Departing briefly from crystal ball gazing, it is salutary to remind ourselves that in the absence of the MFA, introduced in 1973, the present size, shape and distribution of the knitting industry would be very different from that of today. There is no doubt that without the MFA the contraction of the textile, knitting and clothing industries in Britain, the rest of the European Community and the United States would have been considerably more acute. Given the associated adverse social and economic consequences, this would have added to the already record levels of unemployment and balance of trade deficits in each of these countries. For the newly industrialised countries of Hong Kong, Taiwan and South Korea, their pre-eminence as dominant exporters of textile products, established in the 60's, would have been further enhanced throughout the 70's and 80's with no MFA. This would have severely retarded and denied the economic benefits of the diffusion of these industries into a multitude of other, more relatively impoverished nations, eg, India, Pakistan and Indonesia.

Praised Not Condemned

Against this background, the internationally approved MFA is an orderly marketing instrument that should be universally praised and not condemned. Certain nascent textile exporting countries should never forget that they would not have secured a look-in without it. Moreover, the presence of the MFA has unquestionably averted an international trade-war, the consequences of which would have spread way beyond textile products as national governments scrambled for the political lifeboats and the consequential retaliation took its toll to the lasting detriment of the world economy as a whole. Despite the theoretical, academically persuasive arguments of multilateral trade liberalisation, the associated philosophies of the international division of labour and the law of comparative advantage, the abolition of the MFA must not be countenanced if a convolution of world trade on a major and unprecedented scale is to be averted. The return of our industry's products to the normal rules of GATT, the antithesis of the MFA, cannot be contemplated seriously until all the players involved are deploying their skills on the same level pitch.

For the foreseeable future, the distortions to trade brought about by the paradox of exchange rates, penal tariff and non-tariff barriers, soft loans, export subsidies, exploitation of child labour, counterfeiting of designs, models and trade marks, all augment into a manifestly unfair and unacceptable trading scenario. Indeed, the prevailing scenario is tantamount to playing different games, to different rules, in different stadiums. In other words, bluntly stated, the trading nations of the world cannot expect to enjoy free trade without genuine fair trade. For the purpose of this prognosis, it is assumed that commonsense will again prevail and the MFA will not be unilaterally disarmed in the Uruguay Round of MTNs. It is crucial that this timely opportunity will be grasped by HM Government and the European Community to negotiate a better and more equable balance of rights and obligations.

Paramount in this litany of inequities lies the dilemma of exchange rate movements. The abolition of fixed exchange rates, following the collapse of the Bretton Woods Agreements in the early 70's, notwithstanding the virtues of so doing, has created a global economic trading situation which can only be described as perverse in its magnitude and effect. How much longer can the world trading system and, more significantly, the knitting industry, tolerate and be capable of digesting a situation whereby the currencies of many of the industrialising countries in the Far East and South East Asia are linked to the US dollar, regardless of their own individual economic performance? It is an unacceptable corruption of any state of orderliness or fair play if a weak dollar, brought about by the unprecedented trade and budget deficits in the United States, is mirrored in the value of the currency of, for example, South Korea which enjoys a massive balance of trade surplus. This bizarre paradox must be addressed and effectively resolved as a matter of extreme international urgency. Why should jobs and capital invested in the British and European knitting industries continue to be sacrificed on the altar of exchange rate perversity, which compounds the inherent comparative advantage of the low labour cost countries?

Turkey, an aspirant full member of the Community, has already established itself as the major operator but the African, Caribbean and Pacific (ACP) countries also enjoy preferential status as suppliers to the EC, entitling them also to duty free entry. Mauritius is the main supplier but several other countries, such as Zimbabwe, are also growing exporters. In the medium term, an increasing quantity of imports is likely from Caribbean countries such as Jamaica, where production is growing quickly with considerable investment by US and Far East firms. At present, sales are primarily aimed at the USA but their attention is likely to turn to Europe in due course. Haiti and the Dominican Republic, substantial exporters to the USA, are likely to be invited by the EEC to join the ACP Group in the near future. Equally, the recently concluded EC/Gulf States Co-operation Agreement can also be expected to feature in the reckoning as new investment is attracted by the real prospect of preferential access to a Community market with a population of 320m.

Sleeping Giant

Above all, the sleeping giant in the form of China, already rising from its self imposed slumber, with a population of almost twice the size of the EC and the US combined, has the capability of achieving near total destruction of the textile, knitting and clothing industries in both the developed and developing world given unrestrained access to these markets. Faced with such facts, how could anyone of sound mind even contemplate throwing to the wolves the jobs of 480,000 workers in the UK and over 3m in the EC as a whole, with sales of £956bn and external exports of £12bn?

The next major element for analysis is the impact of the much vaunted Single European Market scheduled for completion by the end of 1992. In itself the direct effect of the Single Market on the EC knitting industries is already in place. The tariffs on knitted goods which existed between the Member States have long since been removed. Apart from the effect of flammability regulations in fringe areas, the free movement of knitted goods manufactured within the Community is not restricted by technical barriers of the kind which proliferate and retard trade in many other industrial sectors. However, the secondary effects are likely to be dramatic, always recognising that the drama will evolve gradually and not manifest itself overnight in another 'Big Bang' on 31 December, 1992. For the European knitting industries, the major pre-occupation is the continuing division of MFA quotas between each of the Member States — an arrangement which does not fit comfortably into the Single Market concept with its envisaged abolition of Customs border controls. The British industry will clearly be the most vulnerable, faced as it is, with the most easily penetrated domestic market in the world with access to 60m consumers. The concentration of the channels of distribution in the UK is unique. The adoption of Community quotas must be phased if the worst consequences are to be avoided.

The next most important secondary impact will be the synergy generated by the Single Market. So far, since the creation of the Common Market, this has remained largely dormant but is poised for major change with alliances in the form of takeovers, joint ventures, increased franchising, licensing and other forms of co-operation arrangements being forged between firms within the Member States and the preferential countries. British companies must review their strategic plans and those of their European competitors. They must ensure that they are fully aware of how they will be affected by the Single Market and position themselves accordingly. The need for linguistic capabilities in other Community languages will acquire a new and meaningful dimension, particulary for a disproportionate number of monolinguistic Brits. The strategies of the major High Street retailers, and the impact on their sourcing policies, will also need to be carefully monitored.

Motivated by a quantum leap in technology during the past decade, the new dynamism in fashion, now firmly established, will remain and probably progress still further. Gone for ever are the days of the two basic seasons of Spring/Summer and Autumn/Winter. Styles, designs and colours will change with increasing rapidity. However, the undoubted added burdens that this places on manufacturers are more than offset by the advantages offered to those firms who are able to rise and meet this challenge. The ability to be able to respond quickly to the demands of the market place will be an essential tool of any company which is intent upon staying in the race. The essential concomitant must be that the industry's retail customers give the degree of ongoing commitment to their suppliers which is necessary to ensure that their partnership in Quick Response is allowed to fulfil its potential to their mutual benefit.

What then are the future prospects? Certainly the Knitting Industries' Federation will continue to fight vigorously for the maximum amount of reasonable protection against the unfair competition, at the same time advocating the need for genuine reciprocity in international trading arrangements. But without in any way wishing to be defeatist but always realistic, the extent of the Federation's successes will continue to be measured in its ability to achieve damage limitation rather than a rolling back of the existing damage. That means that the knitting industry in Europe must brace itself for a further growth in imports at levels which will be greater than the growth in demand, ie, greater import penetration.

Individual firms must use every available weapon in their armoury to improve their overall efficiency, particularly in the areas of design, productivity and their ability to service their customers on factors other than price, thereby enhancing their international competitiveness in their own national market, other Community markets and beyond. Concurrently, bodies like the KIF and Mailleurop will not leave a stone unturned in their determination to dismantle the barriers which severely restrict the ability of the knitting industry to export knitted goods worldwide.

Within this framework, individual companies must not only seek to internationalise their business by expanding their exports, but should also be looking seriously at supplementing their own domestic production by themselves sourcing parts of their ranges from overseas and averaging their prices at the manufacturing stage. For over a decade, the German knitting industry has pursued, and is now in the process of fine tuning, this collective strategy induced by its high wage economy. This policy has resulted in maintaining jobs in the German knitting industry which would otherwise have been lost, whilst enabling employers to pay the levels of remuneration needed to attract the required calibre of management and operatives, notwithstanding the competition for labour, particular from the sector of services.

Enforced Dilution

The enforced dilution of origin labelling facilitates the ability of manufacturers, in co-operation with their retail customers, to move in this direction. A significant number of British knitting companies, both large and small, have already begun to move in this direction, but the industry as a whole lags well behind the German and Dutch competition. The other majors in the form of the Italian and French knitting industries are also in the process of pursuing such a course, bearing in mind the Single Market and the accompanying unfettered free circulation of goods. British companies must not find themselves left behind as the disciplines and opportunities of more liberal and wider market forces become more firmly established. While such a strategy is analagous to heresy in the context of traditional values, it should always be remembered that the dinosaur became extinct, in spite of its size and omnipotence, because of its inability to adapt to the changing environment in which it found itself.

The British knitting industry has been tried and tested many times since the time of William Lee, but the inherent entrepreneural skill, the readiness to assimilate new technology, when harnessed to the resolution and determination of everyone at all levels, has always ensured that the industry has won through as a continuing social and economic force of substance. Admittedly, the going has never been tougher. Future prospects in 1992 and beyond have never been more challenging, but I cannot help but feel that when our successors come to celebrate Lee's Quincentenary, they will look back and say that "This was their finest hour".

THE LARGEST RANGE OF KNITTING MACHINES IN THE WORLD

JUMBERCA: 32 CIRCULAR MODELS, FOR SINGLE KNIT, DOUBLE KNIT, SWEATERS AND BODY SIZES.

Jumberca, with 40 years of experience under its belt, offers the widest range on the market, covering all special requirements. Fast, versatile machines, with plenty of creative scope.

Machines which are able to knit anything, from the simplest interior garment to the most sophisticated creations of top designers.

Only a firm with a strong technological base —and a policy of continuous investment into research and development— is capable of meeting the challenging demands of fashion: by providing the right machine at the right time, while guranteeing absolute reliability and high production output.

JUMBERCA

JUMBERCA, S.A.
Jacinto Benavente, 32
08911 Badalona
Spain

☎ 389 12 62*
Fax 389 16 12
TX 59504 Jumb E
✉ P.O. Box 128

PURE NEW WOOL
CERTIFICATION TRADE MARK

A COLOURFUL FUTURE FOR KNITWEAR

With dyes, pigments and auxiliaries from

YCL YORKSHIRE

Yorkshire Chemicals plc Colours Division
Kirkstall Road, Leeds LS3 1LL England.
Telephone: (0532) 443111
Telex: 55366 Y CLLDS G Fax: (0532) 421670

Setting the standards for others to follow

The birthplace of the modern textile industry—Nottinghamshire, is also home to one of the UK's leading centres for textiles and fashion education.

At Trent Polytechnic we are continuing William Lee's tradition of innovation. Our award winning courses in fashion, textiles and knitwear design attract students from around the world. In 1988 Trent won the top 3 places for the Deloitte Haskins & Sells Award for textile design, open to young designers under the age of 26.

For details of our courses, degree shows and consultancy services, contact the Department of Fashion and Textiles, Trent Polytechnic, Burton Street, Nottingham NG1 4BU. Tel. (0602) 418248.

Trent Polytechnic Nottingham

Nottinghamshire County Council

CASHMERE
Pure Luxury Spun in Scotland

For over 120 years we have been spinning fine yarns, and none is more luxurious than our world famous cashmere.

Our spinning expertise gained through the use of the traditional system and enhanced by the introduction of modern electronically controlled machines, ensures we continue to offer an outstanding regularity of yarn levelness, time and time again.

Todd & Duncan Ltd

Lochleven Mills · Kinross · Scotland · KY13 7DH
Tel: (0577) 63521 · Telex: 76168 · Fax: (0577) 64533

Suppliers of Luxury Yarns to the World.

Represented by: Joseph Dawson AG · Baarerstrasse 73
Ch-6300 Zug 2 · Switzerland · Tel: Zug (042) 216066
Telex: (IDAG CH) 868857 · Fax: (042) 215165

Colourful Impressions

For guaranteed colour consistency in your products use VeriVide.

The VeriVide range of inspection equipment includes, Artificial Daylight, U.V., Tungsten and Point of Sale light sources for the visual assessment of colour, in accordance with BS.950, CIE and ISO standards.

Whatever your colour matching needs, VeriVide, the market leaders have the answer.

Contact us today and find out more about our standard range and custom designed equipment.

LESLIE HUBBLE LIMITED
FROG ISLAND, LEICESTER LE3 5AG
TELEPHONE 0533 620228. TELEX 34643 HUBBLE G. FAX 0533 514170

JOHN WILLIAMS
Textile Machinery
Sales Limited
66 Cannock Street
Leicester LE4 7HR

Telephone (0533) 460204
Fax (0533) 460161
Telex 342667 will g

World wide suppliers of Quality Used Knitting Machinery.

We thank all our valued customers for your continued support and welcome hearing from new clients.

Commission dyers and merchants of mercerised cotton, soft cotton, acrylic, polyester, polyamide, blends and fancy yarns.

A stock range of 100 shades available in 3/14 c.c. Combed Cotton.

ELTON COP DYEING Co. Ltd.

WALSHAW ROAD, BURY LANCASHIRE BL8 1NQ
Telephone 061-764 1383. Fax 061-763 1159. Telex 669810.

KLITRA
celebrate 400 years
of knitting manufacture
and look forward to future progress.

SYMBOL OF EXCELLENCE

Your Independent Non Statutory Training Organisation working with you for a better industry.

KLITRA,
7 Gregory Boulevard, Nottingham NG7 6LD.

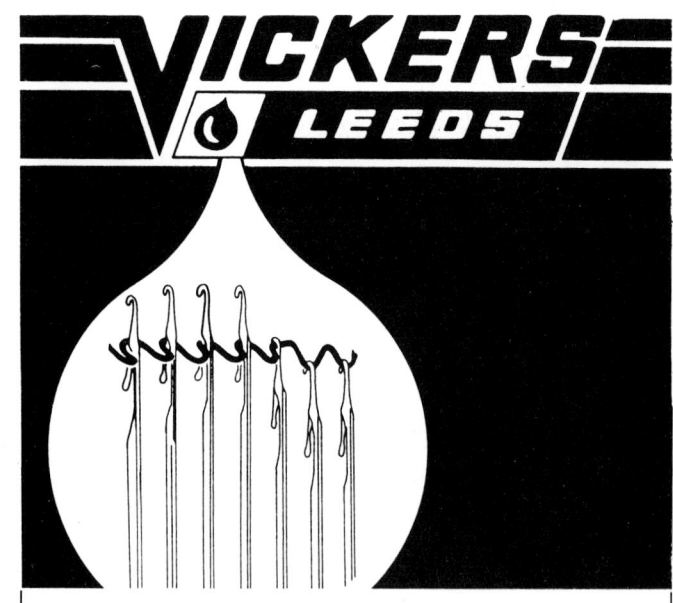

A COMPREHENSIVE RANGE OF QUALITY NEEDLE LUBRICANTS FOR ALL TYPES OF KNITTING MACHINES AND FABRICS.

Benjn R. Vickers & Sons Ltd.
5 Grosvenor Road, Leeds LS6 2EA, England
Tel (0532) 752601. Fax (0532) 304199. Tlx 55250.

A UNIQUE OPPORTUNITY TO AQUIRE A LITTLE PIECE OF HOSIERY HISTORY....

Preceding by more than 25 years the classic two-volume framework knitters' petition, this is a 52 page word-by-word record of the Findings and Minutes of Evidence given before a House of Commons Select Committee "Appointed to enquire into the Petition of the Hosiers and Framework Knitters in the Woollen Manufactuery of the Town and County of Leicester", presented to the House on 12th February 1819.

We are making available a strictly once-only facsimile reproduction edition of 750 numbered copies of this unique document.

Considerable investigation has been carried out to match as closely as possible the hand-made paper of the original: the facsimile is superbly reproduced on Glastonbury Book Antique White Laid paper. Tests have shewn that the faded slate grey cover is likely to have been the cobalt shade of the facsimile. The limited edition is hand-sewn with cotton thread, again to match the original as closely as possible.

A document to be read, re-read, put away and treasured. Then to bring out to delight and suprise your knitting friends.

Write now for your personal numbered copy, price only £5.75 ($14 USA and Canada) including VAT, postage and packaging.

**FERRY PICKERING PUBLISHERS LIMITED,
EASTERN BOULEVARD, LEICESTER LE2 7BN**

1776—1989

THE NATIONAL UNION OF HOSIERY & KNITWEAR WORKERS

General President-David Lambert.   General Secretary-Tom Kirk.

55 NEW WALK, LEICESTER LE1 7EB.
Telephone: (0533) 556703. Facsimile: (0533) 544406.

Our Union has, for more than 200 years, been actively engaged within the hosiery industry: its membership is to be found throughout England, Scotland and Wales.

The NUHKW is affiliated to the Trades Union Congress, The General Federation of Trade Unions and the International Textile, Garment and Leather Workers Federation.

The Union's objective is to promote and encourage the Trade Union organisation of all people working within the industry, to regulate the relations between members and employers and to seek improvements in the industrial and social welfare of the industry's workforce.

Illustrated around the 1890 membership certificate are: Top left, the Head Office of the NUHKW, 55 New Walk, Leicester.
Top right, Saving jobs by lobbying the EEC in Brussels for import controls.
Bottom right, NUHKW conference in session.
Bottom left, Supporting trade union colleagues at GCHQ Cheltenham.

Profits, Exchange Rates And Enterprise In The 1980s

By David Buck, Barclays de Zoete Wedd

IN THE DARK DAYS of 1980 there was genuine belief that UK textile and clothing industries were suffering from terminal illness. Yet between 1981 and 1987 we saw recovery and growth in profits of 25 per cent per annum compound which outperformed average industrial earnings by over 5 per cent per annum. Margins moved from an average 2 per cent to 7 per cent.

In the preceding 15 years quoted textile companies had underperformed average industrial earnings by 4 per cent per annum with a highly cyclical profile. It is no wonder that they were given a high risk, low reward rating by investors.

In 1980 sterling was strengthening towards $2.40 exposing a number of weaknesses in UK textiles which required tough and decisive action, which in turn bred a new style of market-wise profit orientated manager who led the recovery. Although some of the decision making was already in process during the 1970s, we have seen emerge: one of the most technically advanced shirt industries; Europe's leading manufacturing and technology base in ladies' outerwear; probably the world's most sophisticated household textile market place and one of the most successful ladies' tights businesses in the Western World.

Knitting has played a significant part in the success stories of recent years, and the return of circular knitting in fleecewear and fashionable jogging suits plus the success of hosiery so brightly highlighted in the Sock Shops around the travel centres of the United Kingdom have also played their part, but what of knitwear?

It was knitwear which saw us through the 1970s: profits earned and cash generated by the likes of Nottingham Manufacturing and Dawson

UK CLOTHING & KNITWEAR

	1978	1981	1985	June 1988 Annualised
Prices (£ 1kg)				
UK	8.81	10.56	11.21	12.52
"Low cost" imports	6.52	8.54	11.03	9.93
— @ Purchasing Power Parity	6.66	9.95	8.94	11.17
Market share (%)				
UK	70.9	65.6	71.2	63.2
EEC (excl. Spain/Portugal)	5.2	6.9	7.1	6.9
"Low cost"	23.9	27.5	21.7	29.9
Currency (average)				
$/£	1.92	2.03*	1.30	1.75
@ PPP	1.89	1.74	1.60	1.56
DMk/£	3.85	4.56	3.78	3.03

* After 2.33 in 1980

Note: imports from non-EEC countries, together with Spain and Portugal, have been designated "low cost". Although this is not strictly true, low cost, dollar-related countries account for the vast majority of such imports. Spain and Portugal have been excluded from EEC to give consistent figures with the earlier years.

International seemed to fly in the face of even a $2.40 pound and yet in 1988 $1.80 seems to be too much, as consumers switch to more structured, woven garments and only the cheaper imports manage to steal a living whilst closures strike the headlines all too frequently.

So in 1988 we face another crisis of confidence. Again it is currency which has exposed the weakness, but the impact has been felt all the way back up the chain, from the severe contraction of such famous knitwear names as Mansfield Hosiery and Corah through Laidlaw & Fairgrieve and Courtaulds' spinning closures, to the profit agony of Courtaulds' acrylic business.

Action has been taken quickly, which has probably removed 10-15 per cent of UK knitwear capacity. UK textile profit margins will probably fall from average 7½ per cent to 6½ per cent in 1988, the first drop in 7 years. Although fashion has played its part in the knitwear story, currency has been an ever present influence which has cast a shadow over the scene, particularly since autumn 1987. The sharp rise in sterling seems to have been the one *real* influence of The Crash and the shadow is now appreciated to be of much greater significance than any potential loopholes in or even removal of MFA.

To illustrate: between 1978 and 1981 knitwear and clothing importers from low cost countries were able to raise prices by nearly 15 per cent per annum in dollar purchasing terms (and still remain 30 per cent cheaper than the UK) whilst the UK managed only 6 per cent at a time of high inflation: during the period low cost imports gained 3½ per cent market share and the UK was fighting for every ounce of business. Between 1981 and 1985 when the pound fell from $2.40 to under $1.10, importers had to reduce prices in dollar purchasing terms by 2½ per cent per annum in order to hold their sterling price increases down to 6½ per cent per annum at a time when UK price increases were held to 1½ per cent per annum during a period of rapidly improving productivity. The UK clothing industry regained 5 per cent market share, even though import prices were on average 7½ per cent cheaper.

However, since 1985, as the pound has strengthened, low cost (dollar related) importers have taken 8½ per cent increased market share; their sterling prices have fallen by 4½ per cent per annum (whilst the UK has increased by 4 per cent per annum) but they have enjoyed the benefit (no doubt to their profits) of nearly 10 per cent per annum in the prices received in dollar purchasing terms.

It seems to me the lessons are clear. Firstly, the UK industry seems to have lost the ability to make productivity gains which were such a remarkable feature of the post-1980 scene; but perhaps early action, at least in knitwear, will re-inspire that continuous necessity.

Secondly, this country needs a more stable currency. My personal hobby horse is not only to join EMS but to fight for a European currency. This ideal is at last beginning to gather momentum as we reach towards 1992. In my opinion, an ECU would provide a new trading currency which would take some of the international pressure off the US$ and could bring a new stability which would help us all.

The current problems are a timely reminder that consistent textile profits only result from constant vigilance, not only on the broad direction of fashion but also on international competitiveness. The currency lessons may be uncomfortable and unfair but they are lessons to be learnt nevertheless, even if in an ideal world currency stability is an ideal goal.

Wool's Current And Future Role In The Knitting Industry

By Caroline Walker, International Wool Secretariat

BEFORE ADDRESSING THE current and future role of wool in the world's knitting industry, it is interesting to pause momentarily to consider in this Quatercentenary publication that wool has played an integral part in human life and civilisation for over 12,000 years.

Historically, wool's unique properties have made it a fibre ideally suited for use in all aspects of man's bid for survival in a harsh environment. It has provided him with shelter, clothing and protection.

The secret of wool's long and enduring relationship with mankind lies in the very nature of the fibre. Its structure is unique. Unlike any of the other natural and synthetic fibres, wool fibres are covered by tiny scales. The surface of the fibre is as a result water resistant, whilst its interior is highly absorbent. The wool fibre can absorb as much as 30 per cent of its own weight in moisture without feeling wet. Air trapped between fibres gives wool its insulating quality, providing great warmth without weight. But by drawing perspiration away from the body, wool clothing prevents the skin from feeling clammy in warm conditions making it an extremely versatile fibre for both warm and cold weather wear.

Whilst man's needs have changed over wool's 12,000 year history from those of basic survival to the very different requirements of today's more affluent and sophisticated consumer, wool continues to play an important role in satisfying the demands of a modern lifestyle. Where the properties of comfort and style are of primary importance to the modern consumer, wool meets these needs as effectively as ever. And nowhere more so, when coupled with the most advanced spinning and knitting technology, than in knitwear, in which creative opportunities can be unlimited.

Having placed wool in its historical context, it is valuable in establishing wool's current position in knitwear to refer in the first instance to available market data.

After many years of significant expansion the all fibre knitwear market is currently less buoyant, as consumers temporarily show greater interest in other forms of outerwear. The volume of fibre consumed in the knitwear market in the major consuming countries of N. America, Japan and Western Europe amounted to 405m kgs in 1987. To give a sense of proportion slightly less than half the amount consumed in women's outerwear.

The US is by far the largest market for knitwear, as would, no doubt, be expected. It is, in fact, almost three times as large as that of Germany which comes in second. The volume of knitwear consumed in Japan, France, Italy and the UK is roughly similar, although France has replaced the UK as being marginally the smallest of the four.

At a figure of 96m kgs, the volume of virgin wool consumed in knitwear is substantial. Indeeed, it is in knitwear that wool has the highest market share of the three main apparel end-uses. Japan and the USA are the two largest markets for wool. In Japan wool's share is almost 50 per cent of total fibre consumed. Second only to this is Italy, where with the highest level of wool consumption in knitwear in W. Europe wool has a market share of over one third.

In the knitwear market in particular, where the opportunities for creativity in yarns are limitless, virgin wool is used in both pure and blended merchandise. In recent years there has been an increase in the use of wool blends. However, the majority of wool continues to be consumed in pure wool products. In the main consuming countries 58 per cent of virgin wool is consumed in pure wool products, with 30 per cent in wool-rich garments and only 12 per cent in wool-poor garments.

Global Picture

Whilst these figures represent a global picture, there are not surprisingly significant differences in the proportion of virgin wool used in pure wool knitwear between countries. For example, in the UK 100 per cent wool merchandise accounts for 86 per cent of wool consumption with only 12 per cent going into wool rich blends and 2 per cent into wool-poor blends.

After noting the continuing dominance in the major consuming markets of pure wool knitwear it is interesting to look at the Woolmark knitwear market data. The total volume of world Woolmark production amounts to 38m kgs, of which five countries: UK, Italy, Hong Kong, Mauritius and Japan account for 64 per cent. The largest producer of Woolmark knitwear is the UK accounting for 22 per cent of world production in 1987. It is maybe not too much of a surprise then, that the UK is also the world's largest consumer of Woolmark knitwear, 20 per cent of the 1987 figures.

The majority of Woolmark knitwear produced in the UK is fully fashioned — estimated at 87 per cent of the total, with only around 13 per cent manufactured using the cut and sew method. The table below shows the manufacturing structure of the major countries. Whilst this is only an estimated figure, it indicates that with the exception of Japan, each country's industry is more or less dominated by either one manufacturing method or the other. The Japanese knitting industry is split almost equally between fully fashioned and cut and sew knitting, but interestingly also 10 per cent of Japanese machines are hand fashioned. The majority of machine capacity in Hong Kong and China is still also hand-fashioned.

Woolmark Knitwear Manufacturing Method 1985

	% Cut & Sew		% F.F.		% H.F.
Germany	85	UK	87	Japan	19
France	70	Italy	64	Italy	1
US	59	Japan	47	Hong Kong	85
Japan	43	US	41		
Italy	35	France	30		
UK	13	Germany	15		
China	5	China	95	(H.F./F.F.)	
Hong Kong	5	Hong Kong	10		

In terms of yarn consumption the world's knitting industries tend also to be characterised by the yarn type consumed. In France, Italy, Germany and Japan, the majority of wool yarns used in knitwear manufacture are worsted yarns. Whereas, in the US, UK, Hong Kong and China, woollen yarns are more widely used.

Finally in this review of the current situation for wool in knitwear, let us look briefly at world trade in wool knitwear.

In 1987, the total volume of trade in wool knitwear amounted to 88m kgs, a 40 per cent increase on the 1985 figure. International trade in knitwear is dominated by relatively few countries, but the volume of trade accounted for by each is changing rapidly. For example, whilst the US alone accounts for 17 per cent of total wool imports, this figure has, in fact, fallen, from 21 per cent in 1986. Take the US with the other major importing countries of Japan, Hong Kong, Germany and France and you have accounted for two thirds of imported wool knitwear. However, worth noting is the fact that the volume of imports to Germany and France has fallen marginally since 1986, whilst those to Hong Kong and Japan have increased significantly.

On the export side, the market is even more extreme with just 3 countries, Italy, Hong Kong and China supplying 62 per cent of global trade. Again the change in these figures since 1986 is interesting. The volume of Italy's wool knitwear exports has fallen by 2 per cent, whereas Hong Kong's have increased by the same amount and China's by a substantial 4 per cent. With the growing interdependence of production and sales between Hong Kong and China, it is believed that a large proportion of the trade between China and Hong Kong is re-exported from Hong Kong. However, this fact underlines the growing importance of the S.E. Asian area in the world knitwear market.

As the market information which IWS collects regularly from all the major wool consuming countries have adequately shown, wool maintains its position as a quality luxury fibre ideally suited to use in knitwear. Indeed, turning now from the factual to the aesthetic, the fashion forecasts for the coming autumn/winter season of 1989/90 confirm the continuing dominance of wool as the preferred fibre to create the most fashionable and contemporary looks.

The briefest look back over the eight decades of this century, endorses the view that fashion trends reflect the social climate of the time, and never more so than in the affluent 80's. As a new decade begins the fashion forecasters believe that a new wave of authenticity, a search for real values and a need for a more profound quality of life are beginning to permeate the cultural and social scene of industrialised societies to the detriment of the artificial and materialistic way of life, some would say, so characteristic of the 1980's. Translated into styling trends the consumer desire for quality and authenticity obviously favours natural fibres. In knitwear, for autumn/winter 89/90, the desire for softness, refinement and elegance will continue with quality yarns, both fine and smooth and discreet fancies favouring fine gauges and fancy, delicate stitches. Alongside this trend will be a growing interest in rustic, outdoor knits complementing the revival in tweeds in woven outerwear. Yarns will be woollens, Shetlands, tweeds, brushed and hairy, with an opportunity for medium to coarser gauge fancy stitches, Irish stitches, ribs and cables. Knitwear will become once again a focal point, a garment in its own right. The silhouette of previous seasons inspired by ready to wear looks will take a back seat to the new bold, decorative and specifically knitwear effects.

The outlook for spring '90 sees these trends confirmed and evolving, and taking a longer term view, as far as that is wise in fashion, the requirement for comfort, luxury and individuality will be reinforced by the growing importance of the older consumer age group for whom these considerations, it is expected, will be a priority. If this is the case,

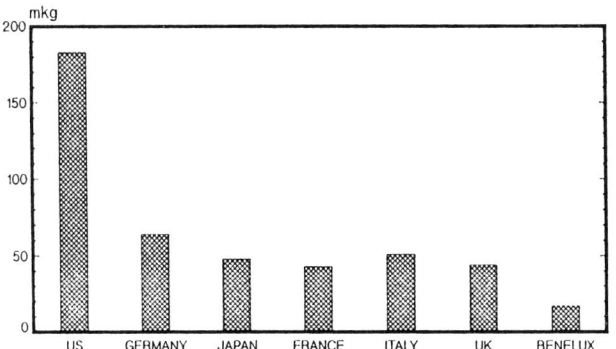

ADULT KNITWEAR
ALL FIBRE MARKET-CONSUMPTION 1987

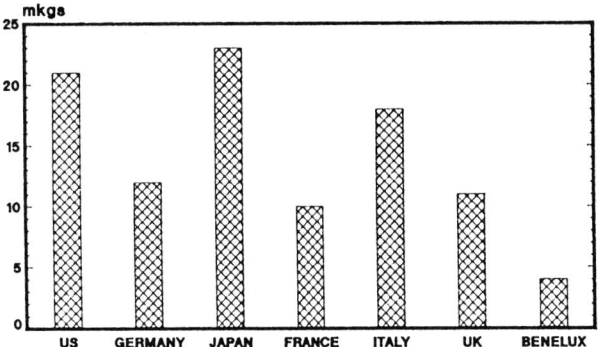

ADULT KNITWEAR
VIRGIN WOOL CONSUMPTION 1987

wool positioned as a quality fibre at the top end of the market will continue to be seen as contemporary and desirable.

But, will the rapidly developing, ever changing world of new machine technology also be so kind to wool? Witness the fact that at the recent ITMA exhibition in Paris in October 1987, all the major knitting machine manufacturers operated their machinery, either entirely or partly, on pure new wool yarns and the answer is clear. Yes, the wool fibre is compatible with the very latest and most technologically advanced machine innovation.

The development of knitting machinery since the invention by William Lee in 1589 has, of course, been enormous. None more so in recent years, than perhaps the introduction of the first electronic controlled flatbed machine by Stoll in 1975. The development of the electronic knitting machine has improved the quality of production and the versatility and flexibility of the knitting process. Improvements have been made for yarn delivery and yarn guiding, carriage and cam angle, needles, racking and take down. Above all the new generation of machine technology is more user friendly thus promoting the greater efficiency and effectiveness of the operator.

To exploit the full potential of today's electronic knitting machinery, computer aided design is a must. With most CAD systems now also including the additional options of non-interlaced screen, hard discs, multi-colour digitiser, video camera, black and white and colour monitor, laser scanner, thermal and colour print and x-y plotters, the opportunities for greater creativity in design have never been better.

The use of advanced machinery in combination with CAD, for example, newly developed presser foots or knock overs, facilitates the production of shaped panels from flatbed machinery which offers considerable benefits for wool as savings in the raw material can be significant. In addition, the development of electronically controlled fully fashioned (cotton type) machinery has created specific advantages for wool, increasing the possibilities of new products in a sector of the industry which has traditionally been a heavy wool user.

With the knitting industry currently leading the textile field in the adoption and utilisation of both computer aided design and computer aided manufacturing, the potential for exploiting new technology to produce innovative products quickly and efficiently and directly tailored to the consumers requirements, should carry the knitting industry firmly forward into the 1990s.

To complete this review of the role of wool in the knitting industry we must look forward to the challenges which will face the wool knitwear industry in the future.

Response

An understanding of and response to the changing world trading environment and the development of new products and new markets for wool will enable wool to retain and consolidate its position as a contemporary fibre.

Whilst wool has always been more closely associated with the autumn/winter season and a traditional customer profile, the IWS believes that wool usage can be considerably increased by the development of new products targeted at specific market segments. In particular markets which present new opportunities are the casualwear market and the spring market.

To look at one example of how new wool products are developed to satisfy new market opportunities let us consider wool in active sportswear. Changing consumer lifestyles in the 1980s have lead to a boom in the casualwear market. The desire for comfortable and stylish clothing coupled with an upsurge of interest in health and fitness naturally benefited knitted fabrics in all fibre types in active sportswear. Wool it is considered has the desired properties to meet the needs of the upper end of this market. Wool's natural properties make it highly efficient at keeping the body warm whilst at the same time transmitting water vapour thus providing wearer comfort over a wide range of sporting activities.

Trade in Wool Knitwear

Imports	% 1986	1987	Exports	% 1986	1987
USA	21	17	Italy	21	19
Japan	12	14	Hong Kong	21	23
Hong Kong	12	15	China	16	20
Germany	11	10	Korea	8	7
France	11	10	UK	6	6
UK	5	4.5	Mauritius	6	5
Canada	5	5	India	4	4
USSR		4	All Other	18	16
All Other	23	20			

Woolmark Production 1987

	m.kgs.	%
U.K.	8,378	22
Italy	6,735	17
Japan	3,380	9
Hong Kong	3,319	9
Mauritius	2,935	8

Virgin Wool Share of Total Knitwear Consumption 1987

	%
US	11.4
Germany	18.75
Japan	48.4
France	23
Italy	34.4
UK	25.4
Benelux	24

Virgin Wool Consumption Pure vs. Blends 1987

	% Total Knitwear	% Women's Knitwear	% Men's Knitwear
Wool poor	12	14	9
Wool rich	30	36	23
All wool	58	50	68

Consumption of Worsted vs. Woollen Yarns in Wool Knitwear Manufacture 1985

	% Worsted		% Woollen
France	75	USA	76
Italy	75	UK	60
Germany	70	Japan	30
Japan	70	Germany	30
UK	40	Italy	25
USA	24	France	25
China	35	China	65
Hong Kong	20	Hong Kong	80

Woolmark Consumption 1987

	m.kgs.	%
UK	7,165	20
USA	5,427	15
Japan	5,149	14
Germany	4,216	12
Italy	3,356	9

Fabrics have been developed specifically for this market by IWS called Aquaduct fabrics.

New developments targeted at the spring market include additional comfort properties for garments worn next to the skin. New processes are being developed which improve the natural flexibility of the wool fibre thereby reducing the feeling of prickle when next to the skin. The process produces a much softer handle which is ideal for wool underwear and spring/summer knitwear. It has the added bonus of imparting machine washability, in one process, on the type of garments for which this will be a pre-requisite for the consumer.

The various different processing treatments applied to wool to give a washable product are also continually being worked upon with the objective of developing a cheaper and quicker application which is of benefit to wool processors and an improved garment which will ensure consumer satisfaction in the aftercare of wool knitwear.

But the development of new products and the creation of new market segments is only one way of facing the future with confidence. Equally important is the understanding of the changing world trade environment. As the data shown earlier in the article demonstrated, knitwear is the most heavily traded product in the world textile industry. Increasingly this trade is coming to be dominated by very few countries and operators. It should come as no surprise perhaps that one of the few truly international companies in the textile industry is the knitwear giant Benetton.

The dismantling of trade barriers in Europe in 1992 creating one single European market of 320 million consumers will facilitate the growth of companies who operate efficiently and effectively across nations. Whilst this will, no doubt, affect changes in global trading relationships, the unified European market is dwarfed by the vast potential offered by the liberalisation of both China and the Soviet Union. Whilst progress in terms of developing domestic consumption is predicted to be relatively slow, China's textile industry, is committed to a policy of export growth. The required technical knowledge and expertise is being built up very rapidly and even now China is the world's second largest producer of wool knitwear. As production capacity in Hong Kong becomes limited, and production costs in Japan become uncompetitive, the investment of foreign capital in China's industry, bringing with it the latest technology and expertise, is becoming more attractive to both Japan and Hong Kong and is of great benefit to China.

Closer To Home

Closer to home and becoming more important is Turkey. Whilst the Turkish knitting industry is currently very varied both in its knowledge and equipment there are several indications such as investment in new production techniques and government incentives to modernise, that this sector is rapidly becoming a more viable modern concern. Coupled with entry to the economic community Turkey looks set to become a much more important player in the knitwear field.

In terms of textile trade, the world is very rapidly becoming a smaller place. A process which is being accelerated by the ever more widespread use of modern communications systems. Recognition of the changes taking place in the industrial environment and the adoption of strategies which will enable individual operators to remain competitive be it in terms of price, quick response or innovative products, will ensure that the wool knitwear industry remains viable.

To conclude this paper, let us look at the key factors which mean that the wool fibre has an important role in the knitting industry of today, and is well placed to meet the challenges of the future.

At the point at which we began, wool as a natural fibre, has unique properties which make it ideally suited to meet the modern consumer's requirements for comfort, style and performance. Wool's innate versatility has established it as the appropriate fibre for the autumn/winter season whilst at the same time new opportunities for Cool Wool are being developed and exploited for spring/summer ensuring that wool is truly a year round fibre. The resources and expertise of IWS will continue to be employed to create new demand for wool by means of market support, product innovation, and the identification of new opportunities for wool products.

Without a doubt, for wool in knitwear, the present looks healthy and the future bright.

Linen In Knitting

By R. R. Franck, International Linen

IT IS NOT INAPPROPRIATE to think of linen on the occasion of the 400th anniversary of the invention of the first knitting machine by William Lee. In his day the only yarns that he and his contemporaries could have knitted would have been spun from either wool or flax. Cotton and silk were known but were esoteric and very expensive imports whilst linen and wool were the common, everyday fibres. Rayon and synthetic fibres, of course, just did not exist.

Even more surprisingly this situation lasted for a further 200 years or so, until the establishment of the American "plantations", which provided the fast developing "New World", with substantial quantities of cotton at much more reasonable prices. At about the same time Arkwright invented the spinning jenny and the mechanical production of textiles in general, which was, with the discovery of steam power, the basis of the Industrial Revolution, gained momentum over most of Europe and North America. The net result was that cotton started to replace linen, and not only in the knitting industry!

However before this happened linen was extensively used for knitting, and most of the ladies' and gentlemen's hose, at that time, was made from linen. Now the situation is changing once again. After a very long absence linen is again making its appearance in knitted products, both in 100 per cent form or in blends and mixtures with other fibres.

Why Linen In Knitwear?

It is perhaps worth asking ourselves what linen brings to knitwear? The answer is, by and large, the same qualities that it brings to woven fabrics, but with an additional advantage in that knitted constructions crease a lot less than woven ones, even in linen.

Linen is cool, comfortable and its appearance gives a sheen or lustre that is unique. These basic qualities are due to the molecular structure of the fibres themselves which consists of highly orientated almost pure cellulose. This structure enables linen to absorb and desorb moisture at a greater rate than any other fibre, hence its comfort. This structure is also the reason for its cool and pleasant handle which in its turn is the basic explanation for the "niche" that linen has found in the knitwear market. In our temperate climate even late spring and summer are not always very warm — especially in the evening, but often wool or acrylic knitwear feels too warm. Linen fits perfectly into this segment of the market.

Again linen's huge moisture absorbancy and cool feel explain the success of linen socks in summer.

100 Per Cent Linen Knitwear And Hosiery

Men's and women's 100 per cent linen knitted outerwear and men's socks have been produced by leading manufacturers and distributors by some of the top fashion names for several years, in fact this trend started soon after linen made its come-back onto the fashion scene some ten years ago.

However, the development of linen knitwear and socks has varied markedly from country to country. As one would expect, the leader has been Italy, the largest consumer market for all linen products in the world. 100 per cent linen knitted outerwear and socks are well distributed at the more exclusive level, to which linen is confined simply because of its price.

Major brands are involved and, especially over the past few years, considerable business has developed.

Although unfortunately no detailed statistics are available, the second biggest market for linen knitwear is probably Japan — at least if one judges by the amount of linen knitwear being offered in the windows of the fashion boutiques and department stores in Tokyo and Osaka.

France also is becoming a worthwhile market, both from a manufacturing and consumer point of view and Germany is not far behind, but mostly as consumers, the garments being imported are mainly from Italy.

Knitted Piecegoods

In all these countries the use of linen is not confined to knitwear but knitted piecegoods are also produced and made up by brand leaders. These are usually jersey fabrics of various constructions but flat bed fabrics are also used for the more open effects.

The variety of knitted articles proposed in linen

can be judged from the suggestions put forward by International Linen with their colour forecasts for spring 1990 concerning knitwear and knitted fabrics:

> fine gauges for tight plain knits
> coarse gauges for "sophisticated rustics"
> mercerised and glacé finishes
> stretch crêpe knits
> écru/colour twists
> single jersey
> double jersey
> milano rib
> raschel lace effects
> bi-coloured shantungs

United Kingdom Trails

However successful knitted linen is becoming on the Continent — and even in the United States some interesting developments are taking place — the UK seem to be lagging in a market that is both growing and profitable. It is true that Jonathan Thorpe have been producing attractive ranges of linen knitted piecegoods for several seasons but one swallow does not make a summer. Why it should be so is difficult to analyse. Perhaps the particular structure of the market, when compared to Continental countries, is at least part of the answer but one would have expected, bearing in mind the demand in Continental countries, that some of our more export orientated companies might have taken up the challenge.

Technical Problems

Another possible reason is that linen yarns are not easy to knit. Flax is a fairly rigid fibre and normal linen yarns do not take kindly to being bent round needles. This problem, however has now been overcome and flax spinners such as Herdmans in this country, Salmon in France and Linificio and Zignago in Italy now produce specially softened linen yarns for knitting.

Linen Blends

Whilst 100 per cent linen articles make the headlines and indeed are now substantial business, in terms of quantity, blends, if only because of price, are in the bulk market. These blends include linen with silk, wool, rayon, cotton, acrylics and polyester in all possible combinations and percentages. It would be idle to deny that one of the reasons for incorporating linen into a blend, and especially a minority blend, is that it enables the finished garment to show the word "linen" on its label. However linen does also bring other advantages especially if the linen content is over 50 per cent for example.

The rustic look, contrasts in lustre between linen and other fibres, cross dyeing effects, etc are all used very effectively by designers with the result that most spinners now include linen blends in their spring ranges, be they cotton, synthetic or wool spinners.

A further important development is the extensive use of pure linen yarns as a component for fancy yarns for knitwear. Again the Italians lead the field and such fancy yarn manufacturers as Linea Piu, Filatura Di Crosa and Overfil all offer interesting ranges of such yarn; interesting both from the point of view of colour and of texture.

The Linen Symbol

The penetration of linen into the knitting industry has certainly received a fillip from the linen industries decision to promote their symbol, not only at trade fairs, in the trade press and by supplying labels and swing tickets bearing the logo, but also by consumer advertising in "up market" media and the fact also that the issue of these sales aids to knitters and garment manufacturers is limited to their being used only with merchandise that meets certain minimum performance standards. This symbol is now also generally becoming known and gives all the companies involved, from manufacturing to retailing, much greater confidence in what is, after all, for many a new article.

Blossoming Renaissance Of World's Oldest Synthetic Fibre

By John Coleman, ICI Fibres

THERE IS A GROWING force influencing all Western European textile markets that cannot be ignored. And the knitting industry is no exception. The new force is an increasingly discerning consumer. This consumer — whether born in the baby boom and now part of the 'yuppie era' or one of the growing band of over-50's — is one of a high spending group of affluent people with the appetite for stylish products designed for specific needs. An important part of ICI Fibres' marketing strategy is to meet these ever changing requirements with a wide and versatile product portfolio.

The knitting industry has undergone huge change since the days of William Lee. Machine speeds and efficiencies have developed beyond belief and the trend is set to continue. ICI Fibres' role within the industry is to provide the right yarns to complement advanced technology. This objective is set against a truly international backcloth where we have strategic partnerships with the key names within the industry around the entire world.

The polyamide business for us began with hosiery and this is still of very great importance in the late 1980s. Hosiery is no longer seen as merely a commodity item but a vital part of a woman's dress and self-expression via fashion.

Other end products from the versatile knitting industry range from fibres for automotive upholstery to curtain nets, and from socks to sportswear.

As a result of high consumer expectations and technologically advanced knitting machines, ICI's family of polyamide (and polyester) fibres have, over the past few years, developed a new identity. Brand names such as Tactel are now synonymous with quality, performance and fine aesthetics.

The hosiery market is an extremely important one for ICI Fibres. In the UK we hold a leading share of that market and are Europe's leading supplier of hosiery yarns, but ICI has global coverage of the hosiery market, selling in North and South America, South East Asia, Australia and New Zealand as well as in Western Europe.

ICI is committed to constantly advancing its technology by sustained investment in research and development to improve efficiency and reduce costs. To create the sheer, sophisticated hosiery that the consumer requires, yarn technology has been developed to the point of producing 10 denier yarn so fine that 1kg stretches one million metres.

The key yarns currently dominating fine hosiery production are a comparatively new development. Partially orientated yarn (POY) is now the basic feedstock of the industry and was introduced by ICI as recently as 1979. The last five years have been the most important for ICI, as the market has accelerated rapidly and has seen knitting speeds leap by 50 per cent from 850 to over 1200 rpm and the crucial introduction of robotics in garment make up. Today production speeds have the theoretical possibility of reaching 1700 rpm, creating 2.6 million stitches every minute.

Spectacular Rate

This spectacular rate of development of course means that ICI and the knitting industry as a whole is better equipped to meet the requirements dictated by the consumers — 110 million women in Europe alone. Extensive consumer research has been carried out by ICI to provide data to effectively segment the European market for fine hosiery and to identify key consumer needs from which to direct new product developments.

Results from this consumer research show that hosiery fashion has received a real boost in recent years. This is a marked contrast from the 1970s 'have to wear' attitude. Hosiery is not only worn as a functional item but is also a major fashion accessory and is part of a total coordinated package of self-expression.

Self expression is of course paramount, with a wider choice of type, colour and pattern readily available. There is a strong psychological element related to buying and a polarisation between 'special occasion' (e.g. evening) purchasing, and hosiery to be worn everyday.

Our new affluent consumer now treats hosiery as a disposable item and has a more considered approach to wearing and purchasing. Hosiery has become a high interest area closely associated with a woman's femininity which furthers her means of self-expression and offers increased versatility to her clothing and her individual style.

ICI produces a complete family of fibres to enable every mood to be taken into account, and as an important part of our offer, there is an ongoing programme of colour and design forecasting. These predictions first showed up the current feeling for more subtle and elegant styles. The two major trends in current fashion are for sheers (finer yarns) and for opaques (heavier yarns), and these both have some way to develop.

Strategic partnerships with key producers, coupled with consumer research, provide ICI with a truly global perspective. The extensive and ongoing investment in technology ensures market leadership and a wide product range showing commitment to innovation, quality and service.

The next few years will see us producing higher quality products which will run on faster knitting machines while meeting the stringent standards that the consumer demands. More attention will be paid to the fit of the garment with opportunity to improve stretch and recoverability of yarns, thus offering the consumer a greater choice of sizing, and so greater comfort.

Knitting machines for basic commodity hosiery will become ever faster continuing the progress over the last few decades. In 1940-50 — the era of fully fashioned knitting — one man operating an F/F frame would produce 30 hose every 45 minutes. In 1988 — with seamless kniting — one man operating 60 machines produces 3150 garments every 45 minutes! This momentum of change is set to continue as knitting technology continues to advance, and robotics become more commonplace.

Warp knitting has progressed in leaps and bounds over the last couple of decades since being the main fabrication route for producing nylon fabrics for shirts, sheets and lingerie.

After the decline of these traditional end uses, warp knitting has developed in two directions. The first was end-use specialisation for applications such as stretch tricot fabrics for swimwear and lightweight foundation wear. (Other end uses included automotive upholstery, furnishing fabrics, sportswear and lingerie). Secondly, warp knitters recognised they could produce large amounts of extremely cost effective lightweight fabrics with high strength to weight ratio (for laminate backings, pocket trims and many other uses) by the use of new knitting machines and faster speeds. The yarn producers could produce consistently high quality yarns to be knitted at high speeds with improved dye uniformity. With the aid of more sophisticated technology, warp knitting can efficiently meet the demand for an increased quantity of fabrics with improved quality.

As the trend towards greater productivity continues (from 800-1000 stitches per minute in the 1970s to present speeds of about 2500 stitches per minute), ICI produces fibres which knit perfectly and so can meet the challenge of progress. This will continue to be our aim in the 1990s.

Our new technology polyester yarns are being used for automotive upholstery and curtain nets (having a high resistance to sunlight and good level dyeing properties) and also for sportswear where polyester gives the desired surface aesthetics at the right cost point.

Major Supplier

ICI Fibres is and will remain one of the major suppliers in Europe of polyamide yarn into lingerie. Our aims in lingerie are, as ever, to supply the market needs and meet the needs of the consumer. When a need was indicated for more sensuous fabrics and finer, lighter, silkier fabrics the warp knitters responded with 40 gauge machinery. ICI in turn responded by developing finer decitex yarns.

We see in the future that the demand for end-use specialisation will continue but there will still be a real need for large volume commodity yarns at competitive prices. Quality standards in both cases must be kept high and focus kept on new aesthetics. Our current new technology yarns are taking us forward into the next decade by meeting these requirements.

Weft knitting continues to provide a very rapid response to changing fashion trends. Rapid response to demands can be achieved — weft knitting is the most versatile fabrication route in this respect — and alterations can be implemented within a few days, if necessary, at the knitting machine.

Even five years ago, the same range may have remained in production for long periods, but now leading knitters launch several ranges a year and are more adept at meeting response, with bespoke knitting being the norm.

ICI is very committed to changing the original end-uses of polyamide (where it was used for its stretch and abrasion qualities) and the role of polyamide in weft knitting has altered drastically with the advent of new products. It will change even more in the early 90's.

The consumer now expects garments to be individually 'made for them' rather than just being mass-production commodities and so the market increasingly requires 'purpose built' fabrics. Historically, this meant meeting performance criteria, but now the discerning consumer expects the addition of design, style and comfort to satisfy his needs. With this in mind, ICI and Western European knitters have introduced Tactel products to meet a real need. These products provide the optimum balance between the advantages offered by natural fibres and polyamide fibres. Fabrics made from these fibre combinations offer garment designers increased scope. In addition, more product flexibility enables the European textile trade to provide a rapid response with a wide range of products and so develop a high degree of protection against garment imports from outside the EEC.

Fabric Groups

The ICI offer of fine denier per filament textured yarns (e.g. 78 decitex/46 filaments) to combine Tactel with cotton, is designed for two quite different fabric groups. Aquator in Tactel is a double faced fabric (Tactel on the inside, cotton on the outside) which enables the wearer to remain cool and comfortable in active and leisure situations by wicking moisture away from the body. This new development in Tactel will be immensely important for some years to come.

The other group of fabrics are a more intimate mix of cotton with Tactel with the advantages of softness, structure and weight. Leading Western European garment makers are already using this commercially. The fabrics are targeted at tops, casual shirts, sleepwear and underwear. These are all areas where an enhanced Tactel/cotton offer will meet the consumer needs for style, comfort and function.

The future will see an ever increasing trend for weft knitted 'purpose built' fabrics. This can only come about with major research and investment into polymers, fibre spinning and fabrication routes. ICI's direction is heavily biased towards the polymer/spinning end of the process in order to meet the trade's demands for production innovation in all sectors.

Within weft knitting, socks are one of ICI Fibres' largest business sectors. ICI is the major supplier of polyamide into the sock business, and makes up a substantial percentage of the total tonnes of yarn supplied into Western Europe and the USA.

As in all other aspects of the knitting industry, machinery has been extensively modernised since the early days. The original flat bed machine has been replaced by circular modern machines leading to much faster knitting speeds. Some of the first circular machines were wound by hand with a few still in use today. Machines are now designed to knit at an increased rate, with a motor driven single cylinder now producing up to 320 revs per minute.

Socks were originally wool based and then also cotton, where the main problem was the durability factor (or lack of it!). When 100% polyamide socks were introduced, the sock trade contracted as the garments lasted much longer. Nowadays, both performance and aesthetics are assured and the polyamide sock is often backed with wool, cotton or acrylic.

Men's socks have exploded into the fashion arena in recent years as ladies' hosiery did in the early 1980s. Men no longer buy the plainest, dull coloured socks they can find, but instead view them as an esssential part of dress and individual expression. There is a marked change in the sock market at retail level with more styles and colours in demand.

Consumer attitudes towards synthetics — influenced by the success of (for example) Tactel — have now changed favourably, and this is beginning to be seen in the trade. It will accelerate, as products are being developed with more exciting properties. Tactel gives improved colour vibrance and ICI yarns enable the industry to respond well to socks as a fashion item. Patterning potential is now enormous and the latest innovation is for a computer jacquard with individual needle selection to give designs with ever-greater variety. As in the ladies' hosiery market, the new consumers discard socks rather than darning them. Gone are the days when a pair of socks would be kept for many months, full of diligently mended holes.

In the future, we will see an even softer handle with synthetics matching and even surpassing the characteristics of natural fibres, such as cotton and wool. Manufacturers will produce innovative socks in a wide variety of styles and colours to respond quickly to fashion changes. This will offer protection to the European sock industry against the cheaper sock-producing markets and will create a higher value, technically-sophisticated and fashion-orientated western European sock.

The changes which have recently affected men's hose, will spread to children's and ladies' socks. Girls socks are now very fashionable and will become more so over the next five years. In the UK and West Germany, an increasing number of women are wearing socks under jeans. This trend, too, is likely to develop.

Rapid Response

ICI provides the necessary rapid response in yarns through its throwster partners. The rate of change can be expected to increase dramatically, leading to new fibres and yarns being produced for a variety of styles and designs. Our aim will be to both lead and support the changes . . .

The hand knitting market has also undergone a considerable amount of change over recent years. The low and declining state of the hand knitting industry worldwide is well known and ICI has made large investments in order to stimulate the market, especially by offering new and exciting products to the UK spinners.

By identifying customer needs we have developed a range of speciality effect fibres which enable the spinners to produce yarns with a luxurious handle and appearance of the exotic natural fibres, with the added bonus of performance and easy care properties associated with polyamide fibres. These new speciality polymaide fibres have been produced and launched under the brand name Tendrelle. They have been designed specifically for the hand-knitting trade and are used instead of (or more often in conjunction with) natural exotics such as cashmere, angora and mohair, to improve performance and benefit handle or appearance, whilst allowing the spinner to control costs.

As with all our other brands, our offer must by dynamic, and have the capacity to adapt to market forces. As requirements develop and consumer needs alter, ICI will develop a range of appropriate products to satisfy these needs, in this as in the other knitting markets.

We will fund a continuous rolling programme of market research and consequential product development. Polyamide products, with our new technologies, will match the handle and aesthetics of natural fibres and will give the significant added bonuses of easy-care and superb wear-performance. Our programme will develop to provide the machine knitting market with a whole range of products to meet customer requirements in the same way.

It is clear that the role of the consumer is an all important one for the success of our business. ICI Fibres has learnt to listen to the marketplace, and the structure of the knitting industry makes it possible to angle our product portfolio as market demands alter. We see this trend set to continue and are confident that our extensive fibre offer and immensely strong technical base will meet our customers' needs throughout the industry for decades to come. We look forward to the start of the next four hundred years of the knitting industry.

Courtaulds And Knitting

By Robert Aitken, Courtaulds Viscose and John Picker, Courtaulds Courtelle

THOUGH NOT HAVING a history dating back to 1589, Courtaulds' association with knitting does go back as far as the turn of the century when they started the man-made fibres industry with the production of viscose fibre. Viscose was quickly exploited in knitted fabrics and to this day it has a significant share of key market sectors. Approximately a half century after the first production of viscose, Courtaulds introduced its acrylic fibre, Courtelle, which has grown to be a very major fibre for knitwear.

Both fibres have long histories but more importantly they also have an assured future as technical and commercial innovations are continually being pursued.

Viscose

The British man-made fibres industry was started in 1905 when Courtaulds first produced viscose rayon commercially in Coventry. Originally viscose was only available in filament yarn form, as "artificial silk", but it was soon realised that the fibre could be cut into staple, for spinning on the cotton, worsted or woollen systems. In the manufacturing process the cellulose undergoes a chemical reaction, and is later reconverted to cellulose in fibre form, and this imparts great versatility with regard to product type. Fibres can be made with a wide range of dtex, staple length, cross-section, crimp and modulus.

In apparel, viscose provides absorption and comfort, drape, softness and lustre, and it contributes a share of these properties to knitted fabrics made from viscose/polyester or viscose-acrylic blends. In blends with polyester the viscose contributes its special aesthetics and the polyester gives durability, wash stability and easy care. The tendency towards leanness exhibited by polyester blend yarns was overcome by the development of a special type of viscose to improve the fabric aesthetics.

Courtaulds achieved this by modifications to the extrusion and regeneration processes so as to optimise the cross-section stiffness and surface properties of the fibre. This new fibre, called Viloft, achieved the breakthrough for viscose/polyester blends in the knitted fabric market. It contributed to a naturalness to complement the ruggedness of the polyester, so that the fabrics had warmth and fullness, absorbency and wicking, and freedom from static. For the first time viscose gained a serious share of the thermal underwear business, with 25% of the market in Britain. This is in second place behind the leaders which are cotton (for men) and polyester (for women). Viloft is also successful in other areas where its special properties gave benefits, in sportswear and in leisurewear.

Viscose Research was then given the task of optimising the performance of the fibre in terms of yarn spinning and knitting efficiency, fabric appearance and stitch clarity, while maintaining the advantages of handle, softness and drape. This was achieved, and the results demonstrated with the assistance of the newly available Kawabata system for instrumental measurement of fabric handle, in terms of bending, shear, compression and surface smoothness. Viloft could now be expanded into knitted nightwear and outerwear.

Another area in which viscose has recently made its debut is hand knitting yarns. Courtaulds Viloft yarns offer the hand knitter bright colours, sheen, warmth and softness. The cross-section and refractive index of the fibre contribute to the lustre, and the softness results from the right combination of density, shape factor, tensile modulus and dtex. The yarns are made from viscose tow over one million denier thick, converted into top by the stretch breaking route. This had originally been developed for viscose, but later the tow-to-top converters were engineered to meet the needs of acrylic tow. Much research attention has recently been directed at refining the viscose tows so that they can be processed on the very latest converters, such as the Seydel 860 Compact Jumbo. In trials at the Seydel plant in early 1988 viscose tows were processed at over 200 metres/minute, and produced exceptionally clean slivers.

Coloured tops are available from a stock of 24 shades, ranging from brilliant white through pastels to full colours and black. The tops are gilled and spun into yarns by the semi-worsted process. In

February 1988 at Harrogate, Courtaulds Viscose Europe showed over 90 Viloft yarns in a variety of textures and blends. Many of the blends were with wool or mohair, and some were with acrylics or other synthetics. Commercial yarns already available are "Supermatch Crepe DK" in 60/40 acrylic/Viloft from Emu, in 10 colours, and "Next Generation" in 50/30/20 acrylic/Viloft/nylon from Hayfield, in 20 colours. Also being launched is "Voyager" in 61% acrylic/27% Viloft/12% nylon from Sirdar.

For the future Courtaulds predicts an increasing participation of viscose fibres in knitted products, and these will be in blends with the prestige natural fibres, and with the high performance synthetics. The new high speed yarn formation processes, as well as high speed knitting developments, will increasingly be brought into widespread use over the next few years. In addition to engineering innovations the new generation of machinery requires an input from the fibre maker, so that the raw materials can continue to be upgraded to match the processing equipment of the future. Courtaulds Research is actively involved in these developments now, so that the products will be ready when the industry needs them.

There was another important introduction in 1966, latent crimp Courtelle. This is a bicomponent fibre which on bulking has a helical crimp which produces a bulky, tough fibre which is very hard wearing. It is used mainly for school knitwear and men's knitwear and of course is produced in Neochrome colours. School knitwear is produced mainly on V bed machines and the menswear generally on 15g fully fashioned machines.

During the seventies, electronic control of both V-bed and jersey machines greatly increased the patterning ability and speed of changeover of patterns. This meant that heavily patterned knitwear and knitted fabrics were available at moderate prices and considerable qualities, thus boosting knitwear as a fashion item. For this explosion of patterning a wide range of coloured yarns was needed and Courtelle Neochrome fibre was used by some of the major spinners in the UK to meet the demand.

To assist the spinners in using Courtelle, a colour and design service was provided and the launch of "Technological Chic" Courtelle in 1980 expanded this area. With the Courtelle colour palette and facilities for yarn and garment development Courtelle supplied a complete service to knitters. This was extended to the final customer, the retailer, by means of retail presentations where new ideas in colours, yarns, fabrics and garments were presented to major buyers in stores and fashion houses.

To extend this fashion image in Courtelle, Design Awards have been introduced over the last few years. These Awards are a joint operation between Courtelle, colleges of fashion and major retailers and encourage young designers to experiment with colour, texture and garment design using the range of Courtelle yarns available and being able to see the winning garments on sale. The three main areas of Courtelle which have Awards are knitwear, knitted fabrics and hand knitting, and over the years they have been successful in promoting Courtelle in fashion.

In addition to the continuing involvement of research into viscose and acrylic fibres for the future, Courtaulds has just begun the production of an entirely new man-made fibre. This is the solvent spun cellulose fibre, which has been given the generic name tencel. It uses the same polymer supply as does viscose, woodpulp, but instead of the chemical reactions of the viscose process the cellulose is dissolved in a solvent and extruded in the form of pure cellulose fibres with an exceptionally high modulus, stronger than cotton even when wet. Fabrics made from tencel have a distinctive crisp handle, and the strength of the yarns offers immediate advantages to the spinner. This development illustrates the commitment by the fibre producers to the textile industry of the future.

Courtelle

Courtaulds entered the field of acrylic fibres in the mid-50's with Courtelle, a fibre which had been developed by their research team. Acrylic fibres have the property of recovering from excessive stretching when heated, and by suitable fibre blending of stretched and unstretched fibre, high bulk, worsted spun yarns can be produced. This bulking process was carried out whilst the garments were being dyed so allowing them to be produced economically and with a soft, wool-like handle. At the time fully fashioned garments were in vogue, usually being knitted from wool or wool blends. By using Courtelle and knitting unrelaxed yarns at slacker stitch lengths knitting production was increased and the garments after dyeing were soft and bulky like the wool ones. Hence, existing fully fashioned machines could knit Courtelle with only minor changes to their operation. This ensured a viable operation, particularly as the Courtelle garments were easy care and so proved very popular. The introduction of stretch breaking systems, the tow-to-top process, made the procedure even more productive and stretch breaking of acrylic tows for knitwear and jersey yarns is now commonplace all over the world. Thus, by the late fifties and early sixties, Courtelle was established in knitwear and jersey areas, being promoted as soft and luxurious. To these markets was added hand knitting as the high bulk yarns, both 100% and in blends with nylon, proved very popular.

However, in the mid-sixties jersey fabrics in polyester, branded Crimplene, became fashionable and acrylic jersey markets declined. To combat this Courtaulds introduced in 1963 their Neochrome process in which the Courtelle fibre is dyed whilst being spun so that coloured yarns can be produced at lower cost. In addition, the colour fastness properties and colour continuity were extremely good. Together with the cotton spinning route this meant that coloured fabrics could be knitted at lower cost than knitting conventionally dyed yarns. The Neochrome process is now an integral part of the Courtelle operation and is now the largest, most versatile dyeing operation in the world. Considerable quantities of Courtelle ponte-roma fabric, branded Neospun, were produced from Neochrome fibre for dresswear, skirts, trousers and children's wear.

A recent introduction to the Courtelle range, a 1.3dtex staple fibre, is proving highly successful in open-end spinning. This combination of Courtelle with the latest open-end spinning technology is enabling spinners to produce high quality yarns very efficiently, so assisting knitters to compete more effectively in the market.

For knitting globally, demand and production will increase but in Western Europe and probably the USA and Japan some restructuring of the knitting industries is likely to occur, with more high added value products and lower volumes in these areas. This, of course, will affect spinners and fibre producers so possibly the UK knitting industry may become more integrated than at present.

In the UK three main factors could have an effect on Courtelle:

1. Fashion changes from coarse gauge cut and sew to fully fashioned knitwear.
2. Imports of low cost yarns, fabrics and garments.
3. Shorter fashion seasons, leading to shorter lead times required by manufacturers and buyers.

Courtelle as a leading name in knitwear for almost 30 years is ready to face these challenges and continue to provide fashionable, colourful knitwear well into the next century.

Aristoc

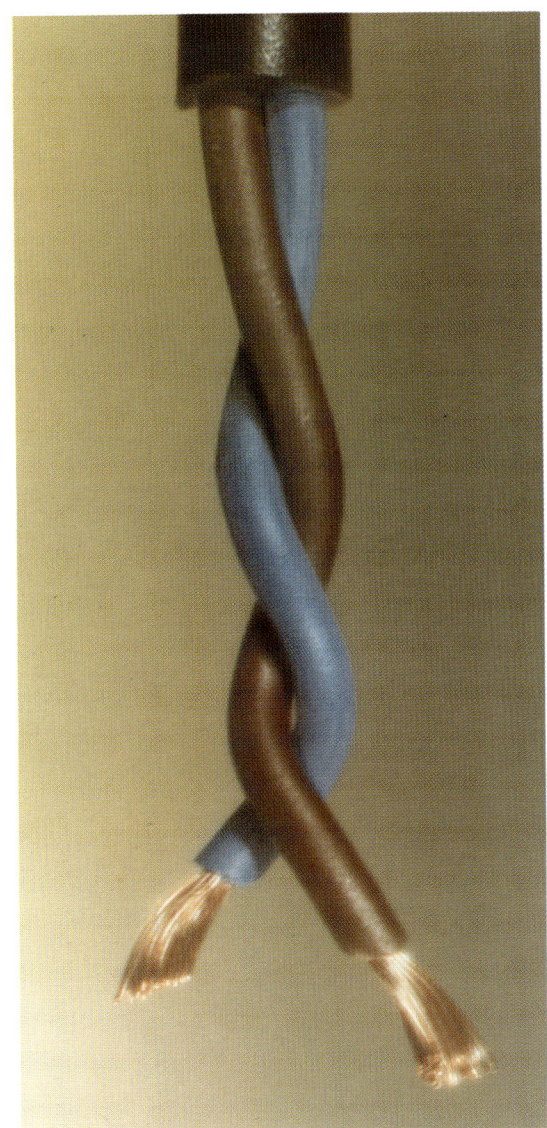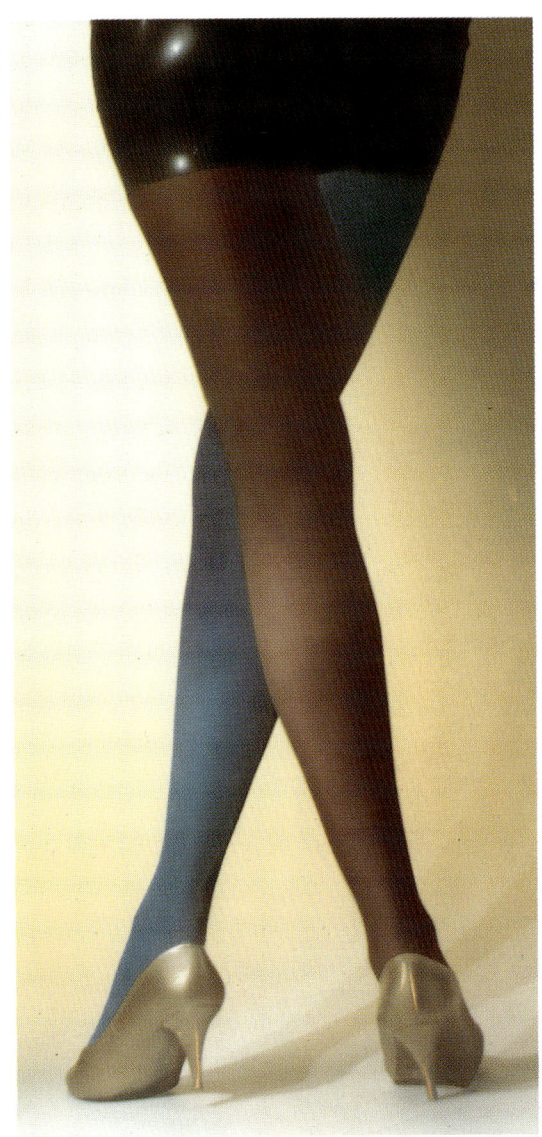

WHERE HIGH TECHNOLOGY MEETS HIGH FASHION.

Aristoc, North Street, Langley Mill, Nottingham NG16 4BT (0773) 716177.

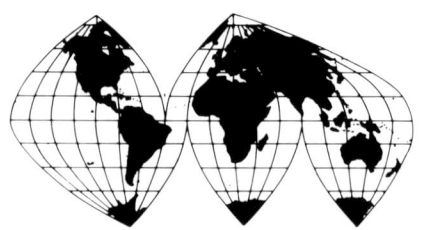

Kurt Salmon Associates — A Worldwide Vision

400 years versus 50 years

We may not be able to boast 400 years service to the knitting industry but over 50 years ago KSA was founded by Kurt Salmon, a textile engineer from the hosiery industry.

From 3 consultants then, we now have over 350 worldwide with offices throughout the USA, Western Europe and in the Far East.

Today we offer specialist services on an international basis to selected fashion consumer products industries, their suppliers and retailers, covering the full spectrum from strategy and marketing, through information technology and control systems to manufacturing operations and distribution.

We plan to be around to celebrate William Lee's 500th anniversary and would like to take this opportunity of wishing all our clients good fortune in their efforts to do the same.

Kurt Salmon Associates Ltd, Bruce Court, 25 Hale Road, Altrincham WA14 2EY, Cheshire

UK   USA   GERMANY   SPAIN   SWITZERLAND   HONG KONG   CANADA

MAGNUM M.3 — The latest woollen card technology from Tatham

A totally new design concept purpose developed to meet the increasing demand for wider card units.

* Modular frame construction mounted on substantial bed plates with unique levelling system.
* Increased diameter cylinders and rollers – statically and dynamically balanced, combined with precision machining to maintain accurate settings under operating conditions.
* New drive arrangements – customer choice of alternative main and ancillary drive systems.
* High speed comb motion assemblies feature individually driven split comb stocks ensuring maximum stability.
* 'Double drive' system assemblies utilizing V or HTD toothed belts give quieter performance, longer life and optimum efficiency.
* New style top covers.
* Undergrid systems with new quick release and pivoting mechanism.
* Unique overhead mobile crane system with motorised two-speed lifting facility.
* Stylised fully interlocked sliding panel guard system for added protection, easier access and better aesthetics.
* Use of latest machine control technology ensures control panels will match most exacting customer specifications.

For a wider perspective on this revolutionary machine, ask for full details.

Our reputation is your re-assurance.

William Tatham Ltd.
Belfield Works, Rochdale,
Lancashire OL16 5AU, England.
Tel: 0706 345888 Telex: 635033 Fax: 0706 354732

To be ahead
For the next 400 years

Never change a winning team

VISCOSUISSE
GROUPE RHÔNE-POULENC

"CONSISTENT
TEXTILE PROFITS
ONLY RESULT
FROM CONSTANT
VIGILANCE"

– DAVID BUCK
TEXTILES ANALYST BZW

*Congratulations
William Lee
on four centuries
of successful vigilance.*

BARCLAYS de ZOETE WEDD
LIMITED

The 'A – Z' of Dyes and Auxiliaries for Knitwear begins and ends with 'I'...

ICI, PO Box 42, Blackley, Manchester M9 3DA Tel: 061-740 1460

STEVENSONS FABRIC DYERS LIMITED

Quarry Road, Somercotes, Derby DE55 4JA
Telephone: 0773 540197 (5 lines) 0773 540208 (2 lines)
Fax: 0773 605118   Telex: 377465 (FABDYE)

Dyers and finishers of weft knit and woven fabrics in polyester, cotton and polyester/cellulosic blends. Open width compacting of cotton a speciality.

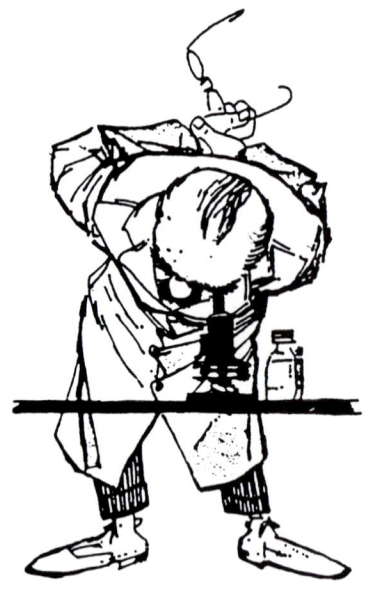

○ **Do you Make:**
Anoraks ❑ Blouses ❑ Dresses ❑ Shirts ❑ Skirts ❑ Trousers ❑ Household Textiles ❑ Upholstery ❑ Carpets?

○ **Do you supply:**
Garment Manufacturers ❑ Distributors ❑ Contractors ❑ Retailers?

○ **Have you ever had problems with:**
Durability ❑ Shrinkages ❑ Colour Fastness ❑ Seaming Slippage ❑ Pucker ❑ Sizing ❑ Quality of make-up ❑ Pile Compression ❑ Flammability ❑ Non-compliance with expected quality?

If not you are very fortunate!!!

SGS Textile Testing Division is the largest independent commercial textile testing house in the U.K. and is a NAMAS approved laboratory. We provide quality assurance testing of fabrics, trimmings and accessories backed by our opinion and advice, quickly and at an economical price. We also carry out quality audits at manufacturer's premises. Send us your enquiries and problems on Performance Testing, Conformity and Specifications, Project Investigations and Technical Training needs. Most probably we can save you money and assist you in your ultimate target -- greater customer satisfaction and the consequent increase in business.

Please contact: R. Croskell   Tel: 01 998 2171
                               Telex: 25658 Corbor
                               Fax: 01 997 9723

SGS TESTING

Quality Control International Ltd
Gaw House, Alperton Lane, Wembley, Middx.

We set Standards In Yarn Preparation and Fabric Manufacture

- Mayer Automatic Cone Winder
    - Improved package quality
    - Versatile scope — from natural silk to linen, from cotton to man-made fibres, from 22 dtex silk to carpet yarns
    - Economic production (up to 1200 m/min)
    - VD/VP link systems ring spinning machine / Mayer Coner

- Tricot machines for an extensive range of end uses, including magazine weft insertion, terry fabrics and terry towels
- Raschel machines for laces, curtaining, elastomeric fabrics, apparel — including fabrics for sports and leisure wear — household textiles, technical fabrics and packaging materials

- Direct warping machines for both warp knitting and weaving sectors
- Draw-warping machines
- Ancillary equipment such as fabric slitting and separating machines

- Technical advice
- Preparation of patterns and pattern programmes
- Assistance with new projects
- Training programmes, information reports, service

Karl Mayer Textilmaschinenfabrik GmbH · D-6053 Obertshausen

☎ 06104/402-0 · 4 10 174 · Telefax: 06104/43574

USA:
MAYER TEXTILE MACHINE CORP.,
310 Brighton Road,
Clifton, New Jersey 07012
7102 Sherwin Road,
Greensboro, N. C. 27410

BRASIL:
KARL MAYER MAQUINAS TEXTEIS LTDA.
Avenida Presidente Castelo Branco, 5949 (Marginal do Tiete)
São Paulo

JAPAN:
NIPPON MAYER CO. LTD.
13, Kageshiro, Kamikitano-Cho
Fukui-City

U.K.:
KARL MAYER TEXTILE MACHINERY LTD.
Kings Road, Shepshed, Leic.

Hong Kong: Karl Mayer Hong Kong Ltd., Room 1204 A, 12/F Tower B, Mandarin Plaza, 14 Science Museum Rd., Tsimshatsui East, Kowloon, Hong Kong

The fibres, today

SNIA UK LTD., 36 Broadway, St. James's, LONDON SW1H 0BH. Tel. 01 222 8696. Tlx. 23377.

New End-Uses Will Broaden Polyester's Prime Position

*By R. J. Woodward, Hoechst UK and
G. D. Myers and J. G. Kilroy, British Man-Made Fibres Federation*

POLYESTER, which was discovered in the laboratories of Calico Printers Association in 1941, was first developed commercially by ICI in the United Kingdom and is now the leading synthetic fibre worldwide in terms of both volume and versatility.

Large scale production began in 1955 under the well known brand name Terylene. Other producers were licensed by ICI to produce polyester and in Europe these included Glanzstoff and Hoechst (in 1953). The latter recently acquired American Celanese and as Hoechst Celanese is the world's largest producer of polyester fibre with 900,000 tonnes. Trevira has long been established in virtually all apparel end uses, as well as furnishings, car upholstery, carpets and industrial end uses. The Trevira brand name was first registered in 1955 and fibre production spread quickly to many different parts of the world. In 1970 production of filament yarn began at Limavady, Northern Ireland. Hoechst's other production units are in West Germany, Austria, Denmark, USA, South Africa and Brazil.

In addition to existing polyester production in Europe from such companies as AKZO, Montefibre and Rhone Poulenc there is growing capacity from the NIC countries, notably Taiwan and South Korea, in both PE filament and staple. Turkey is also becoming a significant polyester supplier. Meanwhile Japan is increasingly concentrating on its technical expertise in the fine decitex and fine dpf areas.

Polyester staple fibres are used in 100 per cent form in fillings for quilts and the like and in nonwoven fabrics. However, their principal use is in blended yarn woven for apparel and domestic end-uses. Polyester filament yarns, both textured and non-textured, go into the knitting and weaving of fabrics, also for clothing and domestic purposes. In industrial outlets polyester high-tenacity yarns have a substantial niche.

The estimated production of polyester fibres in 1986 worldwide was about 7 million tonnes, of which 59 per cent was staple fibre and 41 per cent filament.

Polyester (filament yarn and staple fibre) accounts for about 50 per cent of world synthetic fibre consumption and is second only to cotton in the world fibre consumption league. In reaching this position polyester took the lion's share of the growth of synthetic fibres which increased from 1.5 per cent of world fibre consumption in 1953 to about 39 per cent in 1986. A major factor in polyester's growth has been the pre-eminence of polyester staple fibre for blending with cotton. As a consequence polyester staple fibres alone are used more than any other man-made fibre and also exceed the consumption of wool on a world basis.

In the period 1979–86 polyester production increased slightly in Western Europe (2 per cent p.a.), declined in the USA (−20 per cent), and remained constant in Japan. However, it more than doubled elsewhere, particularly in the Far East. Whereas in 1979 production outside Europe, the USA, and Japan accounted for 35 per cent of the total, in 1986 the proportion had risen to 57 per cent. This growth is expected to continue in these areas, especially in China.

End-Uses

Polyester is one of the most versatile synthetic fibres, providing the excellent easy-care and enhanced performance characteristics which have established a new standard for clothing and domestic textiles. For these purposes, polyester filament yarns, textured and non-textured, are used to produce both knitted and woven fabrics. Polyester staple fibres in 100 per cent form, but more usually in blends with natural fibres, are mainly used in woven fabrics. In blends with cotton (commonly in 50/50 or 67/33 polyester-rich blends) polyester enhances substantially the wash-wear performance and durability of the fabric at a competitive price. Polyester is also blended with wool for use in outerwear, as a means of improving wear properties and appearance retention. Polyester staple fibres are also made with characteristics suitable for fillings and nonwovens whilst polyester filament yarns are well established in industrial applications where physical properties such as high tenacity, high initial modulus, and dimensional stability give the best performance/cost ratio.

The main uses are indicated in Table 1, which gives the mill consumption of polyester by the EEC textile industries in 1986, as estimated by CIRFS — the international trade association representing the man-made fibres industry.

Polyester thus has its largest use in weaving, where the mill consumption in 1986 was 425,000 tonnes. The greatest part of this was for apparel fabrics at 246,500 tonnes made up of:

Non-wool types, e.g. cotton system and filament yarns	185,000 t
Wool types	61,500 t

In the woven furnishing and household sector, the mill consumption of 92,000 tonnes was made up of:

Household	30,000 t
Net curtains	24,000 t
Furnishings	23,000 t
Bedding	12,000 t
Blankets	3,000 t

whilst for woven industrial fabrics, where the mill consumption is 75,500 tonnes in the EEC, the make up is:

Tyre cord fabrics	6,000 t
Webbing/Belting	30,000 t
Filters/Sailcloth	39,500 t

Significant quantities of polyester are also used in the EEC knitting industry (188,000 tonnes) with the largest proportion 140,500 tonnes going to weft knitted end-uses, mainly outerwear, as follows:

Socks	1,000 t
Underwear	8,500 t
Outerwear	120,000 t
Furnishing and household	4,000 t
Industrial	7,000 t

Mill consumption for warp knitted end-uses at 47,500 tonnes comprises:

Apparel	12,000 t
Net curtains	20,500 t
Household and furnishings	14,000 t
Industrial	1,000 t

Other polyester fibre uses not classified under weaving or knitting accounted for a further 192,000 tonnes of mill consumption made up as follows:

Carpets	15,000 t
Sewing thread	21,000 t
Ropes, nets, twines	8,000 t
Fillings/Waddings	89,000 t
Nonwovens	69,000 t

To summarise, more than 50 per cent of all polyester processed in EEC textile mills in 1986 was for weaving, predominantly for apparel manufacture, where it accounted for 23 per cent of all the fibres used, including natural fibres. The knitting sector makes a further substantial contribution to the dependence of the apparel market on polyester fibres, consuming a further 141,500 tonnes, although the share of polyester is lower at not more than 19 per cent of all fibres used in knitted apparel.

In some specific sectors, polyester has a dominant share. In net curtains for example, 45,000 tonnes of polyester fibres account for 75 per cent, and in industrial webbing and belting 30,000 tonnes

Table 1

Polyester mill consumption by main and end-use, EEC, 1986.

	'000 tonnes	% of all fibres
WEAVING (total)	425	21
Apparel	246.5	23
Furnishing and household	92	14
Industrial fabrics	75.5	24
Narrow fabrics	11	27
KNITTING (total)	188	18
Weft knitting	140.5	15
Warp knitting	47.5	31
OTHER USES	192.0	22
TOTAL	**805**	**20**

(Note that final consumption of polyester in EEC in 1986 will in general be a higher figure resulting from mill consumption (as above) less exports plus imports — of textiles and clothing).

Table 2

Estimated mill consumption of all fibres, 1986

	'000,000 tonnes	%
Cotton	16.9	47
Wool	1.9	5
Viscose	3.3	9
Synthetic fibres	13.9	39
TOTAL	**36.0**	**100.0**

Table 3

Estimated mill consumption of synthetic fibres, 1986

	'000,000 tonnes	%
Nylon	3.5	25
Polyester (total) of which	7.0	50
Staple fibre	4.1	29.5
Fil. yarn — Industrial	0.4	20.5
Fil. yarn — Textile	2.5	
Acrylic	2.5	18
Polypropylene/others	0.9	7
TOTAL	**13.9**	**100**

represent 57 per cent of mill consumption. On the other hand, in nonwovens, using 60,000 tonnes of polyester fibres, the polyester share is only 21 per cent of all fibres; in filters, sailcloth, and proofed fabric, consuming 40,000 tonnes, it is 22 per cent; and in household textiles (sheets, etc), 30,000 tonnes of polyester fibres represent only 11 per cent of all fibres used (showing the continuing predominance of cotton in this sector).

Polyester also has a significant share of the synthetic fibre consumption for industrial purposes and a healthy share of the total industrial market (24 per cent).

Other noteworthy end-uses are sewing threads and fillings.

Mill Consumption

Looking at the world scene, the estimated mill consumption of all fibres in 1986 is set out in Table 2 with the make-up of the synthetic fibre element, which includes polyester, shown in Table 3.

A comparison based on estimates of mill consumption in the main areas is set out in Table 4, which confirms the relative importance of polyester fibre in synthetic consumption throughout the world.

From consideration of demographic factors, the significant differences in consumption of fibres per head of population (ranging for example from 4.5 kg in China to more than 25 kg in USA), the potential for economic growth and the increasing trade in textiles and clothing, the mill consumption of fibre will grow at a significantly higher rate in the developing regions and centrally planned (CP) economies than in the developed countries.

Also of importance is the probability that cotton, having declined from a world market share of about 70 per cent of mill consumption in 1953 to 47 per cent in 1986, will at least maintain this share and probably increase slightly as cotton production increases, e.g. in China. It is expected that cotton will be in adequate supply at competitive prices.

This situation is of relevance to the future demand for polyester staple since (as Table 4 shows) the textile industries in the developing regions and CP economies are cotton-orientated and for both internal consumption and external trade it is probable that increasing quantities of polyester/cotton blend fabrics and made-up goods will be produced, the two fibres being complementary rather than polyester replacing cotton.

Other blends, e.g. with wool, may well increase also in these areas, and there is potential for growth of polyester filament yarn consumption which already amounts to some 35 per cent of polyester consumption.

Polyester industrial yarn consumption will also increase with the growth of other manufacturing industries.

Production

The emerging pattern for the distribution of polyester production in the world also confirms the shift from Western Europe, USA, and Japan, to the developing countries and the CP economies. Table 5 sets out the production from 1979–1986 in Western Europe, USA, Japan, and the rest of the world.

Table 4

Comparison of estimated mill consumption in 1986 by main areas

	USA		WESTERN EUROPE		JAPAN		DEVELOPING REGIONS*		CENTRALLY PLANNED ECONOMIES†	
	'000 tonnes	%	'000 tonnes	%	'000 tonnes	%	'000 tonnes	%	'000 tonnes	%
Cotton	1,495	30	1,350	29	695	34	6,150	56	7,105	57
Wool	65	1	465	10	115	5	425	4	705	6
Viscose	410	8	545	11	230	11	655	6	1,430	11
Synthetic	3,065	61	2,345	50	1,015	50	3,770	34	3,305	26
of which										
Polyester	1,425	28	880	19	605	25	2,320	21	1,685	13
Staple fibre	925	18	475	10	220	11	1,230	11	1,165	9
Textile filament yarn	355	7	310	7	230	11	1,065	9.5	465	3.5
Industrial filament yarn	145	3	95	2	55	3	25	0.5	55	0.5
Percentage of polyester in synthetic consumption		48		38		50		62		50.0

*Developing Regions — include S.E. Asia, Indian Sub-continent, Near East (including Turkey), Africa and Latin America.

†Centrally Planned Economies — include USSR, rest of E. Europe, and China.

Table 5

Polyester production (Unit = 1,000 tonnes)

WESTERN EUROPE			USA			JAPAN			REST OF WORLD			WORLD		
FY	SF	TOTAL	FY	SF	TOTAL	FY	SF	TOTAL	FY	SF	TOTAL	FY	SF	TOTAL
386	403	789	779	1,117	1,896	314	318	632	739	1,070	1,809	2,218	2,908	5,126
336	373	708	663	1,146	1,803	305	320	625	791	1,200	1,991	2,094	3,033	5,127
379	412	791	712	1,182	1,894	310	321	631	820	1,329	2,149	2,221	3,244	5,465
365	404	769	550	887	1,437	314	314	628	902	1,370	2,272	2,131	2,975	5,106
373	414	787	617	991	1,608	310	320	630	1,024	1,551	2,575	2,324	3,276	5,600
397	446	843	544	994	1,538	327	320	647	1,235	1,811	3,046	2,503	3,571	6,074
418	453	871	599	916	1,515	329	323	652	1,437	2,096	3,533	2,783	3,788	6,571
402	450	852	532	967	1,499	322	310	632	1,620	2,387	4,007	2,876	4,114	6,990

Source: CIRFS
Abbreviations: FY = Filament yarn. SF = Staple fibre

Production in Western Europe has increased at about 2 per cent p.a. over the period whilst in the USA there has been a step change downward in both filament yarn and staple fibre production of the order of 15–20 per cent. In Japan production remained relatively constant over the period.

On the other hand, production of both filament yarn and staple fibre more than doubled in the rest of the world. Whereas in 1979 these countries, principally the developing countries and CP economies, accounted for 35 per cent of world production, the proportion had increased to 57 per cent by 1986.

According to a recent survey among engineering firms by the German journal Chemiefasern, 70 per cent of planned new fibre capacity is for polyester production, most destined for the developing countries and CP economies, with China emerging as a major producer. Taiwan already has more polyester capacity than Western Europe. By 1990, therefore, the proportion of world polyester production in these areas may well exceed 60 per cent.

World polyester production increased at the rate of 8 per cent p.a. between 1982 and 1986, almost entirely as the result of the high growth rate (15 per cent p.a.) in the developing countries and CP economies. Even allowing for more modest growth rates, world production of polyester fibres will probably exceed 8 million tonnes by 1990.

The Future

Man-made fibres have increased their share of the textile raw materials worldwide to just under 50 per cent. Polyester has developed favourably within this figure and particularly in the sector of "technical" fibres for industrial end uses, where the special nature of polyester offers a number of advantages — strength, dimensional stability, behaviour towards moisture and resistance to ultra-violet radiation, fire and chemicals.

Growth in the technical sector will be achieved through the large number of new products rather than through traditional markets. These new end uses include insulation, motoring safety and functional interior fittings in cars.

Industrial Sector

The range of fibres that Hoechst offers in the industrial sector is particularly wide-embracing; Trevira High Tenacity, Trevira Monofil, Trevira Spunbond, Trevira CS flame retardant and Dolanit (asbestos substitute). The sales opportunities for Dolanit look promising and Trevira CS flame retardant fibre will undoubtedly increase its penetration of the market.

Fine nonwoven material in the Spunbond sector will be produced and modified Trevira monofilament grades will be added to the Hoechst range.

There will also be growth in the more traditional apparel and home textile markets, bearing in mind that about 80 per cent of the production of the European textile industry is still absorbed in these two areas. There will probably be greater expansion in home textiles, where both floor coverings and fillings have much potential for new polyester products aimed at specialist segments. Inevitably the apparel market is more vulnerable to low cost imports but even here there are new opportunities for polyester. For example: the continuing development of finer decitex yarns in both the filament and staple sectors; the growing demand for functional clothing; and the potential of new rotor spun yarns. Only by continually improving and refining its product range in the three areas of apparel, home textiles and industrial end uses can the European textile industry defend itself from the surge in imports.

A Fibre Giant's Chlorofibre Speciality

By Terry Duncan, Rhone-Poulenc

ON ANY BASIS OF assessment, the French Rhone-Poulenc Group must rank high in the first division of the world fibre-producing league. Some find it surprising that the Group is now the world's fourth largest man-made fibres producer, after Du Pont, Hoechst and Courtaulds, and by a very substantial margin retains its position as the leading manufacturer of synthetic texile yarns in Europe.

Not so surprising is that the great bulk of this production is comprised of polyester (43 per cent of total production capacity) and polyamide (37 per cent), the balance of 20 per cent being largely attributable to cellulose and PVC-based products. Whilst many thousands of tonnes of product in each of these areas are sold as "commodity" yarns and fibres, the Rhone-Poulenc Group has gained particular recognition for its numerous yarn and fibre specialities. These extend across a broad spectrum of chemical bases, and across a considerable network of Group subsidiary companies, each operating internationally. These divide into two main geographical groups, based respectively in Western Europe and in South America.

In Europe, the Rhone-Poulenc Group's textile sector embraces the activities of Rhone-Poulenc Fibres, Cellatex and Rhovyl, all based in France, Rhodia AG in Germany, Viscosuisse in Switzerland, and SAFA in Spain, with the South American subsidiaries Rhodia SA and RAQT based respectively in Brazil and Argentina.

Of the particular yarn and fibre speciality products from each of these organisations, a number share the special feature of presenting notably good aesthetics in terms of appearance and handle. Such products include the widely-acclaimed 'Opal' natural-look polyamide 6.6 for the carpet industry, the Tergal 'Pontella' "filament with the aspect of fibre" yarn which uses an outer sheath of fine filaments and an inner core of coarse filaments to achieve a wide range of different "spun" and "natural" looks, and the internationally acclaimed 'Kermel' non-flammable aramid fibre used in high-comfort protective garments.

One of the most remarkable of the Group's speciality products is chlorofibre, which was invented more than thirty years ago by the scientists of Rhone-Poulenc. Today, the Group subsidiary, Société Rhovyl, based in Paris, is the only manufacturer of chlorofibre in Europe, and the continuous programme of research and development which has been pursued in the field of chlorofibre performance and applications in providing major new successes.

In the apparel and fashion markets, Rhovyl chlorofibre has achieved in recent years a virtual renaissance. In only a few years, Rhovyl has advanced from being seen purely as a "thermal" fibre very largely for use in winter underwear, right into the mainstream of fashion-orientated sports and leisurewear.

A constantly expanding network of leading spinners, both in the UK and throughout Europe, spearheads this new impetus, making available a whole range of new blends to open up new fabric possibilities and new options in garment design and performance.

Apparel Spectrum

Rhovyl is moving ahead, right across the apparel spectrum — in underwear, outerwear, active sports and leisurewear, in fine up-market lingerie, in high-performance underwear and "midwear", in sports socks, in safety nightwear, and in footwear. This dramatic expansion of the scope that Rhovyl can offer is largely the result of major advances in the achievable characteristics of chlorofibre-based fabrics. In its original applications, in traditionally-styled thermal underwear — a market where Rhovyl chlorofibre still features prominently — the blend conventionally used is the classic 85/15 with polyester, polyamide or acrylic as the minority fibre.

But increasingly imaginative new blends, together with major advances in the development of Rhovyl chlorofibre itself, have greatly enhanced the aesthetic, tactile and textile appeal of the fabric possibilities now attainable with chlorofibre — without compromising any of its inherent chemical and physical advantages.

These centre on the ability of chlorofibre to

"wick" away perspiration from the body, which is thereby kept both warm and dry — and thus more comfortable — and on its inherently non-absorbent and flame-retardant properties. These combine with the high level of thermal insulation for which chlorofibre first gained special recognition.

It is this combination of comfort, safety and warmth which closely answers the prescription for nightwear, children's wear and babywear, and Rhovyl today is gaining great sucess in these market sectors.

With growing momentum, more and more exciting new looks and styles of fabrics have been achieved with Rhovyl chlorofibre, providing at the same time outstanding thermal protection and specially attractive appearance and handle.

The great variety of fabric types which can now be achieved in Rhovyl chlorofibre and the new Rhovyl blends extends from ultra-fine, delicate lace effects, providing thermal warmth without weight in high-fashion lingerie, to chunky, heavy knitwear.

For summer-weight sports and leisurewear, and with great potential for fashion outerwear and active sports underwear, the newly introduced 70/30 blend of Rhovyl chlorofibre with Modal, based on viscose, is attracting considerable attention. The blend is notable for its combination of practical and comfort advantages — providing at the same time the wicking performance of the chlorofibre component and the controlled moisture-absorbing benefits of the Modal minority fibre.

With its attractive handle, drape, comfort-in-wear, and peformance capabilities, Rhovyl/Modal offers exciting new fabric possibilities. In high-performance sports underwear, Rhovyl/Modal will complement the classic 85/15 Rhovyl blend which has been succesfully used for some years by leading specialist manufacturers in this field.

In the lingerie field, where leading manufacturers are also now working from the 85/15 Rhovyl blend of chlorofibre with polyester, there is also rapidly growing interest at the luxury end of the market in the recently introduced blending of chlorofibre with 15 per cent silk to produce particularly fine and sophisticated fabrics.

In heavy knitwear based on Rhovyl, keen interest has been shown in a 50/50 blend of chlorofibre with wool, for which a good spinner base has been established; and in further blends including chlorofibre/acrylic and 50/30/20 chlorofibre/wool/acrylic.

These blends, together with Rhovyl/Modal are successfully opening up new potential for Rhovyl in the hosiery market.

To meet the special requirements of so wide, and so rapidly increasing, a range of applications, Rhovyl yarn is now available through a considerably augmented network of cotton, worsted and woollen spinners, working with a wider variety of blends and counts, and ensuring the ready availability of yarn from the UK and from major countries throughout Europe.

Strong and sustained international promotion of Rhovyl chlorofibre, involving not just fabric and garment-makers, but also leading names in the retail distribution chain, is now under way to demonstrate the ever-widening capabilities of Rhovyl in fashion applications.

The Expanding Uses For Lycra In Knitting

By Margaret Jacob, Du Pont UK

WHAT WILLIAM LEE would have thought of Lycra, Du Pont's elastane fibre and its dramatic impact on the hosiery industry is hard to imagine. But 400 years later his successors, today's knitters, find the addition of a small percentage of Lycra contributes to a high degree of comfort and freedom of movement, applicable across the whole spectrum of clothing. It also makes possible sophisticated dimensional effects which expand textile design possibilities.

Du Pont announced the trademark Lycra, their fourth truly man-made fibre, in October 1959 and began commercial production just three years later. Since 1962, they and the knitting industry have explored its use with every type of machine and application. It all started with bodywear and expanded rapidly into swimwear, hosiery and socks. Then came outerwear, leisurewear and all forms of active sportswear.

Reviewing current and future developments in the Quatercentenary year of William Lee, it seems appropriate to start with hosiery although this was not in fact the first market to feel the influence of Lycra.

Hosiery

Lycra began to be used for support hosiery during the early '60s and its contribution to improved fit and comfort was appreciated immediately. Du Pont went on to develop finer yarns but it wasn't until the '70s that 22 dtex yarns began to penetrate the wider fashion hosiery market. 11 dtex, the most technically advanced form of the fibre, followed in 1985.

Another major advance was the introduction of fine dtex clear yarns which have the lack of visibility, essential for today's sheer hosiery. These developments enable Lycra to contribute its superior stretch and recovery properties to the wider and most fashionable end of the hosiery industry.

The explosive growth in the use of Lycra is the result of continuous development, best described by grouping hosiery into categories.

Satin Super Sheers with smooth, 'glassy' sheen and soft touch, use single or double covered 11 or 22 dtex yarn knitted alternatively with flat nylon. While the same dtex yarns, this time bare, are plaited or 'laid-in' to make Superfit hosiery ranging from very sheer or less sheer.

For opaques/fancies, fit and shape retention is achieved with 22 or 44 dtex either bare or covered, particularly with spun yarns or heavy dtex nylon, as well as in fancy stitches and laces.

Fashion demands for figure hugging dresses require garments with a perception of control and no visible panty line. The answer is a control top which although well established in the US, has not as yet taken off in Europe. So Du Pont and the hosiery knitters all speculate that there is ample room for considerable growth with this type of product. It uses 44-156 dtex Lycra, mainly covered, in combination with cotton or bright yarns.

Another sector using the same yarns, is support. Today it can be both fashionable and desirable while still providing therapeutic compression. And it can range from heavy 'functional' support to light fashion support.

Lingerie Tops, the final group, has infinite possibilities for development with 22-78 dtex Lycra. It describes tops with a decorative finish and excellent fit. And can include fashionable bikini and tanga shapes, knitted as one with the pantyhose, or cut and sewn.

Although there will be continued developments using existing Lycra yarns, new introductions are equally important. With this in mind, Du Pont recently launched a 17 dtex product which will stimulate the creation of more new styles.

Circular Knits And Tricot

Nowhere has the impact of Lycra been more evident than with bodywear. It was first called corsetry, but as the industry developed lightweight yet figure controlling fabrics and garments, changed into foundationwear, intimate apparel and then bodywear. The changes picked up momentum as 44 and 22 dtex Lycra yarns went into circular knits and tricots, and with the development of core spun cotton/Lycra knits.

A wide variety of the circular knit fabrics is used in close fitting garments such as leotards, swimwear and bodywear where it is essential to have high stretch and recovery. Lycra also adds the same advantages to other fabric constructions used in clothing for skiing, riding, climbing, cycling and athletics.

For the special needs of a growing swimwear market, Du Pont introduced a chlorine resistant fibre in the 80s. The principal fabric, lightweight quick-drying nylon or polyester/Lycra tricot, provides an excellent base for colour and print, and a huge opportunity for garment design.

There are some further areas with development opportunities. Lycra provides a superb route for achieving surface effects in both single and double jersey fashion knits, through the technique for differential collapse. Textured surfaces; fancy patterns; heavy-look, lightweight fabrics — are all within the compass of the imaginative fabric designer.

To ensure that the trimmings of sweat shirts, track suits and leisurewear are functional and keep their shape for the life of the garment, all that is needed is the incorporation of a small percentage of Lycra into the circular knit ribs.

Stretch lace is also showing development potential either as a complete garment or as a trim for other stretch fabrics. In fact the whole area of narrows — bands, edgings and inserts — is becoming increasingly important.

Knitwear

The use of Lycra in knitwear has yet to be developed fully although there are many possibilities. It can be knitted into cuff, waist and neckline to improve shape retention and fit. And used selectively in the body, can create unique styling such as ruching, seersucker or bubble effects.

It is incorporated into the fabric using either covered or core twisted yarns. The latter is made by an extra twisting process, in combination with the yarn already selected for the garment.

Socks

Although socks containing Lycra have been produced for many years, the new generation will use the recently introduced 17 dtex product as the plaiting yarn, rather than just 100 per cent nylon.

The many advantages include cleaner patterns and better cling, cut ends that are more securely locked into the fabric and the use of thicker face yarns. Plaiting is easier and there is consequently less misplaiting. The increase in face yarn content can also be reflected in the labelling. Lycra can be used covered conventionally, air jet textured or possibly bare, the latter only on certain machines and styles.

Outerwear

By 1988 Lycra in outerwear has become an established formula. Take any knitted fabric, add a touch of Lycra and the result is limitless design possibilities with unmatched functionality. From lightest weight cottons and softest silks, to the fanciest wools, it adds performance, comfort and value.

The recent expansion into all areas of clothing has been swift and the advantages endless. For sport clothing, it adds comfort, is protective, hardwearing and practical. In leisurewear it allows freedom of movement and has shape retention. And for fashion it mixes with any fabric, is flexible, allows better fit, moves with the body and is easy to wear.

All these factors have helped Lycra become an established addition to fashion fabrics and garment design will continue to challenge and inspire creativity.

The Future

Consumers continue to change. They are fitter and lead healthier, more active lifestyles. They tend to be more demanding and when looking for knitted clothing — from hosiery to outerwear — have begun to expect the quality and added comfort provided by Lycra.

To prepare for the future and the continued development of both established and as yet unidentified markets, Du Pont is spending over 200 million dollars on increased capacity worldwide. Compared with 1987, Du Pont shipped over 25 per cent more Lycra in 1988 and expects that figure to reach 100 per cent more by 1990.

Anniversary portrait of founder-chairman Geoffrey Macpherson J.P.

Macpherson are privileged to be celebrating their golden, fiftieth anniversary year, 1988-1989, during the quatercentenary of the Reverend William Lee's mechanised knitting revolution.

Geoffrey E. Macpherson Limited
Lenton Lane East, Nottingham NG7 2NT, England.

Telephone: 0602-868701 (Overseas code +44 602) Fax: 0602-864430 (Overseas code +44 602) Telex: 377217 MCPHSN G.

Leading yarn and machinery suppliers with full after sales service to most major processes in the textile and apparel industries.

Associate companies in U.S.A., Canada, Australia and New Zealand. Agencies world-wide.

A Spinner's View Of The '90s

By Robert Shelton, Thomas Burnley & Sons

IN LOOKING FORWARD, it is always wise to take a quick glance back, if only to ensure that something dismissed yesterday is not the way of the future.

With reference to Europe, 1992 and beyond, worsted spinning — and Bradford in particular — has a very special place. Bradford's ties with Europe go back to the early nineteenth century. One only has to look today at the trading names still operating around the area called Little Germany — Mainz, Dewaverin, Heydemann, Jacob Hoare, Blocha Behrends, Provost, etc — many now amalgamated in larger groupings, but evidence of long associations which have survived at least two major European conflicts.

Multilingual trading is a daily occurrence for both merchants and spinning companies, and Bradford has a long established trading record throughout the world. Local companies are now gearing up in marketing, warehousing and distribution to capitalise on this heritage, to supply Europe on an equal timescale to the UK, and so take full advantage of any opportunities which arise.

Looking to the future from an industry in the midst of severe recession needs the kind of optimism and fortitude which conquered the Luddite revolts and made way for the Industrial Revolution. Being part of that heritage, we are ready to take up the cudgels (or micro-processors) again to defend our future in Europe.

It somehow seemed more simple then, without the everyday things we now take for granted — electricity, gas/oil fired boilers, rapid transport, telecommunications and computerisation. These were just not around then to ease (or complicate) life, but neither was world competition — the 'workshop of the world' situation prevailed.

We all have (or should have) learned the lessons of the post-war production-led selling principles; and, glossing over the transitions, have now arrived at a market — or consumer-led — view to the future. The problem is, how high are the levels of automation that can be blended with total versatility in this diverse and fickle industry?

In the past low labour cost countries have used this advantage, coupled with their political need for hard Western currency, to overtake any textile company unwary enough to become complacent. To a large extent, worsted spinning in Europe walked right into this trap during the 1970s. Survivors of this conflagration have since become wary; and today, although wounded and battle weary, they can stand up as being the most comprehensively equipped in the world. In saying this, we must acknowledge the European spinners have had the advantage of the availability of the most up-to-date technology, if they had the courage and foresight to introduce it. UK companies in particular have invested heavily in the future, at their own risk, with little encouragement from Government.

In the last decade, technlogical progress in worsted spinning has been staggering, but it must be said that many of these advances were forced on the industry by the need to cut costs. These changes include a shortening/speeding up of product routes; automation of heavily manual tasks; and de-skilling many crucial operations. This has resulted in productivity levels undreamed of by our fathers, and far in advance of those available to the knitting industry.

Rate Of Progress

However, the advent of this technology has not been universally welcomed — there is always someone somewhere on a volcanic island just risen out of the sea who insists that he can do it the old way cheaper but using subsidies, as long as it suits his purpose, and this does somewhat slow down the rate of progress.

The conventional ring spinning route has benefited from many varied developments — allowing higher maximum speeds; the development of stretch-breaking and blending machinery, resulting in greater control of the fibre, coupled with improved drafting equipment such as electronic auto-levellers; linked winding/electronic auto-levellers; automatic doffing; linked winding/electronic clearing/splicing; two-for-one twisting, etc — all mind-bogglingly modern, and much of it thanks to the micro-chip, but further development of this route is hard to envisage.

The problem with progress of this nature is that it

can all be nullified by a dramatic upward swing in the price of raw material, an example being the current price of wool; or by a significant shift in currency, for example Sterling v DM or US $. The hard-won cut in costs, achieved only by vast investment, can disappear overnight at times like this. The days of the labourless mills are almost with us — cotton spinning systems shown at ITMA '87 incorporating auto-loading -creeling, -doffing, linked systems and even robot cone inspection all confirm it. "This should, once and for all, lay the spectre of cheap labour", we hear you say, but that remains to be seen.

The Yorkshire industry has always had a detailed knowledge of world economics, exchange rates and finance, due to its raw material sources and trading partners. It has now learned the arts of strategy, marketing, design, fashion forecasting and politics. It is not only the yuppies of the city who constantly discuss the value of a currency to three decimal places, or debate which will have the biggest effect on the value of the dollar, the American budget deficit or its massive trade deficit. The fact that the USA has quietly changed from being the world's number one creditor nation in 1983 to the world's biggest debtor in 1988 has escaped few in textiles, because generally the US $ is the currency of imports.

Discussing the situation with fibre producers, spinners, dyers, knitters and retailers, at $1.50 to the £ generally Far Eastern imports are not desperately attractive, at $1.20 to the £ distinctly unattractive, but at $1.80 — "when can you deliver?". With swings of this magnitude, how can sensible long term planning take place? Our own Government with gay abandon, pushes up interest rates to goodness-knows-what by the publication date of this article, in a vain attempt to prop up a desperately overvalued pound; and exacerbates an already critical import situation in all manufactured products, not just textiles. With high interest rates and an overvalued currency, we are not exactly well equipped to take on the world.

Much has also been written about the imports from Mexico and Turkey, and repeating the arguments here will serve no useful purpose, but unless there is recognition by government of the irreparable damage that these artificial prices have caused, and are continuing to cause, to our European manufacturing base, the consequences are dire.

Having looked upon the negatives, let us view the positives. The situation we find ourselves in at the moment is not entirely unique, for the spinning industry at least. Japan was the textile problem after its post-war restructuring, and its near neighbours quickly learned the tricks and followed its example. This posed severe problems for the Lancashire cotton industry in the 60s and 70s, and for the acrylic spinners in the late 70s. Result — re-equip and restructure. The difference then was that we were a little complacent, now we are not. A few recent press cuttings raise a smile on our careworn faces; and show, as Confucius said, "even the monkey fall from the tree":

> "Japan seeking duties on knitted imports — Japanese knitting companies, which have been hit by a flood of imports, will ask the Government today to impose anti-dumping duties on imports from South Korea, their chief competitor. Japan would impose duties only with great reluctance".
>
> "Japanese imports soar — overall imports of yarn and clothing rose by 50.9 per cent, and raw fibres by 15.4 per cent in the first half of 1988".

Factories are now being built within the UK and EEC by S. Korean and Hong Kong based knitwear companies, the reason being that domestic inflation and transport costs will make them uncompetitive in world markets. The old approach of building an economy based in labour-intensive textiles with which to attract world currency, and thus expand other industries, still works. These newly-developed countries can later discard the 'low tech' textiles when labour costs rise. Unfortunately, in Western economies, the governments forget to tell their own textile manufacturers. It is vital that we convince governments not to sacrifice their manufacturing base, not only in textiles, but all manufactured goods. We cannot all work in service industries; and, however much we automate, we still need technicians and personnel to run a business, not matter how few.

World Pressures

Fibre producers were the first to feel the world pressures; and giant multinationals such as Monsanto and Du Pont are no longer in acrylics in Europe. Further amalgamations and takeovers prove that this is a continuing problem. Spinners have felt the changes; and now knitwear manufacturers, who are labour intensive, bear the brunt of world economic changes. The retailers will be next, and a battle will be seen in the High Streets of the EEC.

If we are not vigilant, imports will rule. We, as a textile-consuming society, will be entirely at the mercy of non-European sources, and be forced to pay their price, regardless of the health of our currency. By the way, what is the price of cashmere knitwear today?

The future of the European industry lies in the realisation that, regardless of our function, we are all component manufacturers of garments, each with our own skills, and we must work as one industry. If by 1992 all internal, material, technical and fiscal barriers are indeed removed, this should enable competitive pressures to grow, and also enable the efficient producer to show his real worth within the community. Community-wide opportunities for marketing and specialisation should emerge, and produce an efficient industry to compete on world markets.

For example, the spinner with fully-automated 'lights-out' production on a commodity product would be able to reap the economies of scale by supplying a much-enlarged customer base. The smaller fancy, or specialist, yarn producer with short cycle product lines, would again be able to service a much larger fashion-conscious pool of manufacturers, not necessarily influenced by centrally co-ordinated retailers. The larger integrated spinner may be able to amalgamate both philosophies, given a larger and more accessible customer and retailer base, and therefore significantly improve the pipeline reaction.

For our part, we are looking towards this end, and we felt that an essential weapon in the armoury was to establish a quality standard. To this end we have attained registration under BS 5750, Part 2, and ISO 9002 Quality Assurance Schemes, thus ensuring our working methods are to an internationally accepted level. Participation in Dynamic Response projects, to improve and strengthen raw material to retail links, has been pledged. Investigation and use of the latest computer aids in the planning, forecasting and monitoring of all aspects of our business are constantly under development, together with further investigations of new dyeing and yarn assembly techniques.

Our technology does not protect us; but, with the co-operation of our suppliers, it does give us the knowledge that what we are doing is correct in the world market. We do not seek protection or subsidy, but we are concerned about unfair trade practices and foreign government subsidy. We have held our flag since 1752, and do not intend to relinquish our standard. We look forward to the 21st century; and, if our customers in Europe can survive the onslaught, we will be here to service them.

Just two last questions — If we cannot beat the imports, do we join them? and was Ned Ludd right?

Fully-Fashioned To Seamless: Productivity And Fashion

By Dennis R. Goadby

MANY NAMES ARE associated with improvements and developments to the hand frame but the major credit for the drive into the era of the power machine must belong to William Cotton of Loughborough. He in 1864 combined all these developments and his own into a machine where all the motions for the knitting cycle of reciprocating and undulating were obtained from one rotating cam shaft. The so-called rotary frame had arrived; knitting speeds increased, more knitting sections were added and fabric shaped by widening and narrowing. The number of wales being knitted could not be predetermined and be carried out automatically. Cotton's frame development also marks the point in time where the process of reducing the human skill element began a trend which has continued to the present day.

The knitting principle involved in Lee's frame is paradoxically simple in action but complicated to perform, demanding hands, eyes and foot movement co-ordination and dexterity. In basic terms a length of yarn is laid by hand across the stems of the horizontally disposed needles. The yarn is then kinked to form individual loops around the needle stems by the action bars of the sinkers. These have been pushed down by the action of the jack bars which in turn have been moved by a cam called the slurcock.

The slurcock is traversed across the sinker jack bars by means of a foot operated pedal and drum. With a full complement of loops engaged in the upper throats of the sinkers they are collectively brought forward by the sinker bar operated by both hands until the new loops are beneath the beards of the needles. At this point the presser bar is engaged using another foot pedal to close the beard around the new loops. At this point the forward motion of the sinkers is continued to place the old loops on and over the beards until they are knocked over by the new loops. By a complicated up and over motion and return motion of the sinkers collectively the new loops are engaged in the lower throats of the sinkers to become the old loops when the next course of knitting is produced.

Coarse Gauge

Lee's original frame was by modern standards for hosiery manufacture of coarse gauge having 8 needles per inch (12 gauge). Lee eventually produced a 'silkframe' having some 20 needles per inch (30 gauge) on which up to 1,500 loops per minute could be produced. As an indication of the development of straight-bar knitting technology with respect to fine gauge ladies' hosiery production at the pinacle of progress in the early 1960s one operator could control 2 × 40 section machines running at 100 courses per minute. Assuming the machines were 60 gauge — gauges up to 84 were in fact made — one

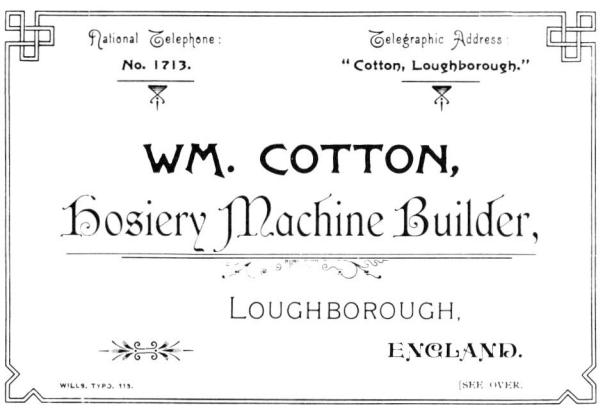

The face side of an early promotional card from Wm. Cotton used to explain the newly designed mechanics of his machine.

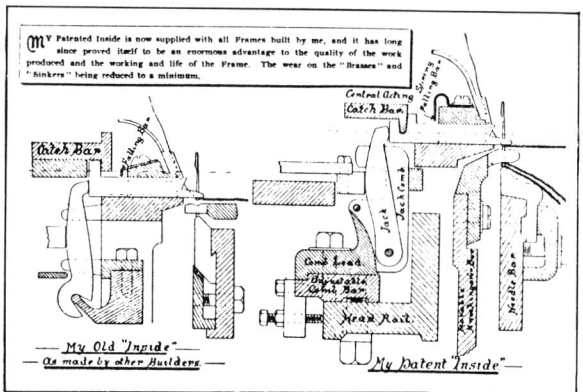

The reverse of the card with the 'old' method on the left and the 'new', patented Cotton's system on the right.

operator could now produce over 5,000,000 loops per minute. An increase in productivity in 380 years of over 5,000 per cent.

Operative skills for the modern fully fashioned machines as they are now being called are just as demanding but in different ways from those necessary for hand frames. Some of the skills remained, pliering of the elements for example, but the basic sitting down dexterous skills had changed to a walking or patroling up and down a long alleyway between two very rhythmic but noisy machines, visually and manually inspecting not one but 80 individual hosiery garments as they were knitted.

Disappeared

It is now sad in a sense to relate that for the production of fine gauge ladies' hosiery the fully fashioned machine based upon Lee's invention 400 years ago has all but disappeared. There are a number of reasons that can be advanced for this, in my view the two most important were a technological one and a fashion or vogue one. The technological reason for the demise of the fully fashioned hosiery machine began when Decroix in France in 1798 built a circular machine having horizontally disposed bearded needles. This was followed by other developments until 1847 when a small diameter machine was built having vertically disposed needles. This trend of development towards knitting tubes of fabric more closely following the shape of limbs received its biggest impetus in 1849 when Mathew Townsend produced a practical 'self acting' needle, the latch needle as we know it today.

In engineering terms this latch needle requires a series of precise and exacting operations to produce. It was therefore sometime before the potential of this new knitting element could be realised. Lee's genius of the bearded needle in my view only stands just proud of Townsend's latch needle if the impact of the latter in just 80 years or so is considered. The knitting action of the latch needle is simplicity itself — yarn is fed into the open hook, the needle is moved through the old loops on its stem, this action causes the old loops to close the latch over the hook which then slips off as the needle with the new yarn passes through to form the new loop. This new loop is then moved down the stem to open the latch and slip over to become the old loop for the next knitting action. A double headed latch needle followed which was to be the basis of men's hosiery production.

The invention of the latch needle was the key which opened up the potential of the small diameter hosiery machine. By 1870 Henry Griswold had perfected a hand operated sock knitting machine. In 1879 a power operated machine was developed and in 1887 needle "pickers" were added allowing the shaping of the heels and toes. In 1915 Scott & Williams did a "William Cotton". They put together all the known circular knitting technology with their own ideas to produce the world famous ladies' automatic hosiery machines known as the Model K. This machine was able to produce a welt, leg, shaped heel and toe and a foot; the product only required one operation of toe closing to complete. For the next 40 years all the developments on this machine and others built by other companies followed an imitative course succeeding the developments of ladies' hosiery produced on fully fashioned machines.

The introduction — with some regulatory controls — of nylon made the situation worse. The wearers of fully-fashioned nylon stockings with the necessary seam at the back were convinced that they were the best (and at the time the most expensive) and anything else was inferior. Meantime circular machinery developments and fully-fashioned machinery developments continued unabated. The imitative course of the circular machinery developers was such that two attempts were made to produce circular fashioning machines.

This race of one against the other came to the beginning of the end in 1954 when a large American ladies' producer said "enough!". As a result they removed from the ladies' stocking all imitation — seams, splicing, mock fashion marks etc and introduced seamfree or seamless ladies' hosiery. The effect of this landmark decision is now legend. By the early 1960s the fully fashioned product was in decline as sales spurred on by this circular machinery development appeared thick and fast.

A 4-feed tube machine, 6, 8 and 12 feed machines, four different versions of automatically closed toe — on the knitting machine that is — higher knitting speeds up to 500 revolutions per minute followed. The introduction of a very successful automatic toe closer machine stopped closed-toe on the machine development. The average gauge of the present day machines is around 32 needles per inch. During 1964/65 the second reason for the demise of the fully fashioned machine appeared in the shape of fashion which decreed the raising of skirt hemlines — the mini-skirt. Wearers of this popular fashion now demanded for appearance's sake theatrical hose or tights.

Moment In Time

For a brief moment in time it looked as though the fully fashion machine would be back in vogue as it was capable of knitting and shaping a complete pantyhose or tights, but not without a seam. The nylon yarn producers rescued the situation for the circular knitters by introducing stretch nylon yarns. These made it possible for a machine of 3¾ins diameter having 370 needles or a 4ins diameter machine having 400 needles, to knit large diameter knitted tubes which when slit and 'U' seamed together produced the panty section of the pantyhose or tights. From the launch in 1966 pantyhose slowly took over from seamless stockings in the same way that seamless stockings took over from the fully fashioned seamed stockings. Today the fully fashioned stocking and the machine which made them have all but disappeared. Having stated that, at the time of writing interest in stockings is growing again in the fickle world of fashion and it is hard to believe but seams (a mock variety) are reappearing, but too late I am afraid to reawaken the fully fashion machine builders because of engineering costs to start building straight-bar machines once again.

Ancilliary

It is not possible when writing about the production of ladies' hosiery in general and pantyhose in particular to ignore the tremendous contribution made by the ancilliary machine builders. Automatic toe-closers, have already been mentioned but the ancilliary machine which made the biggest impact in late 1971 was the line-closer or automated 'U' seamer. The introduction of this machine alongside toe-closers automated the assembly operation of a pantyhose to: knit the leg/panty blanks, close the toes and 'U' seam to complete the dry operations. Today the manufacture of pantyhose can be almost completely automated from yarn to the finished product in its presentation form.

During this time the relatively slow one or two feed circular all mechanical knitting machine of 1968 has been slowly transformed to a 4-feed very high speed machine capable of up to 1,500 revolutions per minute all electro-mechanical microprocessor controlled. With reference to the ultimate achievement on fully fashioned ladies' hosiery machines in the 1960s where one operator was controlling the production of some 5,000,000 loops per minute an operator with 60 of these high speed 4-feed circular machines is controlling the production of 144,000,000 loops per minute. This is some 144,000 times more than Lee's silk frame.

In addition to their high speed and output capabilities these all electronic circular machines have limitless patterning scope to cater for all requirements. Townsend's latch needle which has stood the test of time — some 140 years — may itself also now be under threat by the introduction of 'self acting' compound needles. At least two models have been built and one is proving very successful in the production of support hosiery. The manufacture of ladies' hosiery from Lee in 1589 to 1989 has seen fast progress from the time of William Cotton in 1864 until the 1960's when the switch to the circular machine occurred. From then on it has been the circular machine and the latch needle all the way.

The manufacture of men's hosiery has followed a somewhat different pattern. Men's socks like women's hosiery before have been handknitted and some were knitted on hand frames. Cotton's type rotary machines were also used for the production of men's hose. The probable starting point for machine produced men's hose is again Griswold in 1870 and the shaping potential developed in 1887. This plus Townsend's double-headed latch of 1849 culminated in 1900 with the invention of the double or superimposed cylinder machine, the XL by Stretton and Johnson. It employed internally controlled loop holding down sinkers from the Spiers and Grieves patent of 1895 and featured rotating camboxes for actuating the needles/sliders.

This machine was capable of producing a secure edge — a welt — a rib top, leg shaped heel and toe and the foot. The product only required toe-closing to complete the 'dry' operations. In 1912 the first different version of the XL appeared as the Komet which featured rotating cylinders as opposed to rotating camboxes. This introduction set the standard and the scene for the knitting of men's hosiery to the present day. This concept became the basis for continuous development which includes stripping, multi-feed, jacquard patterning, links-links, embroidery, plating and terry. All double cylinder machine builders world-wide have used this concept upon which to design and produce their own particular versions. A concept in standing equal to the ladies' hosiery machine the Model K.

The knitting and loop transfer actions on a double cylinder machine are mechanically very complicated. The knitting action for the double-headed latch needle is the same as described earlier but it is complicated by the ability to transfer the needle from one cylinder to the other and at the same time transfer the loop from one end of the needle to the other where it knits as before but inverted to produce a rib/purl loop. Double cylinder or superimposed cylinder machines were until quite recently very complex mechanical pieces of equipment requiring high degrees of skills to operate and maintain them. This is one of the reasons why the supremacy of the double cylinder machine for the manufacture of men's and children's hosiery came under attack some twenty years ago by the manufacturer of single cylinder machines. These machines like their ladies' hosiery machine counterparts are based upon a much simpler concept and are therefore easier to operate and maintain.

Two Categories

Single cylinder machines can be divided into two categories; open top for the production of single jersey fabric constructions and mock ribs and cylinder and dial machines which can produce true-rib structures. Both categories have their applications in the field of men's, children's and now ladies' socks manufacture offering a wide range of product possibilities. Since 1975 when electronics on knitting machines became respected again following the double jersey experience and disaster the builders of double and single cylinder sock machines have not been slow in applying this new knowledge.

Today's double and single cylinder machines are almost totally electro-mechanical in operation controlled by a microprocessor in which is located the manufacturing cycle/programme. Included in the programme by the product designer is all the data for the product including patterns and structures. Machines can have one to six feeds and knit tube or conventional socks. The loops per minute per operator is not so spectacular an increase as their ladies' hosiery machines counterpart — they run much more slowly at around 400 revolutions per minute — but is nevertheless a large increase since Lee's invention.

Attempts have been made to close the toe of the sock on the knitting machine with scant success. Automatic toe closing machines have been developed which are very fast and require little skill to operate. Toe closing can be by random sewing of the loops or linked — the former being a quicker operation than the latter.

Finally it would be very remiss not to mention the tremendous contribution made to this story of hosiery knitting development by the yarn producers. Their efforts have made a number of developments possible, fine gauge machines, highspeed machines, product developments, pantyhose, support and comfort hosiery, dyeing effects and so on. From the simple yarn requirements in the early days of: fine smooth, strong and elastic yarns from wool, cotton and pure silk we have moved on from rayon in 1913 to nylon in 1928, terrylene in 1942 and more recently the elastomerics. Families of yarns engineered for specific purposes supporting both knitting machine development and probably more importantly product development.

Brief Sketch

This brief sketch outlining the progress of mechanical knitting of hosiery from the brilliance of Lee, the inventiveness of Cotton, Townsend, Griswold and many others cannot give full justice as there have been many unsung artisans all of whom have made a contribution. To their credit the story does not end here, what will the future bring; robotic knitting rooms controlled by one master computer; completely automated 'dry and wet' finishing or no finishing at all or will a material be developed which can be sprayed onto leg formes to produce the product which will have the same properties as a knitted product whose origins are to be found in the very distant past.

Into The Weft Knitting Future

By David J. Spencer, Leicester Polytechnic

IN THESE TWO DISTINCT areas of knitting machinery, garment length machines include flats, straight bar frames and circulars, whilst fabric machines range in diameter from body width to very large diameter circulars. Between them, these machines knit a wide spectrum of products from simple plain, constant width continuous length fabric, to integrally shaped garments. Although a number of different distinct machine types are thus included in this survey, they nevertheless, share certain trends in machinery development and are subject to many common influences and requirements. The very latest technology is involved in these machines but this in itself cannot be the spur for development. The incentive to build and purchase new machines is the belief that they are capable of knitting the products which the trade anticipates future customers will wish to purchase.

Transformed

As with most aspects of modern life, the market for knitted textiles is being transformed and sales outlets are proliferating and offering a bewildering range of multiple choices. Fashion seasons and production runs have become fragmented and quick response is the order of the day. The new generation of clothes buyers are less interested in value for money, mass-produced clothes. They are more attracted by new design concepts, including personalised styling and added interest features. Consumers are unconcerned as to whether a garment is woven or knitted, but the belief that knitted fabric should imitate woven structures is a thing of the past — the objective of knitters must be to utilise and fully exploit the characteristics and properties of the knitted structure.

Fortunately, the same information revolution (based on the ubiquitous microchip) which is transforming the requirements of fashion is also providing the knitting industry with the facilities with which to match and satisfy these requirements. The automatic V-bed flat machine, recognised as being the most versatile of knitting machines as regards knitted structures, is now freed from the constraints imposed by mechanical controls. Thus the cost of pattern and garment size changing is measured in pence rather than pounds and takes minutes rather than hours to accomplish. The needle bed width has been increased and standardised at about 230cm and precision engineering means that cam parts and elements can easily be replaced and exchanged.

The four system machine is the standard workhorse, with two system machines being used for higher quality work and some types of fashion shaping. Each system in each bed had identical camming and selection facilities so that knit, tuck, miss or rib loop transfer can be achieved as required, with the opposing bed cam system being automatically arranged for the receipt of a loop selected to be transferred from the other bed.

Simplicity, versatility and a reduction in moving parts is the objective in machinery design. Electronic selection posts which employ permanent magnets and pulse selection rather than moving actuators improve reliability and reduce the problems of wear. Fixed knitting cams and compact cam systems which can be used for knitting or loop transfer can be employed if needle control butts are sunk out of action into the tricks, when no movement is required. This arrangement also prevents stress on held loops and reduces element wear and damage.

With electronic control, the machine control is in constant communication with the cam carriage and not just as previously, at the end of each traverse. Stepper motors are now being increasingly used for adjusting stitch cams on many types of knitting machines and this can occur during the traverse so that, for example, tighter stitches can be knitted at the selvedges. The cam carriage drive now has a variable stroke and infinitely variable step-free adjustment is available.

It is now possible to monitor the rate of yarn feed, to adjust the stitch cams and keep the input tension finely tuned. The racking of the needle beds can be adjusted to suit the extensibility of the yarn and the take-down tension can be finely adjusted during knitting.

The microprocessor is ideal for use as a monitor as well as a control device, thus, perhaps in the near future, knitting machines will be able to monitor and report on the knittability of sample yarns before a stitch has been knitted! On multi-feeder circular fabric machines, a central control, particularly for stitch cam adjustment, is a must for the future as are quick methods of reprogramming mechanical selection devices such as pattern keys.

As far as knitting elements are concerned, the two part compound needle has still failed to make its anticipated impact in circular fabric machinery, mainly because of problems of adjustment for different cam settings. However, the surprising appearance of a prototype V-bed flat machine with compound needles indicates that long term, this needle has the capabilities of stitch selection combined with the advantages of a smaller knitting movement. Meantime, the efficiency of the latch needle has been improved by using spring loaded latches so that the latch opens and closes more smoothly and causes less strain as the loops pass over it.

More thought is now generally being applied to assisting the needle in its knitting action using various forms of lifting knock-over surfaces and for holding down fabric loops. While the presser foot device is being more selectively employed, moving knock over bits are offering an alternative solution to the problem. On the straight bar frame, electronic controls are providing flexibility in carrier selection and movement, but the actual bearded needle bar knitting action remains virtually unchanged from the days of William Cotton. One wonders whether the compound needle might not be able to offer the chance of electronically controlled movement and individual needle selection.

At the moment the flat machine is not fully exploiting the potential for garment shaping, although the fabric take-down systems and set up combs are being developed to cater for the set-up of garment pieces. Eventually perhaps an auxiliary transfer point bed will be more fully developed for use in fashion shaping as the present use of rib loop transfer and needle bed racking appears to be a rather laborious process

The knitting machine still has the appearance of a mechanical device, but there is little doubt that as more and more of the mechanical controls and movements are taken over by electronic devices, this aspect will be changed. Already the machine is rapidly becoming involved in the supply of management data directly on line providing information such as output and stoppages and efficiency and there is also the potential for preprogramming machines from a distance either by a telephone link or even by radio control.

Generally it is advantageous to have stationary yarn packages (even garment length circular machines will probably be of the revolving needle cylinder type in the future). With a stationary yarn creel, it is possible to separate it from the main frame of the machine and house it in a conveninetly situated free standing framework, in conditions which prevent contamination of lint and maintain the yarn in peak condition, whilst providing a simple route to the feed guides. Ease of threading is an important consideration on all machines and the use of sliding package stands which can be pulled to within the operator's normal reach when loading, are very advantageous.

Ergonomical

As far as mechanical attention is concerned, the ergonomical positioning of controls and the designing of the machine to reduce unnecessary and unnatural human movements to a minimum is now at a premium, as is the careful illumination of areas such as the fabric take-down, the use of indicator stop lights and information display panels.

As already mentioned, micro-electronics is providing a bewildering array of alternative possibilities, for example, at the sampling stage; how much sample knitting is required in view of the fact that true-to-scale-and-colour computer print-outs of designs are now readily available? We are now in a situation where customers designs could be accepted by the machines' computerised design system and converted into a knitted article with, in some cases, little intervention from the design staff. We are, in fact, rapidly approaching the day when a customer might be able to walk into a store and via a computer link, produce his own design on a knitting machine in a suppliers' factory.

Thus, as the knitting machine becomes ever more closely linked into the information system of the knitting company, the opportunities for individually tailoring its operating environment to specific needs and conditions increase. These facilities include monitoring of all aspects of its operation, guidance and assistance in machine changes, production control and all aspects of information transfer which can occur with two-way communication links. The knitting machine is no longer viewed as a mechanically operated production tool, it is a versatile production process within a fully integrated production system.

The Warp Knitting Story

By R. Wheatley, Leicester Polytechnic

WARP KNITTING is the mechanical equivalent of hand crochet knitting and remained as a hand operation until almost 200 years after the invention of the weft knitting machine in 1589.

The invention of the warp knitting machine in 1775 is attributed to Crane of Ilkeston in Derbyshire who applied warp guides to the hand frame and so modified the original invention by William Lee which had itself developed by that time from the original concept.

The production of the hand frame was mainly for stockings, so the warp knitting machine followed this type of product, with the manufacture of zig zag stripes as a fabric variation, but the fabric had to be cut and sewn and suffered from bursting at the seams plus a lack of elasticity compared to the weft knit counterpart. Production was thus severely limited.

The warp knitting machine developed for the production of flat fabrics from which garments could be cut and the products were used for underwear and outerwear made from cotton and wool, the latter being fulled to make a more compact and stable construction for outerwear.

Notable inventions which paved the way for the development of the warp knitting industry are too many to be outlined in the short space of this article. However, some are worthy of note. The first was the simplification of the sinker head to use one set of sinkers and to use the foot pedal, normally associated with the 'draw', to operate the guide bar swinging movement, an invention by Tarrot of Nottingham in 1785.

By 1797, Barber of Bilborough in Nottinghamshire took out a patent for the invention of a moveable needle bar. This is a patent which is interesting in itself as it refers to weft insertion as standard practice on hand warp frames, the manufacturer of loop pile, including carpets, and refers to a double needle bar machine by the application of the Derby Rib frame to Barbers' invention. Therefore weft insertion was known and practised before the use of two guide bars, an invention attributed to Brown in 1804.

The Dawson's wheel, equivalent of today's pattern wheel, was invented in 1791 and the first warp lace frame in 1795. Power was applied to warp knitting machines, referred to as rotary warp frames, in 1807 by Orgil. This allowed wider frames up to 72ins to be produced and two frames to be coupled together running at 30 cpm and operated by one man. Before this, one man operated one machine, 44ins wide, at about 10 cpm. In about 1830, Whitely invented a machine for the production of taffeta which was milanese as we know it today.

1839 saw the introduction of a jacquard machine with individual guide control by Draper and the first latch needle double needlebar machine in 1859, the latter being known at the time as 'Fang Kettenstuhl Raschel Machine' in Germany and Polka machine or double loom in England.

Up to this point in the development of the warp knitting trade, the products from the machine were many and varied, including openwork constructions, plain nets, braids, tattings, galloons, warp lace, velvet pile, woollen cloth, elastic hat bands and glove fabrics, the latter taking on more importance towards the end of the 19th century, being manufactured in a variety of sizes and types from simple thick hand coverings to keep the hands warm to elbow length dance gloves with elaborate jacquard patterns for fashionable evening wear.

Continuous Filament

The beginnings of the 20th century saw the introduction of the Simplex machine for the production of double faced glove fabric by Preston in 1915 and the introduction of continuous filament yarns, the latter being a significant development which led to fine gauge machines becoming standard in the tricot section at 28 npi and the introduction of atlas looms or fast warp frames with vertical needle bars and an increase in machine speed from 200-300 courses per minute.

The continuous filament materials, mainly acetate, led to new lightweight fabrics, both underwear and outerwear, and had a disastrous effect on the use of cotton, wool and fibrous yarns in general, as they could not be produced in sufficiently fine counts for the fine gauges and could not compete with the sheer smooth appearance of the new, fashionable 'art-silk'.

The end of the '30s saw two developments which had significant influences on the future warp knitting industry; one was in yarn development and the second in machine development. The yarn development consisted of the invention of nylon by Du Pont in the USA, the first synthetic yarn with the unique properties of thermo-plasticity, strength and elasticity to extents which had not before been known. This invention of synthetics led to the development of polyester, polyurethane and polyacronitrile as completely new materials with unique properties and to the development of bulked and textured yarns making use of the thermo-plastic properties.

The second major development of this time was the introduction of the F.N.F. warp knitting machine which achieved a production speed of 1,000 cpm. This influenced machine development for the future by introducing the first commercial use of the compound needle, incorporating eccentrics as a driving medium using a positive let-off and much more accurate engineering standards, together with dynamic and static balance of machine parts.

The importance of these two major developments did not become apparent until after the Second World War and the technical industrial development of a post-war boom.

The years from 1945 to 1968 saw the unprecedented development of the warp knitting trade with the use of the new thermoplastic yarns in lingerie, outerwear, automotive seat fabrics, raschel lace, bedsheets and elaborate curtains, table cloths, etc, as the public demanded easy-care fabrics, and the use of the new yarns showed no bounds. However, this frantic development did come to an end as the public craved for the return of fibrous yarns to give bulkier, softer fabrics and the everchanging fashion demands caused a decline in the number of warp knitting machines employed which led to the leaner and more competitive warp knitting industry we know today.

Computers

Possibly the most significant development over the last decade has been the use of computers, both for machine control and computer aided design.

The development of computer control became commercially viable with the advent of the bubble memory. This is a small lightweight and efficient computer store capable of holding a maximum amount of information in a limited space. It will not lose the information in the event of a power failure and is sufficiently robust to stand the running conditions in a factory. It also works on a small number of 'plates' so that a minimum of spares are required. At the present state of the art, six areas have received attention for computer control. (1) jacquard control, (2) guide bar control, (3) design preparation, (4) warp let-off, (5) fabric take-up, (6) weft insertion.

The application of computers to jacquard machines was desirable to replace the wirework by a series of electro-magnets to form an interface between the computer and the harness cords. If the magnet is energised, a particular cord is raised, if not, it is left in the low position to effect guide deflection for patterning. With this technique it is

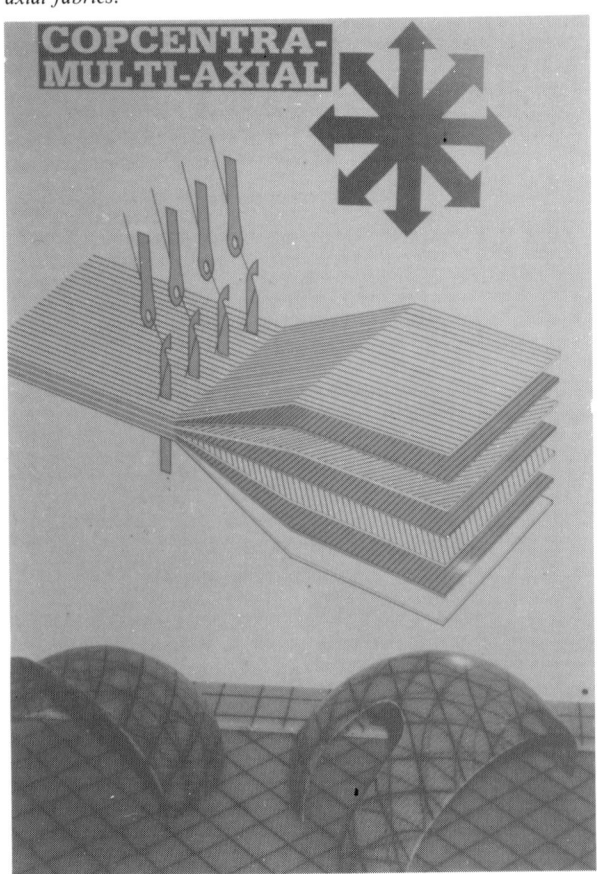

Diagrammatic representation of a multi-axial fabric construction for the manufacture of protective helmets for military and sporting use — one of many non-apparel applications of multi-axial fabrics.

Liba Copcentra multi-axial weft insertion warp knitting machine viewed from the side. This type of unit is designed to produce a variety of technical-textile fabrics.

possible to increase the speed of jacquard machines by as much as 30-40 per cent.

While the application of electronic jacquard control gave increased commercial speeds, the replacement of the pattern chain for guide bar movement was a more spectacular innovation. This replaced chain links which are costly and time consuming in preparation and machine down time. The development first took place on multi-bar raschel machines where the problems of chain building are the greatest, but is now available on tricot machines. It was after the availability of the bubble memory that the feasibility of guide bar control by computer became apparent and an ingenious interface between the computer and the guide bar was developed to effect this achievement.

Thus the elimination of chain links gave the following advantages — saving in capital costs, elimination of costs of chain building, link grinding, dismantling, washing and sorting chain links; reduction of machine down time for pattern change, therefore greater machine efficiency, easier design correction by VDU and less costs in pattern storage, together with the ability to fulfill small orders.

A further advantage of electronic control is the increase in design scope; with normal chain links the maximum number of guide bars is 42, but with electronic control, this can be extended to 56. Also, it is possible to combine jacquard with multi-bar work, machines being available with 56 and 78 bars plus a jacquard. Additionally, a 36 bar machine is available with jacquard, laying-in bars and fall-plate bars, there being 12 or 16 bars in front of the fall-plate, as required. This now opens up tremendous pattern potential for raschel lace producers. The freedom offered to the designer is outstanding. The design may be constructed with guide bars for gimp work introducing different density with different counts, or for the use of outline threads, and the jacquard may be used for gimp work. To this may be added the fall-plate bars to give a three-dimensional effect.

The use of computers in design preparation has also simplified this area of operation, both for multi-bar and jacquard work. The system programmes a magnetic tape which is then used to programme the computer on the machine. The design unit consists of a micro-computer, a VDU with keyboard, a printer, a cassette deck and a drafting table. The system can be used to prepare jacquard designs on the older type of jacquard and then used to cut cards by programming the card cutting machine.

Another area of computer application is the control of beam movement by the electronic beam control system. This system not only controls beam movement, but can also be coupled to the take-up rollers and, in addition, provides a collective data system for organisational and statistical control.

The electronic warp control section consists of a DC motor driving the axle of the beam. Thus, as the warp unwinds, the speed of the beam in terms of revolutions per minute must be increased to keep the run-in constant. This is achieved by the computer which compensates for the decreasing diameter of the beam.

The system gives a more accurate control of warp speed than the conventional mechanical mechanism and is also more versatile since it will deliver up to 85 different warp speeds in any one design compared with the two speeds for a mechanical warp let-off mechanism. The warp speed may be changed on any course and at any point in the design by the introduction of the pre-programmed speeds.

The fabric take-up roller section of the system is programmed in a similar way so that the speed of the take-up roller may be varied during the production of a design. Both these points are new tools to the fabric designer and offer a new dimension in terms of fabric development.

The third part of the EBC system is the data collection section. With this system it is possible to obtain accurate information on fabric length, warp length, and time of warp change, etc., and, by coding

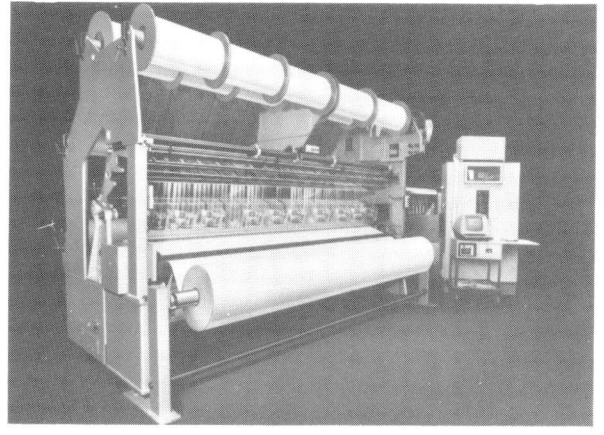

Karl Mayer type KS4 SU 4-bar tricot warp knitting machine with computer control of the guide bars.

State-of-the-art electronic lace making, the Karl Mayer Jacquardtronic MRSSJ 78/1, a 78 guide bar computer controlled raschel machine for knitting lace fabrics.

fabric faults, a complete fault analysis can be obtained from the printer which is incorporated with the computer.

The final area in which computer control has been introduced is that of weft selection on weft insertion machines.

The magazine holding the weft yarns is situated at the side and to the back of the machine to feed the weft ends to a reciprocating weft carriage which supplies the weft to the conveyor chains projecting out of the back of the machine. The weft carriage takes 24 yarns across the machine, but the magazine has 4 ends available for each of the 24 positions in the weft carriage. The computer selects the required weft, (positions 1-4), or no weft, (position 5), at each weft position.

Since the weft selection is determined by microcomputer, the weft repeat is only limited by the size of the computer memory which is equal to 50,000 courses giving a repeat of 50 metres of fabric at a standard quality of 10 courses per cm. The programming of the computer is by means of magnetic tape cassette which is programmed by a VDU and keyboard. This technique gives the biggest and most versatile weft selection mechanism and is ideal for the production of curtains in which the weft consists of many different types of yarn with long pattern repeats.

What of the future? The future depends on the continued development of machinery, the introduction of new yarns and fabric structures and on fashion trends which prevail. On tricot machines, equipment has already reached a high degree of sophistication in running efficiency and on the application of computer control. Speeds in the region of 2,500 cpm are now available on the latest machines and the technology is already developed for the use of 40ins diameter beams to reduce the frequency of re-loading in the interests of efficiency and this, together with large packages in the warping process, increases warping efficiency and reduces yarn waste to streamline the industry for the future.

Electronic Beam Control

Tricot machines are already equipped with electronic beam control and computer guide bar control. The former is well-established and the latter will be adopted more and more as future developments take place and will allow the designer to create new products to enlarge the fabric types available. Well-established products will continue to develop in such end uses as automotive seats, headliners and door panels, wearing apparel, (both ladies' lingerie and outerwear), suedes, boucles, etc, terry towelling, sportswear, tracksuits, etc.

Raschel lace has perhaps shown the most technical development in the last decade and it is now well equipped to face a bright future in terms of machine design, machine efficiency and pattern potential. Machine design is highly advanced with the use of compound needles, elimination of guide bar swing to improve warp control, and computer controlled guide bars which lead to increased efficiency at pattern change.

The pattern potential has never been greater and will improve even further. The use of 100 guide bars will become a reality in years to come. The greater use of jacquards will occur, as this technique becomes more established in the production of banded laces and as the home furnishing market, in which the jacquard is already established, develops to produce more elaborate designs.

Double Needle Bar

Double needle bar machines, which already produce pile fabrics for car upholstery, will develop further for acceptance in home furnishings in terms of upholstery and velvet curtains; while the double needle bar machine, used for special products in the geo-textile and industrial fields, will continue to develop in the production of specially shaped fabrics, many of which will require no finishing operation and go straight from the machine into use for such outlets as drainage, prevention of soil erosion and bank protection. The bank erosion technique consists of knitting a double needle bar fabric with 'pockets' which is laid on the river bank and the 'pockets' filled with concrete to form the bank protection. Double needle bar pile fabrics, while still in the 'face to face' form before cutting can be laid at strategic points to effect drainage or to allow gases to escape which would otherwise build up and cause damage to the foundations of dams, river, road and railway banks.

Areas into which warp knitted raschel fabrics have penetrated and which will most certainly extend in volume for the future, include nets for bird and wind protection, greenhouse shades and horticultural and agricultural protection, particularly in desert regions for guarding vegetable and fruits from excessive ground temperatures in the day and cooling at night, while allowing free movement of the air. The use of heavy nets will expand future uses extending further to container covers, building protection nets and landfall nets, etc.

Weft insertion machines, both of the tricot and raschel type, have now established themselves for products as diverse as sheetings and shirts on the one hand, to conveyor belts and tarpaulins on the other. The stability of these fabrics, together with the machines' ability to handle different yarns makes them suitable for a range of fabrics not normally associated with the warp knitted product and again offer possibilities in the industrial textile field. In fact, the prospects of development in this field of textiles are so encouraging that manufacturers have developed machines with multi-axial yarn insertion to prepare for the future in this area.

Multi-axial machines not only introduce straight yarns in weft and warp, but also introduce two sets of yarn running diagonally in opposite directions, the angle of these yarns being variable between 45 and 60 degrees to the horizontal. This allows such fabric to take strains in all directions making them ideal for industrial fabrics, particularly composites for the formation of plastic laminated components, where strength and lightness are key factors in such end uses as aircraft construction, buildings, ships' decks, hulls for mine sweepers and car bodies.

It must be concluded that raschel machines with weft insertion, multi-axial yarn insertion and double needle bars offer a formidable fabric production capacity to produce industrial cloths of the future.

COURTAULDS FABRICS

Courtaulds Jersey

PO Box 407
Churnet Works
Leek
Staffordshire ST13 8UT
Tel (0538) 399300
Fax (0538) 387564
Telex 367340

Courtaulds Jersey

Portadown Road
Lurgan
County Armagh
Northern Ireland BT66 8RB
Tel (0762) 325123
Telex 74261

Meridian Fabrics

PO Box 54
Haydn Road
Nottingham NG5 1DH
Tel (0602) 608131
Telex 377618

Literary Legacy
The Top 200 Knitting Books

By Jack Smirfitt, Hatra

THOUGH THERE ARE several good and recent bibliographies on hand-knitting, machine-knitting is not so well served. There is the excellent Nottingham University Library bibliography of the East Midlands hosiery trade up to 1920 (Susan Robinson and Michael Brook, 'An introductory bibliography of the hosiery and lace industries in Nottingham and district to 1920', Nottingham, 1982 iv, 14p) but it is limited in time and space. The 1957 bibliography appended to the Suchet and Tremelloni 'Tessuti a maglia in trama', is by far the most international and wide ranging guide to machine knitting, but it contains errors and omissions which have tended to increase in its subsequent editions.

As part of its contribution to the William Lee Quatercentenary, the Hatra Library is to publish a classified listing of over 2,500 books, pamphlets and journals on industrial knitting, based primarily on its own holdings, but giving other locations for some of the older, rarer material.

The selection which follows is strictly limited to 200 items, including a few of the modern 'classics' of hand knitting. To bring it down to this size some rigorous selection criteria had to be applied. Firstly, regardless of their merit or significance, all directories, reports, pamphlets and unpublished theses were excluded: 'books' were admitted only if they were of more than a 100 pages and primarily, if not exclusively, concerned with knitting or knitted goods. Secondly, special emphasis was given to books that had proved their worth by going through several editions or reprints, or being translated into other languages. Beyond this, there was a natural preference for English language books and ones that were widely distributed and still relatively easy to obtain — how else could one explain the inclusion of two titles that on their first appearance received some of the most unfavourable reviews ever written.

The references are arranged chronologically within broad subject headings. With few exceptions, they refer to the first edition of each title, in its original language.

DICTIONARIES AND ENCYCLOPEDIAS

Meiner, H and Willkomm, O. Technische Fachausdrücke im Wirk-Strickmaschinenbau und in der Wirk- und Strickwarenfabrikation. Deutsch — Englisch — Französisch. 4th ed. Apolda, 1927. 156p.

Lesykova, Eva. Nemecko-csky pletarsky slovnik. Brno, Vyzkumny Ustav Pletarsky, 1956. n.p.

Dury, J. Vocabulaire textile trilingue: francais — allemand — anglais. Troyes, Centre de Recherches de la Bonneterie, 1962. vii, 139p + 166p.

Sammler, Günter (editor). Wirkerei- und Strickerei-Fachwörterbuch: Englisch-Deutsch, Deutsch-Englisch. Coburg, Prost & Meiner-Verlag, 1965. 300p.

Reichman, Charles (editor). Knitting dictionary: basic trade terms. New York, National Knitted Outerwear Association, 1966. 131p.

Markert, Dietrich. Maschen ABC. 6th ed. Frankfurt, Deutscher Fachverlag, 1967. 196p + pattern cards.

Hamilton-Hunt, Margaret. Knitting dictionary: 800 stitches, patterns and knitting, crochet, jacquard technics. Paris, Mon Tricot, 1970. 154p.

Reichman, Charles (editor). Knitting encyclopedia. New York, National Knitted Outerwear Association, 1972. 390p.

Uhlmann, H. R. Terminologie in der Wirkerei und Strickerei. 2nd ed. Heidelberg, Melliand Textilberichte, 1973. 320p.

Gartshore, Linda. The machine knitter's dictionary. London, Batsford 1983. 192p.

Weaver, Mary. Japanese for machine knitters: an aid to reading Japanese knitting patterns. Sidcup, Weaver Publications, 1983. ii, 124p.

HISTORICAL WORKS

Origins, precursors

Nordland, Odd. Primitive Scandinavian textiles in knotless netting. Oslo, Oslo University Press, 1961. 154p.

Seiler-Baldinger, Annemarie. Maschenstoffe in Süd- und Mittelamerika. Basel, Pharos-Verlag Hansrudolf Schwabe, 1971. 280p + charts.

Hand knitting

Hartley, Marie and Ingilby, Joan. The old hand-knitters of the dales; with an introduction to the early history of knitting. Clapham via Lancaster, Dalesman Publishing Co, 1951. 128p.

Groves, Sylvia. The history of needlework tools and accessories. London, Country Life, 1966. 136p.

Kiewe, Heinz Edgar. The sacred history of knitting: recent discoveries by Heinz Edgar Kiewe. Oxford, Art Needlework Industries Ltd, 1967. xii, 114p, 87pl.

Wintzell, Inga. Sticka mönster: historiskt om stickning i Sverige. Uddevalla, Nordiska Museet, 1976. 111p.

Harvey, Michael. Patons: a story of handknitting. Ascot, Springwood Books, 1985. 144p.

Rutt, Richard. A history of hand knitting. London, B. T. Batsford, 1987. viii, 248p.

Machine knitting

Henson, Gravenor. The civil, political and mechanical history of the framework-knitters in Europe and America. Vol. 1. Nottingham, Richard Sutton, 1831. 425p.

Felkin, William. A history of the machine-wrought hosiery and lace manufactures. London, Longmans, Green & Co, 1867. xxvi, 559p.

Grass, Milton N and Grass, Anna M. Stockings for a queen. The life of the Rev. William Lee, the Elizabethan inventor. London, William Heinemann, 1967. xvi, 188p.

North, Marcel. La maille et ce qui s'ensuit: Dubied 1867-1967. Neuchâtel, Edouard Dubied & Cie SA, 1967. 173p.

English, Walter. The textile industry: an account of the early inventions of spinning, weaving, and knitting machines. London, Longmans, Green & Co, 1969. xiv, 242p.

Lagarrigue, Jean-Claude. Quatre cents ans de maille. Paris, Editions ATIT, 1983. 279p.

Knitting industry

Steiniger, Kurt. Die Apoldaer Wirkwarenindustrie seit 1914. Weimar, Weimarischer Verlag, 1927. 208p.

Irmscher, Felix. Die Strumpfindustrie in Chemnitz und im Chemnitzer Kreise: eine historische Studie. Berlin, Textil-Praxis Verlagsgesellschaft, 1929. 206p.

Christoph, Alfred. Die nord- und westböhmische Strick- und Wirkwaren-Industrie. Leipzig. Apolda, Rob. Birkner, 1933. 141p.

Wells, F. A. The British hosiery trade: its history and organisation. London, George Allen & Unwin, 1935. 252p.

Pickering, Arthur J. The cradle and home of the hosiery trade. Hinckley, W. Pickering & Sons, 1940. xi, 136p.

Leclercq, René. Historique de la bonneterie dans le Tournaisis. Tournais, (Ecole Supérieure des Textiles), 1958. 141p.

Erickson, Charlotte. British industrialists: steel and hosiery 1850-1950. Cambridge, Cambridge University Press, 1959. xxi, 276p.

Hünger, Heinz. 50 Jahre; Gesamtverband der deutschen Maschen-Industrie, 1916-1966. Stuttgart, Gesamtverband der deutschen Maschen-Industrie, 1966. 111p.

Carpenter, Kenneth E. (editor). The framework knitters and handloom weavers; their attempts to keep up wages. Eight pamphlets, 1820-1845. New York, Arno Press, 1972. n.p.

Gurnham, Richard. A history of the trade union movement in the hosiery and knitwear industry 1776-1976. Leicester, National Union of Hosiery and Knitwear Workers, 1976. xiii, 197p.

Turnau, Irena. Historia dziewiarstwa europejskiego do poczatku XIX wieku. Wroclaw, Zaklad Narodowy Imienia Ossolinskich Wydawnictwo Polskiej Akademii Nauk, 1979. 193p.

Poisat, Jacques. Histoire de la bonneterie en France et dans le Roannais. Roanne, 1983. 167p.

Gulvin, Clifford. The Scottish hosiery and knitwear industry 1680-1980. Edinburgh, John Donald Publishers, 1984. ix, 163p.

— British Parliamentary Papers

Report of the Commissioner appointed to inquire into the condition of the frame-work knitters, with appendices. London, 1845 (609) Vol. XV, viii, 138p.

Appendix to Report of the Commisioner appointed to inquire into the condition of the frame-work knitters. Part I. Leicestershire. London, 1845 (618) Vol. XV, vii, 505p.

Appendix to Report of the Commissioner appointed to inquire into the condition of the frame-work knitters. Part II. Nottinghamshire and Derbyshire. London, 1845 (641) Vol. XV, vi, 379p.

Report from the Select Committee on stoppage of wages (hosiery); together with the proceedings of the Committee, minutes of evidence, appendix and index. London, 1854-4 (421) Vol. XIV, xxiv, 704p.

— Firms and individuals

Blandford, Thomas and Newell, George. History of the Leicester Co-operative Hosiery Manufacturing Society Ltd. Leicester, Co-operative Printing Society Ltd, 1898. 116p.

Thomas, Frederick Moy. I. and R. Morley: a record of a hundred years. London, Chiswick Press, 1900. x, 103p.

Hodder, Edwin. The life of Samuel Morley. London, Hodder & Stoughton, 1887. vii, 510p.

Webb, C W. An historical record of N. Corah & Sons Ltd manufacturers of hosiery, underwear and outerwear, St. Margaret's Works, Leicester. Leicester, N. Corah & Sons Ltd . . . for private circulation, (1941). 120p.

Pasold, Eric W. Ladybird, ladybird: a story of private enterprise. Manchester. Manchester University Press, 1977. xv, 668p.

Knitted garments

Taylor, Wesley. The story of hosiery . . . written for May Hosiery Mills, Burlington, NC, High Point, Houck & Co, 1931. 100p.

Grass, Milton N. History of hosiery: from the piloi of ancient Greece to the nylons of modern America. New York, Fairchild Publications, 1955. 283p.

Haskell, Ira J. Hosiery thru the years. Lynn, Mass, Ira J. Haskell, 1956. iv, 124p.

HAND KNITTING

Tillotson, Margory. The complete knitting book: with patterns and easy-to-follow diagrams for knitting and designing every garment . . . 4th ed. London, Sir Isaac Pitman & Sons, 1940 (reprinted 1947). ix, 234p.

Thomas Mary. Mary Thomas's knitting book. London, Hodder & Stoughton, 1938. xiii, 256p.

Thomas, Mary. Mary Thomas's book of knitting patterns. London, Hodder & Stoughton, 1943. xi, 329p.

Norbury, James. The knitter's craft. London, Patons & Baldwins Ltd in association with Brockhampton Press, 1950. 116p.

Norbury, James. Traditional knitting patterns. London, Batsford, 1962. 240p.

Thompson, Gladys. Patterns for Guernseys and Jerseys. London, Batsford, 1969. 162p.

Harlow, Eve (editor). The art of knitting: garments for today from patterns of the past. Glasgow & London, Collins, 1977. 158p.

Fanderl, Lisl. Bäuerliches Stricken: alte Muster aus dem aplenländischen Raum. 6th ed. Rosenheim, Rosenheimer Verlagshaus Alfred Förg, 1980. 160p.

Hollingworth, Shelagh. A compendium of knitted stitch patterns. London, Batsford, 1985. 192p.

Stanley, Montse. The handknitter's handbook. Newton Abbot, David & Charles, 1986. 288p.

MACHINE KNITTING

General works

Leblanc, V and Preaux-Caltot. Manuel du bonnetier et du fabricant de bas, ou traité complet et simplifié de ces arts, d'après les renseignemens fournis par plusiers fabricans. Paris, Librairie Encyclopédique de Roret, 1830. 320p.

Willkomm, Gustav Adolf. Technology of framework knitting . . . Translated and adapted from the German by William Tertius Rowlett. Part I, containing instruction in hand frames and hand warp looms . . . Part 2, containing instruction in power frames and warp looms, the manner of forming framework knitted articles, and the seaming of hosiery. Leicester, F. Hewitt for the Leicester Technical School, (1885). vi, 136p. + vii, 137-368p. +22p.

Reh, Franz. La fabrication de la bonneterie. Manuel practique . . . traduit de l'allemand par André Simon. Paris, Edmond Rousset & Cie, 1893. 160p.

Hesser, Wilhelm. Die Fabrikation der Trikotwaren und Strumpfwaren und deren Kalkulation. Wien & Leipzig, Hartlebens Verlag, 1903. viii, 215p.

Renouard, Alfred. Traité complet de bonneterie mécanique. Paris, Renard-Morizot, (1905). viii, 700p.

Metcalf, M. A. Knitting: a manual of practical instruction in the mechanical details of all types of knitting machinery, their operation, adjustment and care. Chicago, American School of Correspondence, 1909. 378p.

Quilter, James Henry and Chamberlain, John. Frame-work knitting and hosiery manufacture: a practical work on all branches of the knitting industry. Leicester, Hosiery Trade Journal, 1911-1914. 304p + 352p + 416p.

Worm, Josef. Wirkerei und Strickerei. 2nd ed. Leipzig, Dr. Max Jänecke, 1920. 240p.

Chamberlain, John. Knitting mathematics and mechanisms. Leicester, J. W. Hemmings & Capey, 1923. 207p.

Chamberlain, John and Quilter, James Henry. Knitted fabrics. London, Sir Isaac Pitman & Sons, 1924. xi, 145p.

Chamberlain, John. Hosiery yarns and fabrics. Leicester, J. W. Hemmings & Capey, 1926. 213p.

Metcalf, M. A. (editor). American knitting machines. Boston, Textile American Publishing Co, 1928. 502p.

Udé, Georges. Étude générale de bonneterie: le vade-mecum du bonnetier. Paris, L'Edition Textile, (1930). 267p.

Miller, Max G. Principles of knitting. New York, McGraw-Hill, 1931. viii, 234p.

De Prat, D. Nouveau manuel complet de fabrication de bonneterie et de tricotage mécaniques. Paris, Société Francais d'Editions Litteraires et Techniques, 1931. 283p.

Aberle, Carl. Die Wirkerei und Strickerei, das Netzen und die Filetstrickerei. Berlin, Julius Springer Verlag, 1934. 615p.

Dalidovich, Aleksandr Semenovich. Osnovy teorii vyuzaniya. Moskva, Gizlegprom, 1948. 422p.

Lipkov. Iosif Abramovich. Obshchaya tekhnologiya trikotazhnogo proizvodstva. Moskva, Gizlegprom, 1950. 406p.

Chamberlain, John. Principles of machine knitting. Manchester, Textile Institute, 1951. 108p.

Suchet, J. Théorie de la maille dans les tricots trame. Paris, Editions la Maille, 1951. 276p.

Rius Sintes, Isidro. Tisaje, tintura y acabado de los géneros de punto. Barcelona, Bosch, 1952. 477p.

Gili, Michele. Tecnologia della maglieria e della calzetteria. Milano, Editore Ulrico Hoepli, 1951-1954. x, 461p, + x, 484p.

Schaller, Christoph and others. Technologie Flach- und Rundstricker. Berlin, Volk und Wissen Volkseigener Verlag, 1957. 387p.
Suchet, J and Tremelloni, Attilio. Tessuti a maglia in trama: intrecci, analisi, costruzione. Milano, Centro di Studio per l'Industria Tessile, 1957. 544p.
Dittrich, Heinz and Hähnel, Kurt. Atlas fur Gewirke und Gestricke: Teil I, Kuliergewirke und Gestricke. Teil II, Kettengewirke Rechts/Links. Leipzig, Fachbuchverlag, 1959-1965. 11p + 8p + fabric samples.
Vékássy, Alajos. Hurkolò-és konfekciópar. Budapest, Tankönyvkiadö, 1960. 483p.
Reichmann, Charles (editor). Principles of knitting outerwear fabrics and garments: a manual on basic stitch formations and machine types. New York, National Knitted Outerwear Association, 1961. 193p.
Wignall, Harry. Knitting. London, Sir Isaac Pitman & Sons, 1964. xi, 132p.
Reichmann, Charles (editor). Advanced knitting principles. New York, National Knitted Outerwear Association, 1964. 222p.
Reichmann, Charles (editor). Knitted stretch technology. New York, National Knitted Outerwear Association, 1965. 156p.
Stajniak, Konstanty. Technologia dziewiarstwa: maszyny szydelkujace. Warszawa, Wydawnictwo Przemyslu Lekkiego i Spozywczego, 1966. 380p.
Garbaruk, Vladimir Nikolaevich. Raschet i konstruirovanie trikotazhnykh mashin. Moskva & Leningrad, Izd. Mashinostroenie, 1966. 524p.
Reichman, Charles, Lancashire J. B. and Darlington K. D. Knitted fabric primer. New York, National Knitted Outerwear Association, 1967. 89p + fabric samples.
Shalov, Ivan Ivanovich. Proektirovanie trikotazhnykh fabrik. Moskva, Izd. Legkaya Industriya, 1968. 286p.
Lancashire, J. B. Jacquard design and knitting. New York, National Knitted Outerwear Association, 1969. 140p.
Gallemaert, L, Leclercqz, M. and Meuris I. Initiation à la bonneterie. Paris, Editions la Maille, 1972. 127p.
Reichman, Charles (editor). Electronics in knitting. New York, American Society of Knitting Technologists and National Knitted Outerwear Association, 1973. 115p.
Reichman, Charles, Darlington, Kenneth, D. and Goldberg, Steven. Knitted fabric technology. New York, National Knitted Outerwear Association, 1974. 240, 42p.
Weber, Klaus Peter. Die Wirkerei und Strickerei: Technologie und bindungstechnische Grundlagen. Heidelberg, Melliand Textilberichte, 1974. 183p.
Tremelloni, Attilio and Ceriani, Leonardo (editors). Manuale tecnico per l'industria della maglieria. Milano, Industria Pubblicazioni Audiovisivi-NIG Editrice, 1975-1976. vi, 299p + 402p.

Offermann, Peter and Tausch-Marton, Harald. Grundlagen der Maschenwaren-technologie. Leipzig, Fachbuchverlag, 1977. 240p.
Koci, Vladimir. Vazby pletenin. Praha, SNTL, 1980. 510p.
Spencer, David J. Knitting technology. Oxford, Pergamon Press, 1983. xviii, 349p.
Mann, Gerhard (editor). Technologie der Strickerei und Kulierwirkerei. Leipzig, Fachbuchverlag, 1985. 260p.

Straight-bar knitting

— hosiery

Noble, Emile. Le métier Cotton. Paris, Editions la Maille, 1930. 307p.
Gunther, Rudolph. Entwicklung und Getriebe der Cottonmaschine. Würzburg, 1934. 114p.
Miller, Max C. Knitting full-fashioned hosiery. New York, McGraw-Hill, 1937. viii, 259p.
Vandecasteele, Emile. Le métier Cotton. Paris, Editions la Maille, 1951. 317p.
Bradley, Stanley Bernard. Fully-fashioned hose manufacture. Manchester & London, Harlequin Press, 1953. vii, 172p.
Miquel Soler, Acisclo. El telar Cotton y sus predecesores. 2nd ed. Barcelona, Bosch, 1953. 222p.

— outerwear

Mills, Ralph W. Fully-fashioned garment manufacture. London, Cassell & Co, 1965. xii, 276p.

Circular knitting

Shinn, William E. Principles of knitting. Charlotte, Clark Publishing Co, 1946-1949. xvi, 177p + xix, 271p.
Vandecasteele, Emile. Métier interlock et métiers circulaires à côtes. Paris, Editions la Maille, 1947. 280p.
Mishcon, Lester and Abrams, Abraham. Pattern wheel designing for circular jersey knitting machines. New York, Supreme Knitting Machine Co. Inc, 1949. 165p.
Miquel Soler, Acisclo. Los telares circulares a recogida. Barcelona, Bosch, 1953. 306p.
Palomer Pons, Jorge. Los telares circulares de gran diámetro. Tomo I, Las circulares con agujas de prensa. Tomos II y III, Las circulares con agujas de lengüeta. Barcelona, Bosch, 1954-1956. 376p + 385p + 395p.
Reichman, Charles. Double knit fabric manual. New York, National Knitted Outerwear Association, 1961. 160p.
Palomer Pons, Jorge. Tricotosas circulares. Barcelona, Bosch, 1964. 415p.
Moyer, Earl D. Principles of double knitting. Brooklyn, Montrose Supply & Equipment Co, 1972. 121p.

— **beard-needle machines**

Jungblut, Albert. Étude et réglages du métier circulaire francais: les métiers circulaires a aiguilles a bec. Métier francais et métier Berthelot. Paris, Editions la Maille, 1925. 226p.
Michael, Emil. Der Rundwirkstuhl: Technologie der Rundwirkerei. Leipzig, Fachbuchverlag, 1951. viii, 152p.
Spittler, Ernst. Die Rundwirkmaschine: der mailleusen-Rundstuhl. Göppingen, Werner Müller Verlag, 1955. 107p.

— **hosiery**

Davis, William. Hosiery manufacture. London, Sir Isaac Pitman & Sons, 1920. x, 136p.
Chamberlain, John. Manufacture of knitted footwear. Leicester, Alfred Tracey, 1930. 288p.
Huleux, M. Les machines rondes automatiques à bas et chaussettes. Paris, Editions la Maille, 1930. 852p.
Huleux, M. Étude de machines circulaires à bas et chaussettes et des machines a bords-côtes. Paris, L'Edition Textile, (1930). 416p.
Diebler, Albert. Technologie der Rundstrickerei: Der Rundstrick-Strumpfautomat. Berlin & Stuttgart, Konradin Verlag, (1942). 289p.
Eley, A. W. Stockings: silk, cotton, rayon, nylon. Leicester, A. W. Eley, 1946. iii, 167p.
Vandecasteele, Emile. Les machines rondes automatiques à double cylindre. Paris, Editions la Maille, 1946. 339p.
Shalov, Ivan Ivanovich. Ustroistvo i obsluzhivanie kruglochulochnykh mashin. Moskva, Gizleprom, 1952. 210p.
Wignall, Harry and others. Hosiery technology. New York, National Knitted Outerwear Association, 1968. 151p.
Modig, Nils. Hosiery machines: their development, technology, and practical use. Bamberg, Meisenbach, 1988. x, 170p.

Flat knitting

Buck, H. D. Flat machine knitting and fabrics. New York, Bragdon, Lord & Nagle, 1921. 147p.
Jungblut, Albert and Huleux, M. Les machines à tricoter rectilignes à main et automatiques. 3rd ed. Paris, Editions La Maille, 1948. xvi, 834p.
Fischer, Hans. Technologie der Flachstrickerei: die Mustereinrichtungen an Spezialhandflachstrickmaschinen. Berlin & Stuttgart, Konradin Verlag, (1946). 160p.
Benz, Ernst. Die Links/Links-Strickmaschine. Stuttgart, Konradin Verlag, 1950. 208p.
Weigkricht, Alfons. Strickerei in Industrie und Handwerk; praktisch-technologisches Handbuch der Flachstrickerei. Wien & Heidelberg, Rudolf Bohmann Industrie- und Fachverlag, 1951. 152p.
Fischer, Hans. Technologie der Flachstrickerei: die einfache Flachstrickmaschine. Berlin & Stuttgart, Konradin Verlag, (1951). 135p.
Dury, J. Métiers rectilignes et rectilignes a mailles retournées: technologie des métiers et des tricots. Paris, Editions la Maille, 1954. 744p.
Hähnel, Kurt. Flachstrickerei. Leipzig, Fachbuchverlag, 1959. viii, 272p.
Neumann, Helmut. Die Handflachstrickerei: Technologie und Warenherstellung. Coburg, Prost & Meiner Verlag, 1959. 198p + fabric samples.
Neumann, Helmut. Die automatische Flachstrickerei. Coburg, Prost & Meiner Verlag, 1962. 196p.
Edouard Dubied & Cie SA. Dubied knitting manual. Neuchatel, Edouard Dubied & Cie SA, 1967. 199p.
Tollkühn, Dieter. Flachstrickautomaten: Techniken, Aufbau und Arbeitsweise moderner vollautomatischer Flachstrickmaschinen. Bamberg, Meisenbach, 1979. 251p.
Tollkühn, Dieter. Elektronisch Steuern, Mustern, Stricken: die Musterausarbeitung und Musterfestlegung für elektronisch gesteuerte Universal- Flachstrick-Automaten. Bamberg, Meisenbach, 1986. 166p.

— **domestic machines**

Silver Knitting Institute. Bible for machine knitting. Guide to knitting techniques. How to knit garments. Tokyo, Silver Knitting Institute, 1977. 207p + 223p.
Holbourne, David. The book of machine knitting. London, Batsford, 1979. 120p.
Kinder, Kathleen. Techniques in machine knitting. London, Batsford, 1983. 144p.
Nabney, Janet. An illustrated handbook of machine knitting. London, Batsford, 1987. 200p.

Warp knitting

Merril, Gilbert R, Murden, Edward and Rowan, Joseph. Warp knitting and glove manufacture . . . compiled principally from articles in Textile World. New York, Bragdon, Lord & Nagle Co, 1925. 125p.
Michael, Emil. Technologie der Kettenwirkerei. Berlin & Stuttgart, Konradin Verlag, 1943. 128p.
Johnson, Thomas H. Tricot fabric design. New York, McGraw-Hill, 1946. viii, 124p.
Huleux M. Métiers chaine a aigules a bec: technologie et étude des tricots. Paris, Editions la Maille, 1948. xiv, 554p.
Weigkricht, Alfons. Technologie der Kettenwirkerei: Hilfs- und Nachschlagewerk für Wirker in Schule und Betrieb. Wien & Heidelberg, Rudolf Bohmann Industrie- und Fachverlag, 1949. 156p.
Paling, Dennis F. Warp knitting technology. Manchester & London, Harlequin Press, 1952. vii, 232p.

Rogler, Max and Humboldt, Martin. Der Kettenwirkerei. Band 1: Kettenstuhle. Band 2: Bindungslehre. Obertshausen, fachbuchverlag Martin Humboldt, 1954-1955. 160p + 138p.
Reisfeld, Aaron. Warp knit engineering. New York, National Knitted Outerwear Association, 1966. 467p.
Weber, Klaus Peter. An introduction to the stitch formations in warp knitting: technological and structural rudiments in simple and basic stitch formations. Obertshausen, Karl Mayer e.V., 1966. 107p + pattern cards.
Stajniak, Konstanty. Technologia dziewiarstwa: maszyny osnowowe. Warszawa, Wydawnictwo Przemyslu Lekkiego i Spozywczego, 1968. 341p.
Meuris, I. Tricot et métier rachel. Paris, Editions la Maille, 1968. 211p.
Renz, Rudolf and Fleckeisen, Michael. Bindungslehre der Ketten- und Nähwirkerei. Leipzig, Fachbuchverlag, 1976. 143p.
Nippon-Mayer Co. Ltd. Warp knitting. Fukui City, Nippon-Mayer Co. Ltd, 1982. vii, 389p.
Kopias, Kazimierz. Technologia dzianin kolumienkowych. Warszawa, Wydawnictwa Naukowo-Techniczne, 1986. 178p.
Raz. S. Warp knitting production. Heidelberg, Verlag Melliand Textilberichte, 1987. 548p.

— raschel machines

Jungblut, Albert. Le métier Rachel. Paris, Editions la Maille, 1930. 682p.
Rotenstein, Charles. Manufacture of raschel wool and cotton outerwear. New York, National Knitted Outerwear Association, 1954. 138p.
Wheatley, B. Raschel lace production. New York, National Knitted Outerwear Association, 1972. 266p.

— stitch-bonding machines

Kemter, Heinz. Neue Textiltechnologien: Malipol. Leipzig, Fachbüchverlag, 1965. 117p.
Sobotka, Ladislav (editor). Textilni technologie proplétáni. Systém Arachne. Praha, SNTL, 1971. 427p.
Ploch, Seigfried, Böttcher, Peter and Scharch, Dieter. Malimo-Nähwirktechnologien. Leipzig, Fachbuchverlag, 1978. 464p.

DYEING AND FINISHING

Meyer, Erich. Appreturkunde Wirk-und Strickwaren. 2nd ed. Berlin, Volk and Wissen Volkseigener Verlag, 1952. 135p.
Abramov, Sergei Aleksandrovich. Khimicheskaya tekhnologiya otdelki trikotazhnykh izdelii. Moskva, Izd. Legkaya Industriya, 1966. 418p.
Kertész, Pál and Kertész, Pálné. Kötött-hurkolt cikkek szinezése és kikészitése. Budapest, Müszaki Könyvkiadó, 1968. 204p.
Haigh, D. Dyeing and finishing of knitted goods. Leicester, Hosiery Trade Journal, 1970. 165p.
Rius Sintes, Isidro. Aprestos y acabados de los géneros de punto. Barcelona, Bosch, 1971. 352p.

MAKING-UP

Loweth, Charles F. (compiler). The Singer handbook for the hosiery trade. London, Singer Sewing Machine Co. Ltd, (1920). 240p.
Pashkov, Konstantin Pavlovich. Kettel'nye mashiny. 2nd ed. Moskva, Gizlegprom, 1950. 200p.
Huleux, M. Les machines à coudre employées en bonneterie. Paris, Editions la Maille, 1951. 428p.
Kluge, Guntram and others. Grundlagen der Trikotagen-Konfection. Berlin, Volk und Wissen Volkseigener Verlag, 1960. 183p.
Berger, Ruth and others. Schnittkonstruktion Trikotagen. Leipzig, Fachbuchverlag, 1970. 120p.
Sirghie, Viorel and Schnitzer, Beno. Masini de cusut confectii din tricot. Bucuresti, Editura Tehnica, 1971. 370p.
Barth, Ingeborg (editor). Erzeugnislehre Trikotagenkonfektion. Leipzig, Fachbuchverlag, 1978. 140p.
Turbett, Pam. Cut & sew: working with machine-knitted fabrics. London, Batsford, 1985. 120p.

TESTING AND PROPERTIES

Tompkins, Ernest. The science of knitting. New York, John Wiley & Sons, 1914. xiii, 330p.
Ban, Masataka. Meriyasu amiji no riron to jissai. (The theory and practice of knitting fabric). Osaka, Textile Machinery Society of Japan, 1964. v, 199p.
AATCC. Symposium — knit barré — causes and cures, New York, American Association of Textile Chemists and Colorists, 25th-26th May, 1972. Research Triangle Park, NC, AATCC, 1972. 131p.
Koblyakov, Aleksandr Ivanovich. Struktura i mekhanicheskie svoistva trikotazha. Moskva, Izd. Legkaya Industriya, 1973. 240p.
AATCC. Symposium — knit shrinkage — cause, effect and control, American Association of Textile Chemists and Colorists, New York, 24th-25th October, 1973. Research Triangle Park, NC, AATCC, 1973. 113p.
AATCC. Symposium — sense and nonsense in knit testing, American Association of Textile Chemists and Colorists, New York, 18th November, 1975. Research Triangle Park, NC, AATCC, 1975. iii, 96p.
Korlinski, Wladyslaw. Podstawy dziewiarstwa. Warszawa, Wydawnictwa Naukowo-Techniczne, 1976. 318p.
Teodorescu, Ion and Bucurenci, Ion. Tehnologii privind stabilitatea dimensionala a tricoturilor. Bucuresti, Editura Tehnica, 1976. 340p.

Kudryavin, Lev Aleksandrovich (editor). Laboratornyi praktikum po tekhnologii trikotazhnogo proizvodstva. Moskva, Izd. Legkaya Industriya, 1979. 432p.

KNITTING INDUSTRY

Mill management

Merrill, Gilbert R. Manual of knitting mill practice for superintendents and overseers in knitting mills. New York, Textile World, 1929. 209p.

Withaar, A. Organisatie en planning in de tricotage-industrie. Doetinchem, C. Misset NV, 1952. 126p.

Patrick, A. Weyman. The theory and technique of cost accounting in the hosiery industry. Ann Arbor, University of Michigan, 1956. ix, 299p.

Podbereski, T. A. Production planning and control manual for knitwear and swimwear firms. New York, National Knitted Outerwear Association, 1965. 116p.

Industry surveys

Fahrländer, Ernst. Die schweizerische Wirkerei- und Strickereiindustrie. Ihre Entwicklung und ihr Stand am Ende des zweiten Weltkrieges. Bern, Verlag A. Francke, 1946. xiv, 183p.

Board of Trade. Working party reports: hosiery. London, H.M.S.O., 1946. 224p.

De Haan, J. D. The full-fashioned hosiery industry in the USA. The Hague, Mouton & Co, 1958. 188p.

Economic Development Committee for the Hosiery and Knitwear Industry. Hosiery and knitwear in the 1970s; a study of the industry's future market prospects. A report prepared by Associated Industrial Consultants Ltd for the Marketing Action Group of the . . . Committee. London, H.M.S.O., 1970. xx, 182p.

Directory Of Advertisers

Aristoc 145
Atkins of Hinckley 46
BASF (UK) 74
Barclays de Zoete Wedd 148
Benson Turner & Sons 102
British Coal 103
Thomas Burnley & Sons 99
Camber International 77
Vernon Cooper 54
Courtaulds Fabrics 176
Couture Marketing 53
Dawson International 73
Du Pont (UK) 98
Elton Cop Dyeing Company 124
Exeltor 80
Ferry Pickering Publishers 41
Framework Knitters' Petition 126
Gedling Borough Council 78
Glen Alva 54
Leslie Hubble 124
G. H. Hurt & Son 48
ICI Colours & Fine Chemicals 149
ICI (UK) Fibres 44, 45
International Wool Secretariat 122
Jumberca 121
KIF/Hatra 99
KLITRA 126
Kennedy Wagstaff 50
Labtest Inspection Services (UK) 54
W. K. Lowe & Company 76
Geoffrey E. Macpherson 161
Marks & Spencer 75
Martins (Leicester) 128

F. & C. Mason 46
Karl Mayer 151
Midland Bank 51
Monk-Dubied 52
National Union of Hosiery Workers 127
Patons RTN 104
Pretty Polly 97
Profitex 79
Roberts of Dumfries 79
Ruddington Framework Knitters' Museum 42
SGS Quality Control International 150
Kurt Salmon Associates 146
Sandoz Chemicals 104
Scottish College of Textiles 42
Shima Seiki Manufacturing 100, 101
Sildorex Company 125
Snia (UK) 152
South Pacific Textile Industries Berhad 96
Stevensons Dyers 150
Stoll 49
Sun Ray Spinners & Dyers 99
William Tatham 146
The Textile Institute 43
Textured Jersey 74
Derek Tiney 102
Todd & Duncan 123
Trent Polytechnic 122
Benjn. R. Vickers & Sons 126
Viscosuisse, Group Rhône Poulenc 147
John Williams 124
Worshipful Company of Framework Knitters 47
Yorkshire Chemicals 122